HANDBOOK TO THE GOSPELS

Handbook to the Gospels

*A Guide to the Gospel Writings
and to the Life and Times of Jesus*

John Wijngaards, M.H.M.

SERVANT BOOKS
Ann Arbor, Michigan

Copyright © 1979 by John Wijngaards

Cover photographs by Gerry Rauch and Stacy Whitfield
Jacket and book design by John B. Leidy

U.S. edition available from Servant Books, Box 8617,
Ann Arbor, Michigan 48107

Published in Great Britain in three volumes under the title
Scripture Comes Alive by Mayhew-McCrimmon, Ltd.

Most scripture quotations are from *Today's English Version,*
copyright © American Bible Society 1966 and 1976, and used
by permission.

ISBN 0-89283-118-9
Printed in the United States of America

Nihil Obstat: Adrian Graffy
Imprimatur: Christopher Creede V.G.

Contents

Introduction

The gospels have a special pre-eminence among all the books of Scripture. And this is rightly so. For the gospels are the principal witness for the life and teaching of the incarnate Word our Savior.
(Vatican II, Decree on Divine Revelation, No. 18)

The Gospels tell us of Jesus Christ. They describe his character, narrate his life and his miracles, preserve for us his sayings and parables. The Gospels present the most important part of human history—the way God redeemed mankind. If we want to be mature Christians, to love Jesus Christ more and serve him better, to bring him to others, we will have to make a thorough study of the Gospels. To get to know the Gospels well, there is no substitute for reading the Gospels, however profound the books or learned the commentators. Even when reading *about* Scripture, we should turn to God's word itself at every opportunity.

We do not read the Bible as we read other books. In the Gospels God himself speaks to us; only prayerful reading will open our ears to what he wants to tell us. It is best not to read too much at once, nor to read in a hurry. When you open the Bible, put yourself in God's presence. While you read, remain aware of the sacredness of the text. When a good idea strikes you, reflect on it and pray over it. Five minutes' reading of this kind soon becomes a necessity for daily life. Our spiritual life as Christians is nourished by Jesus' teaching. As we absorb his message, our life will more closely resemble his. Jesus Christ himself insisted that we remain united to him through his word.

> You will be truly my disciples only if you remain in my word.
> (Jn 8:31)

> Remain in my love. You will remain in my love, if you follow my instructions. (Jn 15:9)

> Whoever loves me will keep my word. (Jn 14:23)

To be close to Jesus, to become his disciples, and to show our love for him we should fill our minds and our hearts with his word.

We need background knowledge, however, to understand the Gospels fully. This book will provide information to make it easier to understand the meaning of passages more fully, but only the Gospels themselves can bring us into contact with Jesus Christ, who is our life, our truth, and our happiness. With an increased awareness of what made up his earthly life will come an increased opportunity to touch his person. No other person has occupied such a central place in the history of mankind. Who was this carpenter of Nazareth who died in Jerusalem on a cross and is now accepted by so many as Son of God and way of salvation? The Gospels alone can show us this Jesus.

Jesus' message reaches us through the living witness of his first disciples. To them he entrusted the task of preserving his teaching, of reflecting on it with joy, and of passing on the good tidings of redemption. The result of those disciples' preaching is the four Gospels. We will study the whole process of how the Gospels came about, paying special attention to the evangelists in order to know their minds. By analyzing some key passages in depth, we will deepen our insight into how Jesus' words and deeds came to be expressed in writing. May all of this help us to treasure his words, for however useful knowledge may be, it is no substitute for love. The gospel will be truly ours, if we learn how to listen to Jesus' word and remain in that word.

ONE

Gospel and Gospels

THE WORD *gospel* is derived from the Greek term *eu* (meaning "good") and *aggelion* (meaning "message"). In Latin this became *evangelium*. Many English words have been derived from this: evangelist, evangelical, evangelize. The English term itself is a translation (good spiel, or good tidings) which has been corrupted through usage.

In the Old Testament, we find the term being used with a purely nonreligious meaning. When Joab, the general of David's army, defeated the rebel Absalom, he wanted someone to take the message of victory to David.

> Then Ahimaaz son of Zadok said to Joab, "Let me run to the king with *the good news* that the Lord has saved him from his enemies." (2 Sm 18:19)

But, in the language of the prophets, the term *good news* began to mean much more. The prophets pointed to the Messianic future. Then, when God began to redeem his people, they heard the good news of Messianic salvation:

> Go up on a high mountain
>   and proclaim the good news!
> Call out with a loud voice, Zion;
>   announce the good news! . . .
> The Sovereign Lord is coming to rule with power,
>   bringing with him the people he has rescued. (Is 40:9)

The Jews were waiting anxiously for this good news. That is why, when Jesus began his preaching, he announced his message as the good news of salvation.

> He said to them, "I must preach the Good News of the Kingdom of God in other towns also, because that is what God sent me to do." (Lk 4:43)

> After John had been put in prison, Jesus went to Galilee and preached the Good News from God. "The right time has come," he said, "and the Kingdom of God is near! Turn away from your sins and believe the Good News!" (Mk 1:14)

> [Jesus said to Peter, James, John, and Andrew] "You will stand before rulers and kings for my sake to tell them the Good News. But before the end comes, the gospel must be preached to all peoples. (Mk 13:9-10)

> And every day in the Temple and in people's homes they continued to teach and preach the Good News about Jesus the Messiah. (Acts 5:42)

"The good news" came to mean the happy announcement of all that Jesus said and did (see also Acts 8:35, 11:20; Rom 1:1ff), as he brought to pass the redemption God had promised through the prophets (Mt 11:5; Lk 4:18-19, 7:22).

In the New Testament *gospel* always refers to the whole message about Jesus. In this sense there is only one gospel.

> I am surprised at you! In no time at all you are deserting the one who called you by the grace of Christ, and are accepting another gospel. Actually, there is no "other gospel," but I say this because there are some people who are upsetting you and trying to change the gospel of Christ. But even if we or an angel from heaven should preach to you a gospel that is different from the one we preached to you, may he be condemned to hell! (Gal 1:6-8)

In actual fact, this one gospel preached by the apostles has come down to us in four different editions. In the early centuries Christian writers stressed the unity of the gospel underlying these four versions. They did not speak of "Gospels" in the plural, but rather "the four books of the one gospel" (Muratorian Canon) or "the four-form gospel" (Irenaeus). To make clear that all four editions present one and the same gospel, they spoke of them as "the gospel *according to* Matthew," "the gospel *according to* Mark," etc. It is only in later times that Christians started to speak of the four Gospels, and refer to them individually as the Gospel *of* Matthew, etc. We should always remember that strictly speaking they are four editions of the one undivided gospel of Jesus Christ.

The word *evangelist* has undergone a change of meaning in much the same way as the word *gospel*. Originally, the term meant one who brings good tidings. All preachers of the gospel therefore were called evangelists. We find Paul using the word with this meaning (see Eph 4:11; 2 Tm 4:5), as does Luke (Acts 21:8). In later times the expression was used only of Matthew, Mark, Luke, and John. After the Reformation, some of the Protestant churches returned to the earlier meaning, and so the term is sometimes used to mean preacher, minister, or catechist.

Gospel Formation: From Jesus' Words to Gospel Writings

The Gospel texts surpass the work of human authors because through the Gospels God himself speaks to us. We express this by saying that the Gospels have been "inspired." God himself is their author because he moved the human authors to write what they wrote. How did God do this? In the case of the Gospels we can distinguish three stages.

1. Jesus Christ revealed divine truth to the apostles. He taught them by parables and instructions what they should believe and practice. He showed them by his deeds what God's salvation means. Finally, he gave them the commission

to preach this salvation everywhere.

2. After Jesus' Resurrection and after receiving the Holy Spirit at Pentecost, the apostles fulfilled the commission Jesus had given them. By their oral preaching, by their example, and by their counsels they handed on the apostolic tradition. The greater part of this tradition they had received directly from Jesus. In some matters of interpretation they were assisted by the Holy Spirit so that they could pass on Jesus' gospel faithfully.

3. The apostolic preaching was written down by zealous disciples. What Jesus had said and done was put on paper. First, collections were made of passages that belonged together. Then the time came for a complete written expression of Jesus' message, and the Holy Spirit prompted four writers to compose written accounts.

The Holy Spirit was at work in all these stages. He helped the apostles understand Jesus' teachings. He guided the early church in the faithful expression of apostolic tradition. And he moved and assisted the evangelists during all their work of writing. The work of inspiration embraced the formation of the Gospels in all their stages.

For the Gospels are not the product of the four evangelists alone. The Gospels are the product of the church's preaching. Some individuals, it is true, had an important hand in giving the final shape to the Gospels: that was the special task of the evangelists. But what they wrote down was not their own personal opinion. They wrote as representatives of the church and drew their information from the church.

The Date of Writing

This process of formation began with the preaching of John the Baptist and ended with the death of the apostle John. We can approximate it this way:

27 A.D.—The preaching of John the Baptist. The beginning of Jesus' public ministry.

30 A.D.—On the eve of the Passover, the death of Jesus. On Pentecost, the outpouring of the Spirit on the church.

36-37 A.D.—Martyrdom of Stephen. Paul's conversion.

45-49 A.D.—Paul's first missionary journey.

50 A.D.—The Council of Jerusalem. Matthew's Gospel (Aramaic edition).

50-52 A.D.—Paul's second missionary journey.

53-58 A.D.—Paul's third missionary journey.

61-62 A.D.—Paul imprisoned in Rome. James stoned to death in Jerusalem.

64 A.D.—Mark's Gospel.

65 A.D.—Luke's Gospel? Matthew's Gospel (Greek edition)

67 A.D.—Martyrdom of Peter and Paul in Rome.

68-70 A.D.—The Romans wage war against the Jews, defeat them, and destroy Jerusalem.

70-80 A.D.—Another possible date for Luke's Gospel and the final edition of Matthew.

95 A.D.—John's Gospel.

100 A.D.—John, the last apostle, dies at Ephesus.

Apocryphal Gospels

The Gospels of Matthew, Mark, Luke, and John were not the only gospels that were written. Many others tried to compose lives of Christ. None of these were inspired, as they were the work of individuals and not of the whole church. We call these the "Apocryphal Gospels." Many of them had some devotional value in their own time. Others were downright heretical. Here we may mention some of the better known ones:

The Gospel According to the Hebrews
The Gospel of Peter
The Gospel According to the Egyptians
The Gospel of the Twelve Apostles
The Gospel According to Philip

The Proto-gospel of James
The Gospel of Pseudo-Matthew
The Gospel of Thomas
The Arabic Gospel of the Infancy
The Gospel of Nicodemus
The Story of Joseph, the Carpenter
The Transition of the Blessed Virgin Mary

Right from the beginning, the church exercised teaching authority by clearly indicating which Gospels were inspired and which were not. Some of these apocryphals could be used for private reading, but none of them could be read during a public service. Only the Gospels of Matthew, Mark, Luke, and John were put on the list (the *canon*) of the writings to be used in church and for public instruction. These four Gospels have, therefore, also been called the "canonical Gospels," to distinguish them from the apocryphal ones.

Textual Tradition of the Four Gospels

The apostles and evangelists used the normal writing material of their day, papyrus, a rather primitive sort of paper. This was apt to decay quickly, especially if constantly used. No wonder, then, that the original manuscripts of Matthew, Mark, Luke, and John no longer exist. But from the earliest days copies were made. Each of these copies was written out by hand and checked for accuracy. After some years, copies were made on parchment, that is, on the skins of animals, and these copies were practically indestructible.

The accurate transmission of the text throughout the centuries has been proven by scientific research. Even now we possess many ancient copies of Gospel texts: thirty-five papyrus fragments of the most ancient times, containing parts of the Gospel text; sixty-six uncial manuscripts, parchments belonging to the centuries when all letters were written in capitals; 1,000 minuscule manuscripts, parchments from later centuries

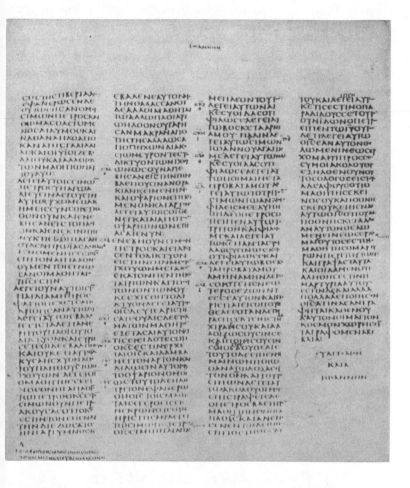

A page from the Codex Sinaiticus shows the final page of the Greek text of the Gospel of John.

when the letters were written smaller; 300 church lectionaries, collections of readings meant for the Sunday service (some of them very old). We have, moreover, abundant material for comparison of the early Gospel texts in ancient translations

(Latin, Gothic, Syriac, Coptic, Armenian, etc.) and in the quotations of the Fathers.

Since so many copies had been made and preserved in so many different places, it was impossible for any individual to change the text. The differences would soon be noticed and corrected by others. Modern scientific research on the Bible has gathered all the information found in the manuscripts and compared it with the actual text used in the church. The result of this investigation has confirmed the Christian claim that the Gospel text has been handed on in all its purity. In fact, the Gospels are the best preserved writings of antiquity. For no other secular or religious writing of the same age can such abundant proof of integrity be produced.

The old manuscripts do differ in some smaller details. Such differences are called "variant readings." Compare two variant readings of Matthew 22:30 in two major manuscripts:

Codex Vaticanus
When the dead rise to life, they will be like the angels of heaven.

Codex Sinaitcus
When the dead rise to life, they will be like the angels *of God in* heaven.

Careful study of all the available information proves that the reading of the Codex Vaticanus (and other manuscripts) was the original one. This reading is, consequently, followed in our translations. In any case, the meaning of both variants here is the same.

Reading Aids to the Gospel Text

At the time when the evangelists wrote, it was customary to write all letters as capitals without intermediate spaces. This kind of text was difficult to read. Consider this illustration of an unpunctuated English sentence:

PETERTOOKHIMASIDEANDBEGANTOREBUKE
HIMGODFORBIDITLORDHESAID

After some centuries an easier way of writing and reading was introduced, including the spacing of words and the use of punctuation.

Peter took him aside and began to rebuke him. "God forbid it, Lord!" he said.

Since all the Gospel passages were written without any divisions, it could be extremely difficult to find any particular passage. For this reason the four Gospels were divided into chapters by Stephen Langdon, in the thirteenth century, and into verse by Robert Estienne, in the sixteenth century. To indicate any passage we now have only to mention the evangelist, chapter, and verse. The text quoted above will be found in Matthew 16:22. In many editions of the Gospels it also became customary to print subtitles and footnotes. All these things are not an essential part of the text, but they serve a good purpose since they make the reading of the Gospels so much easier for us.

Translations of the Gospels. Christ preached in Aramaic, the language of the Jews in Palestine. The early apostolic traditions were first formulated in that language. Matthew, too, wrote his Gospel originally in Aramaic. But as the church spread over the then-known world, Greek soon became the language of communication, for Aramaic was only known to the Jews, whereas Greek could be understood by everyone. Greek was the *lingua franca* for all educated classes, for business and trade, for politics and culture. Thus we find that all the books of the New Testament were eventually composed in Greek. From the third century on Latin became more important, and the Gospels were consequently translated into Latin. In 383 A.D., Jerome was commissioned by Pope Damasus to revise these translations. His work, the so-called Vulgate, became the standard Latin translation.

Throughout the centuries the Gospels have been translated into the languages spoken by people who embraced Christianity. At present, Gospel translations exist in more than 1,200 languages, making it the most widely circulated book in the world. A special word of praise should go to the Protestant Bible Societies who have contributed so much to spreading the Bible text to all continents.

Of course, it will not do to have only one translation in a living language. We need translations for the learned, for children, for use in church, and for devotional use. Moreover, the language we speak changes with the course of time. New translations are, therefore, essential from time to time. If we take English as an example, there have been more than 250 independent translations of the Gospels into English. Some of these translations are outdated, but many of them are still used. Here I shall discuss some that we are sure to come across. They are Catholic, unless stated otherwise.

The Rheims-Douay Version. By English scholars, mainly following the Vulgate. The first edition appeared in 1582, but many revisions have been made since then. It was widely used by Catholics in England. The translation has a certain beauty, but it is now considered outdated because of its antiquated language. Here is an example from Matthew:

> You are the salt of the earth. But if the salt loses its savour, wherewith shall it be salted? It is good for nothing anymore but to be cast out and to be trodden on by men. (Mt 5:13)

The Confraternity Edition. A new, quite accurate, simple, and expressive translation by American scholars and approved by the hierarchy in 1941.

> You are the salt of the earth; but if salt loses its strength, what shall it be salted with? It is no longer of any use but to be thrown out and trodden underfoot by men.

The Knox Version. In 1945, Msgr. Ronald Knox published a new translation which he had made at the request of the English

Catholic hierarchy. Since Knox was a great scholar and writer of English, his translation possesses a majestic style of speech. Though of outstanding merit for people who know English very well, those not acquainted with English literature would find it difficult to understand.

> You are the salt of the earth; if salt loses its taste, what is there left to give taste to it? There is no more to be done with it, but throw it out of doors for men to tread it under foot.

The Catholic Revised Standard Version. This version comes as the conclusion of a long history. In 1611, the Anglican Church brought out an English translation which is known as the King James Bible or the Authorized Version. For many centuries it remained the principal version in Protestant churches, and even today it is still in wide circulation. In 1870, a revision was begun which went through many stages, but eventually received a definite shape and was widely accepted as the Revised Standard Version. Some Catholic scholars went through the text and prepared an edition for Catholics, now known as the Catholic Revised Standard Version (1966). This version has the good quality of being exceptionally faithful to the original diction of the inspired books. It is, therefore, well suited for professional students of scripture. But its tendency to give literalistic translations makes it less readable for the average reader.

> You are the salt of the earth; but if salt has lost its taste, how shall its saltness be restored? It is no longer good for anything except to be thrown out and trodden underfoot by men.

The Jerusalem Bible. Following the example of the scholarly edition of the French Dominicans in Jerusalem (1955), English Catholic scholars produced a very fine new version. They translated the French text into English, with frequent reference to the Greek and Hebrew originals:

You are the salt of the earth. But if salt becomes tasteless, what can make it salty again? It is good for nothing, and can only be thrown out to be trampled underfoot by men.

Today's English Version. The American Bible Society experienced the need of an English translation which would be both very accurate and at the same time extremely clear and easy to read. Dr. Robert G. Bratcher and other scholars achieved this in Today's English Version. Since its appearance in 1966 it has sold millions of copies all over the world. The translation is very well suited for those who have learned English as a second language. It has been approved for Catholic usage.

You are the salt for all mankind. But if salt loses its saltiness, there is no way to make it salty again. It has become worthless, so it is thrown out and people trample on it.

The New English Bible (Protestant, 1961) and the *New American Bible* (Catholic, 1970) may also be recommended for accuracy and readability.

Having considered the general process of Gospel formation and transmission, we may now move to each of the evangelists in turn.

TWO

The Gospel of Matthew

PAPIAS, BISHOP OF HIERAPOLIS (about 130 A.D.), wrote about the various Gospel editions. He tells us that the apostle Matthew put together the discourses of Jesus in Aramaic, the language spoken by Jesus himself. Irenaeus (about 180 A.D.) reports the same tradition: "Matthew preached among the Jews [in Palestine]. He also produced in their language a writing of the gospel. This he did while Peter and Paul were preaching and founding the church in Rome." Many other outstanding writers of the early church confirm this testimony—Pantaenus (about 200 A.D.), Clement of Alexandria (150-215 A.D.), Origen (186-254 A.D.), Tertullian (160-240 A.D.), Eusebius of Caesarea (265-340 A.D.), and so on. It is evident, therefore, that from the earliest times great men in the church have ascribed the edition of the first Gospel text to Matthew the apostle. They were in a good position to trace the authorship, and we have no reason to doubt the accuracy of their information.

The Author and Composition of the Gospel

Does the Gospel of Matthew itself say anything about its author? Not directly. But when we read the text carefully, we can recognize many characteristic traits of the evangelist. Every author quite naturally leaves the imprint of his personality on his writing. In this way we see that the author of the first Gospel must have been a close disciple of Jesus, must have known

Palestine well, must have had a personal knowledge of Jewish customs and practices, must have made a thorough study of the Old Testament, and was a skilled teacher. In one passage, we find the story of a conversion:

> Jesus left that place, and as he walked along, he saw a tax collector, named Matthew, sitting in his office. He said to him, "Follow me."
> Matthew got up and followed him.
> While Jesus was having a meal in Matthew's house, many tax collectors and other outcasts came and joined Jesus and his disciples at the table. (Mt 9:9-10)

In those days tax collectors were looked down upon since they were usually dishonest and not religious. Luke 5:27-29 and Mark 2:13-15 also mention Jesus' calling of the tax collector, but they call him "Levi." Why this difference in name? It may be that Matthew, before his conversion, was called Levi. Perhaps Jesus himself gave him the new name Matthew (gift from God), just as he had given the name Peter to Simon (Mt 16:17-18; Jn 1:40-42). In any case, among Jesus' disciples and in the early church, he was known as Matthew. It may be that Mark and Luke wanted to avoid mentioning that Matthew had been a tax collector and called him by his previous name, Levi. Matthew himself, however, would not mind speaking about it. He would never forget how great God's mercy had been towards him! He would always reflect on Jesus' special love. When enumerating the list of apostles, Matthew says:

> These are the names of the twelve apostles: first, Simon (called Peter) and his brother Andrew; James and his brother John, the sons of Zebedee; Philip and Bartholomew; Thomas and Matthew, *the tax collector.* (Mt 10:2-3)

The Gospel of Matthew went through at least two distinct stages of composition:

Aramaic Matthew. About 50 A.D., Matthew composed the first Gospel in Aramaic. He made ample use of the texts (the words of Jesus) which people had learned by heart under the instruction of the apostles. In fact, the Gospel itself was nothing else but a summary of that instruction arranged for the particular purpose of proving Jesus' divine Messiahship to the Jews of Palestine. Aramaic Matthew has been entirely lost, since there were very few people who spoke Aramaic in later times. What the church canonized was the complete Greek Gospel which we know today.

Greek Matthew. Modern Bible scholars think that Matthew's original material was worked on by disciples and so they speak of the "School of Matthew" to which we owe the Gospel in its present form. They translated it into Greek, added some sections, and cut others short. The Gospel may have reached its final form between 80 A.D. and 90 A.D.

We know very little about Matthew's further life. Tradition has it that he first preached to the Jews in Palestine and then to other nations outside the Holy Land. Some ancient writers say that he went to Ethiopia. Others mention Persia, Syria, Greece, and even Ireland. The circumstances of his death are also uncertain, but we may presume that tradition is correct in calling him a martyr.

Of the four Gospel editions, Matthew's was the one most frequently used in the early church. The Fathers of the church quote with preference from this Gospel. Even in the very early Christian writings, texts from Matthew are cited extensively: the Didache (120?), Clement of Rome (c. 95), the Epistles of Barnabas (c. 120), the martyr Ignatius (c. 107), Polycarp (c. 120), Justin (c. 150), etc. We may conclude from this that Matthew's Gospel enjoyed a special place in the church and that, in fact, it was used as a textbook for catechetical instruction.

His liturgical feast is celebrated on September 21.

The Organization of Matthew's Gospel

When composing his Gospel edition, Matthew decided not to follow so much the actual sequence of events in Jesus' life (putting first what happened first), but to make an artificial arrangement of the material (grouping together what belongs together). He wanted to present Jesus as the new Moses, the new Messianic teacher. He arranged the material around five central sermons, no doubt in analogy to the five books of Moses. Schematically it looks like this:

Narrative	**Sermons**
ch. 1-2	
Jesus' infancy	
ch. 3-4	
The beginning of Jesus' public life	
	ch. 5-7
	Sermon on the Mount: Sanctity in God's Kingdom
ch. 8-9	
Ten miracles show Jesus' power and love	
	ch. 10
	The Apostolic Sermon: The apostles' mission to spread the Kingdom
ch. 11-12	
The Pharisees oppose Jesus' preaching	

Narrative	Sermons
	ch. 13
	The Sermon of Parables: The nature of the Kingdom explained
ch. 14-17	
Jesus trains Peter and the other apostles	
	ch. 18
	Hierarchical Sermon: The role of authority and its function in the Kingdom
ch. 19-23	
The Jews increasingly oppose Jesus	
	ch. 24-25
	The Sermon on Things to Come: The future of the Kingdom foretold
ch. 26-27	
Jesus sacrifices his life to initiate the Kingdom of the New Covenant	
ch. 28	
Jesus rises from the dead and promulgates the Kingdom	

Notice the similarity in the way each of the Sermons ends: "When Jesus finished saying these things . . ." (Mt 7:28); "When Jesus finished giving these instructions . . ." (Mt 11:1); "When Jesus finished telling these parables . . ." (Mt 13:53); "When Jesus finished saying these things . . ." (Mt 19:1); "When Jesus had finished teaching all these things . . ." (Mt 26:1).

Purpose and Principal Doctrines

Matthew wanted to impress on his fellow Jews in Palestine the important truth that Jesus Christ is the Messiah, promised in the Old Testament. Matthew shows this in a variety of ways. First, Jesus came from the family of David, thereby fulfilling the prophecy that the Messiah (the Redeemer) would be a descendant of David (see 2 Sm 7:8, 16; Mt 1:1, 6, 17, 20). Christ is often called "Son of David" in this Gospel (Mt 9:27, 12:23, 15:22, 20:30-32, 21:9, 15). Moreover, Matthew stresses that Jesus is the new Moses, sent in fulfillment of the prophecy by which God had promised that he would raise the Messiah as a new Moses (Dt 18:15-19). Just as Moses had promulgated the old Law on Sinai, so Jesus promulgates his law on a mountain (Mt 5:1). Instead of the Ten Commandments, he gives eight beatitudes (Mt 5:3-10). He explicitly refers to the old Law, perfecting the ancient precepts (Mt 5:17-48). Moses appears as Jesus' forerunner on the Mount of Transfiguration (Mt 17:3-4). Jesus abrogates the permission to divorce granted by Moses (Mt 19:3-9).

Further, when relating Jesus' words and actions, Matthew keeps pointing out Messianic prophecies that have been fulfilled in them. He frequently says that a certain event happened "in order to make what the Lord had said through the prophet come true." This list displays passages in Matthew which fulfill Old Testament prophecies:

Mt 1:22, 23	Jesus' birth of a virgin	Is 7:14
Mt 2:15	the flight to Egypt	Hos 11:1

Mt 2:18	the murder of the innocents	Jer 31:15
Mt 4:15-16	Jesus' ministry in Galilee	Is 9:1-2
Mt 8:17	Jesus' miraculous cures	Is 53:4
Mt 12:17-21	Jesus' unassuming leadership	Is 42:1-4
Mt 13:14-15	the blindness of the people	Is 6:9-10
Mt 13:35	Jesus' preaching in parables	Ps 78:2
Mt 21:4-5	Jesus riding on a donkey	Is 62:11; Zec 9:9
Mt 27:9-10	Judas' treachery	Zec 11:12

Matthew often cites the Old Testament in other ways:

This is what the prophet wrote. . . . (2:5)

The Scripture says. . . . (4:4, 5, 6, 7, 10, 11:10, 26:31)

It is written in the Scriptures. . . . (21:13)

Haven't you read the Scripture that says . . . ?
(19:4, 21:16, 42)

Haven't you read what God has told you . . . ? (22:31)

God said. . . . (15:4, 19:5)

The Jews for whom Matthew wrote his Gospel would have been very familiar with the writings of the Old Testament, and Matthew does his utmost to point out how those prophecies are fulfilled in the details of Jesus' life. For a similar reason he often quotes those sayings of Jesus in which Jesus himself refers to the Old Testament.

Matthew takes care to stress that Jesus is not a political Messiah (which many Jews were expecting), but that he is a Messiah with divine power. These are some of the themes in Matthew which bring out Jesus' divinity and equality with God the Father:

Jesus is greater than the Temple (Mt 12:6), than Jonah and Solomon (Mt 12:42), than David (Mt 22:41-46).

Jesus performs miracles, which only God can do, such as

stilling the storm (Mt 8:23-27) and raising Jairus' daughter (Mt 9:23-25).

God the Father testifies about him, "This is my Son" (Mt 3:17, 17:5).

Jesus knows all that the Father knows (Mt 11:27).

Jesus will judge mankind as only God can judge (Mt 16:27, 19:28, 24:27, 30-31, 25:31-46).

Jesus is, with the Father and the Holy Spirit, Almighty God, in whose name all men should be baptized (Mt 28:19).

Jesus also founded God's Kingdom, the church, which—in typical Jewish manner of speaking—is called "the Kingdom of heaven." He laid down many conditions for membership in this kingdom, and described the sanctity required in it. All five sermons in Matthew's Gospel speak of the Kingdom of heaven.

Gospel Passages Found Only in Matthew

The Gospel of Matthew contains much valuable information about Jesus and about his teaching which we do not find in the other Gospels. The following events in Jesus' public life are proper to Matthew alone:

The healing of the two blind men	(Mt 9:27-31)
The promise of the primacy to Peter	(Mt 16:17-19)
The tax paid by Jesus	(Mt 17:24-27)
The story of Judas' suicide	(Mt 27:3-10)
The guard at Jesus' sepulchre	(Mt 27:62-66)

Matthew also provides reflections on Jesus' infancy (Mt 1-2) and testimonies about the Resurrection (Mt 28:9-20) not found in other Gospels.

Moreover, Matthew has preserved for us parables and other teachings of Jesus which we would not otherwise know:

Parables

The City on a Hill (Mt 5:14)
The Pearls before Swine (Mt 7:6)

The Wolves in Sheep's Clothing (Mt 7:15)
The Fruit of the Fig Tree (Mt 7:16-20)
The Weeds Sown among Grain (Mt 13:24-30)
The Merchant Who Finds a Hidden Treasure (Mt 13:44)
The Merchant Who Finds the Pearl (Mt 13:45-46)
The Net Full of Good and Bad Fish (Mt 13:47-48)
The Householder and His Storeroom (Mt 13:52)
The Debtor Who Did Not Forgive His Fellow (Mt 18:23-35)
The Laborers in the Vineyard (Mt 20:1-16)
The Willing and Unwilling Sons (Mt 21:28-32)
The Wise and the Foolish Virgins (Mt 25:1-13)
The Division of the Sheep from the Goats (Mt 25:31-46)

Other Teachings

On Reconciliation before the Sacrifice (Mt 5:23-24)
On Avoiding Oaths (Mt 5:33-37)
On Practicing Virtue in Secret (Mt 6:1-8, 16-18)
On Taking Up His Yoke (Mt 11:28-30)
On Authority in the Church (Mt 18:15-20)
On the Value of Celibacy (Mt 19:10-12)

Matthew's Interest in Jesus' Words

We have already seen that Matthew composed his Gospel around five sermons of Jesus. This by itself shows how important in his eyes is Jesus' teaching. Furthermore, there are very few passages unique to Matthew which deal with events of Jesus' life. He did, however, preserve parables and instructions which we do not find in the other Gospels. All this demonstrates that Matthew was more interested in Jesus' teaching than in the details of Jesus' life. In his Gospel he gave precedence to Jesus' sayings and used the narrative sections mainly as the setting for these sayings. That is why Papias could say that Matthew made a collection of Jesus' words.

It is of the greatest importance to recognize Matthew's interest in Jesus' words, lest we misunderstand his purpose. For example, did Jesus really speak all the beautiful sayings found in

Matthew 5-7 on one occasion? The answer is no. Matthew collected many sayings spoken on different occasions, and put them in the Sermon on the Mount. The teaching is truly Jesus' teaching, but the setting and the organization is Matthew's. Matthew condensed many sermons on sanctity spoken by Christ into the one Sermon. This is nothing extraordinary. We in the same way collect poems of great writers, letters of politicians, and speeches of leaders. The Sermon on the Mount is such a collection of selected sayings of Jesus.

Matthew's special interest in Jesus' sayings also led to another characteristic trait of his writing. Whenever he narrates events, he tends to abbreviate them. See how Matthew and Mark tell of the same event:

Matthew 9:1-8	*Mark 2:1-12*
Jesus got into the boat and went back across the lake to his own town,	A few days later Jesus came back to Capernaum, and the news spread that he was at home. So many people came together that there was no room left, not even out in front of the door.
where some people brought to him a paralyzed man, lying on a bed.	Jesus was preaching the message to them, when four men arrived, carrying a paralyzed man to Jesus. Because of the crowd, however, they could not get the man to him. So they made a hole in the roof right above the place where Jesus was. When they had made an opening, they let the man down, lying on his mat.
When Jesus saw how much faith they had, he said to the paralyzed man,	Seeing how much faith they had, Jesus said to the paralyzed man, "My son, your

"Courage, my son! Your sins are forgiven." Then some teachers of the Law said to themselves, "This man is speaking blasphemy!"

sins are forgiven." Some teachers of the Law who were sitting there thought to themselves, "How does he dare to talk like this? This is blasphemy! God is the only one who can forgive sins!"

Jesus perceived what they were thinking, and so he said, "Why are you thinking such evil things? Is it easier to say, 'Your sins are forgiven,' or to say, 'Get up and walk?' I will prove to you, then, that the Son of Man has authority on earth to forgive sins."

At once Jesus knew what they were thinking, so he said to them, "Why do you think such things? Is it easier to say to this paralyzed man, 'Your sins are forgiven,' or to say, 'Get up, pick up your mat, and walk?' I will prove to you, then, that the Son of Man has authority on earth to forgive sins."

So he said to the paralyzed man, "Get up, pick up your bed, and go home!"

So he said to the paralyzed man, "I tell you, get up, pick up your mat, and go home!"

The man got up and went home.

While they all watched, the man got up, picked up his mat, and hurried away.

Many details are purposely omitted by Matthew. He does not tell us about the great rush to hear Jesus' preaching. He does not say that the paralyzed man was carried by four friends. He does not even mention the extraordinary way in which they bring the paralyzed man to Jesus' feet. Matthew makes the story as short as possible. His real interest does not lie with the first part of the narrative, which recounts the circumstances, but with Jesus' words, which are not at all abbreviated.

The following passages of Matthew, with their parallels in Mark, also demonstrate Matthew's tendency to shorten narration:

Exorcizing the Gadarenes	(Mt 8:28-34; Mk 5:1-20)
Raising Jairus' daughter	(Mt 9:18-26; Mk 5:21-43)
John the Baptist's death	(Mt 14:1-12; Mk 6:14-29)
The cure of the epileptic	(Mt 17:14-21; Mk 9:14-28)
The question of the Law	(Mt 22:34-40; Mk 12:28-34)
Preparing the Last Supper	(Mt 26:17-20; Mk 14:12-17)

Matthew's Gospel presents us with a complete life of Jesus, from his birth to his death and Resurrection, but throughout the Gospel we should remember to pay special attention to Jesus as the great teacher, for this is what Matthew—under the inspiration of the Holy Spirit—wanted to stress in his edition of the Gospel.

Typically Jewish Ways of Speaking

In his preaching Jesus would have used many typically Jewish ways of speaking. Matthew composed his Gospel for Jewish readers. Small wonder, then, that he preserved many sayings of Christ in the characteristic Jewish form.

The Jews had great respect for and fear of God's name. Had not God commanded them not to take his name in vain? Taking this commandment very literally, the Jews avoided pronouncing God's name at all times and in all circumstances. Instead, they used indirect ways of speaking about God. Matthew preserves Jesus' indirect references to God very carefully (Mt 4:17, 6:9, 7:11, 16:1, 21:9, 25, 25:31, 26:64). Instead of saying "God," Jesus would use words such as "Heaven," "Power," "Glory," "Name," "the Highest," etc. The Jews (to whom Jesus was speaking) would immediately understand the meaning of such expressions.

Another way in which the Jews avoided using God's name in speech was to phrase the sentence in the passive voice. If, for instance, a father wanted to bless his daughter at marriage, he would not say, "May God give you many children!" but rather "May many children be given to you!" In the second form,

"God" is not mentioned, but, because of the passive voice, the Jews would immediately understand that God was meant, and that his name had been omitted out of reverence and respect. Such a passive is called a theophoric passive, i.e., a passive which in its meaning carries God as the author. Jews used this way of speaking quite often, and Matthew has preserved it (Mt 5:4, 7, 6:7, 6:33, 7:1-2).

The following example illustrates Jewish phrasing well. To "loose" and to "bind" means to "declare something forbidden or allowed." "In heaven" stands for "with God." Moreover, there is the theophoric passive. Finally, the statement is repeated (appearing both in its negative and positive forms), another characteristic of Jewish speech.

Text
Whatever you bind on earth shall be bound in heaven, and whatever you loose on earth shall be loosed in heaven. (to Peter, Mt 16:19; to the apostles, Mt 18:18)

The Meaning
Whatever you forbid, God also forbids. Whatever you allow, God will allow.

THREE

The Gospel of Mark

PAPIAS, A BISHOP of the early second century, gives some information about Mark's Gospel in a fragment of writing about the Gospels. The Presbyter he cites may be the apostle John:

> The Presbyter said this also, "Mark, having been the interpreter of Peter, wrote down carefully, though not in order, all that he remembered, both words and deeds of the Lord! For he had neither heard the Lord, nor followed him, but only at a later date, as I have already said, followed Peter. Peter arranged his instructions according to the needs [of his audience] and not as making [a continuous and exhaustive] arrangement of the Lord's words. So Mark was not wrong to write down some things as he remembered them, for he took care to omit or falsify nothing which he had heard [from Peter]."

Notice the chain of tradition—Papias, who writes in 130, testifies to what The Presbyter (the apostle John) had said, probably in the period from 80-90. John goes back to Mark's own time. The tradition notes that the occasion of the edition was to preserve Peter's teaching; that Mark's source was Peter, not Jesus himself; that Mark's way of writing was to arrange the material not in time sequence but in sequence of memory; and that Mark is reliable—he did not omit or falsify anything. This testimony of Papias is confirmed by the other early Christian writers—Clement of Alexandria (150-215), Origen (186-254), Tertullian (160-240), and others. They tell us that Mark assisted Peter in his preaching at Rome and that the Roman converts requested Mark to write down what Peter was preaching. Internal evidence from the Gospel itself harmonizes with this information from tradition.

Mark's Life

We know much about Mark from the other New Testament writings. Piecing together all the bits of information provided in these writings, we can attempt a reconstruction of his life.

John (Acts 13:5), also called John Mark (Acts 12:12, 15:37), was a cousin of Barnabas (Col 4:10). Like Barnabas, he must have been a Levite, that is, belonging to a priestly family, and his home may have been in Cyprus (Acts 4:36f). We can be fairly sure that he received a strictly Jewish education at home and that he learned to speak both the Aramaic of his Jewish parents and the Greek spoken in Cyprus. Mark's absence from Palestine during his youth may account for the fact that he had never heard Jesus (see Papias' testimony). At some later date, however, the family must have moved to Jerusalem. No doubt, they had some family property there. At Jerusalem, Barnabas accepted the Christian faith. He sold his property and gave it to the apostles for distribution among the poor (Acts 4:36-37).

The Acts of the Apostles does not tell of Mark's conversion, but we may assume that it must have taken place at about the same time as Barnabas'. Mark was converted by Peter, perhaps in 38 A.D. This we know from Peter's first letter, in which he calls Mark his "son," which—in the language of the apostles—indicates a person who received the faith through them (1 Pt 5:13). From the beginning, the newly converted family proved very active followers of Christ. Barnabas was a great help to Paul immediately after Paul's vision of Christ on the way to Damascus (Acts 9:27), and Mark's mother, Mary, had offered her house in Jerusalem as a meeting place for the early Christian community. After his miraculous escape from prison, Peter went straight to this house, knowing that he would find the others there (Acts 12:12-17).

In the meantime Barnabas and Paul had begun their apostolate in Antioch (north of Palestine). On one of their trips to Jerusalem, around 45 A.D., they must have met Mark and requested him to join them. Mark left his mother's home in Jerusalem and went to Antioch (Acts 12:25).

Paul and Barnabas were ordained (Acts 13:1-3) and went on a missionary tour to the island of Cyprus. We need not be surprised that they took Mark with them; both he and Barnabas must have been well acquainted with conditions there (Acts 13:4-5). After some time, they left Cyprus and sailed to Asia Minor. For some unknown reason Mark left them there and travelled back to Jerusalem (Acts 13:13). Had he been disappointed by the difficulties of the apostolic work? Did he receive news about his family which made his return essential? We do not know.

Whatever the reason for Mark's departure may have been, Paul disapproved of it. So, in 50 A.D., when the planning for another missionary tour began, some argument arose between Paul and Barnabas. Paul—who was apparently very strong-willed—refused to take Mark as a companion a second time. Barnabas, however, insisted that Mark should be taken. As a result, two different itineraries were decided upon. Paul and Silas went to Asia Minor; Barnabas and Mark sailed for Cyprus (Acts 15:36-41).

Exact information about Mark's life after 60 A.D. is lacking. All we know is that he became Peter's helper. In the letter which Peter wrote from Rome to the Christians in Asia Minor, he said, "Your sister church in Babylon [i.e., Rome] . . . sends you greetings, and so does my son Mark" (1 Pt 5:13).

At about the same time, around 61 A.D., Paul was taken to Rome and put in custody on account of the accusations made against him by the Palestinian Pharisees. Mark was a great help to Paul, and it is a joy to see how these two great men remained intimate friends, in spite of their earlier misunderstandings. Paul writes warmly of Mark:

Aristarchus, who is in prison with me, sends you greetings, and so does Mark, the cousin of Barnabas. (You have already received instructions to welcome Mark if he comes your way.) (Col 4:10)

Epaphras, who is in prison with me for the sake of Christ Jesus, sends you his greetings, and so do my fellow workers Mark, Aristarchus, Demas, and Luke. (Phlm 23-24)

Mark must have composed his edition of the gospel during his stay in Rome, around 64 A.D. Clement of Alexandria recounts the following tradition:

This was the occasion of Mark's Gospel. When Peter had publicly preached the word in Rome, and had taught the gospel in the Spirit, his numerous hearers are supposed to have asked Mark to write down the things which Peter preached. For he had accompanied Peter for a long time and remembered his words. Mark is said to have agreed to their request, and to have given them the Gospel. When Peter learned of it, he neither forbade it, nor encouraged it.

The last sentence is interesting. For the early Christians the memorized learning of the gospel was the most important thing. Peter did not mind Mark writing down such memorized traditions, but he would expect Christians to learn the gospel by heart nonetheless.

By 66 A.D., Peter had been killed under the persecution of Nero. Paul was in Rome, undergoing his second imprisonment. It seems that Mark was away in Asia Minor, probably on some apostolic work. Writing to Timothy, bishop of Ephesus, Paul says, "Only Luke is with me. Get Mark and bring him with you, because he can help me in the work" (2 Tm 4:11).

This is the last information we have about Mark. He is said to have founded a church in Alexandria, and to have been its first bishop, but there is no certain evidence of this. An even less reliable tradition suggests that Mark was the young man who fled from Gethsemane (Mk 14:51), and that Mark's mother's house was the scene of the Last Supper. This, however, would seem to contradict most of the available information concerning when Mark entered into the Christian fellowship.

Though Mark was not an immediate disciple of Jesus, he was well qualified to write his Gospel. His conversion took place in the first years after Christ's Resurrection. Since his family was then living in Jerusalem, he could ascertain the Lord's deeds and statements from the very best sources. For more than twenty years he worked in close cooperation with the leading apostles—Peter, Paul, and Barnabas. He must have been extremely familiar with their catechetical teaching.

Mark's liturgical feast is celebrated on the 25th of April.

The Organization of Mark's Gospel

Everything in his Gospel points to the fact that Mark adhered as closely as possible to the oral preaching of the apostles. There are no clear divisions in it, and commentators disagree as to how Mark himself wants us to group the material. But all are agreed on the fact that Mark arranged the material on a geographical basis, according to the regions in which Jesus worked. The most probable division for the Gospel is 1) an introduction (1:1-13); 2) Jesus' ministry in Galilee (1:14-6:6a); 3) the missionary journeys (6:6b-10:52); 4) Jesus' ministry in Jerusalem (11:1-15:47); 5) the Resurrection (16:1-8); 6) an appendix (16:9-20).

Characteristic phrases help us identify the beginning of the journeys:

After John had been put in prison, Jesus went to Galilee.
(1:14)

Then Jesus went to the villages around there. (6:6b)

He said to them, "Let us go off by ourselves to some place where we will be alone. (6:31)

Then Jesus left and went away to the territory near the city of Tyre. (7:24)

He left them, got back into the boat, and started across to the other side of the lake. (8:13)

Then Jesus left that place, went to the province of Judea, and crossed the Jordan River. (10:1)

Peter's Testimony

The special merit of Mark's Gospel lies in the fact that it contains the preaching of Peter. No doubt, the content is almost identical with what was generally preached in the early church by all the apostles, but we can still discover the special flavor of Peter's own testimony.

In Mark, the public life of Jesus begins with the call of Peter (1:16-18). The detailed description of Jesus' first appearance in Capernaum, the great impression he made in the synagogue when preaching (1:21-22) and when curing the possessed man (1:23-28), Jesus' stay in Peter's house (1:29-32), the miracle he performed that same evening (1:32-34), Jesus' prayer outside the city and how he went to preach in other villages in spite of Peter's objection—all these reflect the manner in which Peter recounted his first contact with Jesus. We can well imagine how enthusiastically the old apostle would speak about it: "I still remember how he came once along the side of the lake. . . . We were fishing. . . . He called us. . . . The next Sabbath he preached in our synagogue. . . ," etc.

Peter ranks first in the list of the apostles; and Mark specifically mentions that Peter received his new name directly from Jesus (3:16). The apostles are sometimes referred to as "Simon and those with him" (1:36). Peter was also chosen by Christ to be—along with James and John—the witness of certain special events—the raising of Jairus' daughter (5:37), the Transfiguration (9:2), Jesus' sermons on the future (13:3), Jesus' agony in Gethsemane (14:33-37). Only the immediate eyewitnesses could be the ultimate source of preaching on these events. Though these events were the common content of the apostolic preaching, in Peter's own preaching they must have been especially vivid.

Mark frequently relates particular statements Peter made.

When Jesus questions the disciples about himself, it is Peter who declares, "You are the Messiah!" (8:27-30).

At the Transfiguration, it is Peter who speaks up and says, "Teacher, how good it is that we are here" (9:2-9).

It is Peter who says to Jesus, "Look, we have left everything and followed you" (10:28).

And again, it is Peter who points out to Jesus, "Look, Teacher, the fig tree you cursed has died!" (11:12-14, 20-21). In Matthew's account, this remark is attributed to the disciples in general.

At the Last Supper Peter boasts, "I will never leave you, even though all the rest do!" and later says even more strongly "I will never deny you, even if I have to die with you" (14:29, 31).

We may also see a trace of Peter's own testimony in Mark's Gospel in the fact that certain praiseworthy actions of his are omitted, such as his walking on the water (Mt 14:28-32). Similarly, Peter's shortcomings are stressed. Mark relates how Jesus has to rebuke Peter (8:31-33), and gives many details of Peter's denial of Jesus (14:27-31, 66-72).

Peter's testimony influenced and shaped Mark's presentation of Jesus' life. Mark's Gospel, then, is an introduction to Jesus Christ by an eyewitness (Peter) through the typical process of oral tradition.

Characteristics of Mark's Gospel

Of all the Gospels, Mark's is the shortest. It concentrates on Jesus' deeds rather than on his words. As a result, it has very few passages which are not also found in the other Gospels. However, there are some—Jesus' relatives' concern for him (3:20-21), the parable of the seed growing by itself (4:26-29), healing of the deaf and dumb man (7:31-37), the cure of a blind man at Bethsaida (8:22-26), the young man at Gethsemane

(14:51-52). Even when Mark narrates the same events as those narrated in other Gospels, he often gives many more details (as in the story of the paralyzed man).

When Mark describes the calming of the storm, he adds that "Jesus was in the back of the boat, sleeping with his head on a pillow" (compare Mk 4:38 with Mt 8:24 and Lk 8:23).

When describing the choosing of the Twelve, only Mark says of James and John, the sons of Zebedee, that "Jesus gave them the name of Boanerges, which means 'Men of Thunder'" (compare Mk 3:17 with Mt 10:2 and Lk 6:14).

Only Mark tells us that the blind man at Jericho was "named Bartimaeus, son of Timaeus" (compare Mk 10:46 with Mt 20:30 and Lk 18:35).

When describing the cure of the man with the withered hand, only Mark relates that "Jesus was angry as he looked around at them, but at the same time he felt sorry for them, because they were so stubborn and wrong" (compare Mk 3:1-5 with Mt 12:9-13 and Lk 6:6-10).

Phases of Introducing Christ. Christ is introduced to us in two distinct phases by Mark. During the first phase we follow Christ as he performs his miracles and preaches his message. In this phase we are amazed by Jesus' greatness, but we do not understand what or who he is. Jesus does not reveal himself as the Messiah, but, on the contrary, he avoids all popular propaganda.

In this first phase, the people react to Jesus with surprise:

The people who heard him were amazed at the way he taught. (1:22)

The people were all so amazed that they started saying to one another, "What is this? . . . This man has authority to give orders to the evil spirits, and they obey him!" (1:27)

[They said] to one another, "Who is this man? Even the wind and the waves obey him!" (4:41)

All who heard it were amazed. (5:20)

When this happened, they were completely amazed. (5:42)

And all who heard it were completely amazed. "How well he does everything!" they exclaimed. (7:37)

Jesus' words and actions gradually revealed to others that he was more than just a man. But, in this first phase of his ministry, Jesus wanted to keep his Messiahship a secret:

> Whenever the people who had evil spirits in them saw him, they would fall down before him and scream, "You are the Son of God!"
> Jesus sternly ordered the evil spirits not to tell anyone who he was. (3:11-12)

> Then Jesus ordered the people not to speak of it [the miracle] to anyone; but the more he ordered them not to, the more they told it. (7:36)

> Jesus sent him [the blind man] home with the order "Don't go back into the village." (8:26)

> [Jesus said to the cured leper] "Listen, don't tell anyone about this." (1:44)

Jesus did not want his ministry to be mistaken for a political movement. Since the Jews were expecting a political Messiah who would liberate them from the Romans, Jesus first wanted everyone to grasp his spiritual message and his interest in spiritual salvation before revealing his true nature.

The turning point in Jesus' mode of action came with a frank discussion Jesus had with his disciples. In this discussion he made them think about his own person, and he drew from them the first acknowledgment of who he really is.

> Then Jesus and his disciples went away to the villages near Caesarea Philippi. On the way he asked them, "Tell me, who do people say I am?"
> "Some say that you are John the Baptist," they answered,

"others say that you are Elijah, while others say that you are one of the prophets."

"What about you?" he asked them, "Who do you say I am?"

Peter answered, "You are the Messiah."

Then Jesus ordered them, "Do not tell anyone about me."

(8:27-30)

We may imagine the tremendous impact this conversation had on Peter and the other disciples. Jesus had admitted that he was the promised Redeemer who would save his people. The disciples understood that Jesus did not have any political ambitions. They realized that Jesus was going to be a Messiah of a different type than the one expected by the people. But what precisely was his salvation going to be?

The second and final phase of Jesus' self-revelation may be called the phase of the "Son of Man." For in explaining the true nature of his Messianic mission Jesus chose this particular term, rather than any other.

The term *Son of Man* (*Bar enosh* in Aramaic) is derived from the prophecy of Daniel, in which the glorious Messiah is called "Son of Man" (Dn 7:13). But the picture of the Son of Man that Jesus applied to himself embodies features taken also from the prophecies of Isaiah, where it had been foretold that the Messiah was to be a suffering servant (Is 42-53). Thus the term, as used by Jesus, includes both the glorious dignity of the Messiah (Daniel) and his sacrificial task (Isaiah).

When Jesus used this term he always used it about himself:

The Son of Man must suffer much and be rejected by the elders, the chief priests, and the teachers of the Law. He will be put to death, but three days later he will rise to life. (8:31)

If a person is ashamed of me and of my teaching in this godless and wicked day, then the Son of Man will be ashamed of him when he comes in the glory of his Father with the holy angels. (8:38)

Why do the Scriptures say the Son of Man will suffer much and be rejected? (9:12)

The Son of Man will be handed over to men who will kill him. Three days later, however, he will rise to life. (9:31)

We are going up to Jerusalem where the Son of Man will be handed over to the chief priests and the teachers of the Law. They will condemn him to death and then hand him over to the Gentiles, who will make fun of him, spit on him, whip him, and kill him; but three days later he will rise to life. (10:33-34)

The Son of Man did not come to be served; he came to serve and to give his life to redeem many people. (10:45)

Compare these passages, and especially the last, with this passage from Isaiah:

He was arrested and sentenced and led off to die,
    and no one cared about his fate.
He was put to death for the sins of our people . . .
    his death was a sacrifice to bring forgiveness. (Is 53:8, 10)

Other passages in Mark echo the vision of Daniel 7:13 (see Mk 13:26; 14:61-62).

Mark introduces Jesus gradually, following the pattern of Jesus' own self-revelation. He shows us Jesus' marvelous deeds, which catch our attention and amazement, so that we want to know more about him. Then he puts before us a picture of Jesus' mission as the Son of Man. This could well reflect Peter's own experience of Jesus: Peter first came to know Jesus because of his marvelous deeds; gradually he came to see and acknowledge that Jesus is the Messiah (8:27-30); then he began to appreciate Jesus' true mission as the Son of Man.

Style. Another characteristic of Mark's Gospel is his very spontaneous and lively style of portraying events. He presents them as scenes in a drama. It is not very hard to imagine many extracts from Mark as dramatic scripts.

> (It happened in Jericho. Jesus with his disciples and a large crowd are all leaving the city. A blind man named Bartimaeus, son of Timaeus, sits begging by the roadside.)

Bartimaeus:	(hearing that it is Jesus of Nazareth, shouts) Jesus! Son of David! Have mercy on me! (The passersby scold him and tell him to be quiet.)
Bartimaeus:	(shouting even more loudly) Son of David, take pity on me!
Jesus:	(stops, says to bystanders) Call him.
Bystanders:	(calling to blind man) Cheer up! Get up, he is calling you. (Bartimaeus throws off cloak, jumps up, comes to Jesus.)
Jesus:	What do you want me to do for you?
Bartimaeus:	Teacher, I want to see again.
Jesus:	Go, your faith has made you well. (At once Bartimaeus is able to see and follows Jesus.)

(Mk 10:46-52)

Almost everything in the above extract is as it appears in Mark's Gospel.

The characteristic features of Mark—the extra episodes, his interest in descriptive detail, and his dramatic presentation— would all be consistent with the influence of an eyewitness. Irenaeus, writing around 180 A.D., says, "Mark, the disciple and interpreter of Peter, left us Peter's teaching in writing." When reading Mark, we are listening to Peter.

FOUR

The Gospel of Luke

ANCIENT TRADITION is unanimous in ascribing the third Gospel to Luke. Unfortunately, we do not have the complete text of Bishop Papias' testimony on the gospel editions, so we do not know what he said about Luke. Irenaeus (c. 180) tells us, "Luke, Paul's companion, put down in his book the gospel which Paul preached." We find more information in a second-or third-century treatise known as the Anti-Marcionite Prologue:

> There is Luke, a native of Antioch in Syria, a medical doctor by profession, a disciple of the apostles. Afterwards he was a companion of Paul until Paul's martyrdom. He served the Lord with full dedication. He died at eighty-four years of age without wife or children, in Boeotia, full of the Holy Spirit. Gospels had already been written by Matthew in Judea and by Mark in Rome. Luke, inspired by the Holy Spirit, wrote this Gospel in the neighborhood of Achaia [near Athens in Greece].

Luke is distinguished from the other evangelists in many ways. He was not a Jew, but a Gentile convert from Antioch. He was a highly cultured man. As a medical doctor he knew Greek science. He wrote his Gospel in the center of Greek civilization (Achaia). We find more, similar information about Luke in the so-called Muratorian Canon (120?), in the writings of Clement of Alexandria (150-215), Tertullian (160-240), Origen (186-254), and others. All agree that Luke himself was not an eyewitness of Christ's ministry, but that he took great care to find out the facts from the apostles and from others who did know Christ in his lifetime.

Luke's Life

We learn a considerable amount about Luke from the New Testament itself. Especially helpful in this regard are the passages in the Acts of the Apostles which are written in the first person plural. In these, Luke writes about events at which he himself was present (see Acts 16:10-17, 20:5-21:18, 27:1-28:16). The letters of Paul are another source of information, and, of course, Luke's Gospel itself adds some detail to the picture we can build up from the other sources. In this way we can reconstruct Luke's life.

His writing shows him to have been an educated Greek, and as such he would have enjoyed sports, discussions, poetry, and art. He may have moved in literary circles. He also seems to have had a kindly nature.

The town of Antioch was one of the first great Christian centers outside Palestine. After the martyrdom of Stephen, Jewish converts moved to Antioch to avoid persecution. There they began to spread their new faith to non-Jews, and many were baptized (see Acts 11:19-21). As the community grew, the apostles at Jerusalem appointed Barnabas and Paul to look after this young church. Antioch became the missionary center for the conversion of non-Jews. It was from here that Paul and Barnabas started on their journeys (see Acts 13:1-3). Because of the circumstances of its own beginnings, Antioch became identified with the "progressive" attitude that converts did not need to become Jews before they could become Christians. It was in Antioch itself that the famous argument between Peter and Paul took place (see Gal 2:11-21). At the Council of Jerusalem, the "progressive theologians" were the delegates from Antioch (see Acts 15:1-5 and Gal 2:1-10). When James settled the matter, saying it was not necessary to be a Jew before becoming a Christian, the council sent a letter of encouragement to Antioch (see Acts 15:22-35).

It was in the atmosphere of this dynamic church community that Luke himself became a Christian, possibly about 45-50 A.D. This would help to explain the missionary enthusiasm in his writing, which was probably first sparked into life by contact with Peter, Paul, Barnabas, and Mark. From Antioch, Luke must have moved to Troas.

When Paul and Silas started out on their missionary trip to Asia Minor, around 50 A.D., they met Luke in Troas. It was here that Paul had the vision of a man who begged them to come to Macedonia. Luke records their enthusiasm:

> As soon as Paul had this vision, we got ready to leave for Macedonia, because we decided that God had called us to preach the Good News to the people there. (Acts 16:9-10)

It was at this point that Luke's vocation as a missionary began. He accompanied Paul and Silas by boat to Macedonia, then inland to Philippi.

Luke himself recounts how the Christian community came to be established at Philippi (Acts 16:11-40). The first converts were pious Jews, among them a woman called Lydia, at whose house the apostles stayed. By casting out an evil spirit, they incurred the hostility of the local people, and Paul and Silas ended up in prison. They were miraculously delivered, which led to the conversion of their jailer and his family. Later, the authorities released Paul and Silas, and they continued on their way through Greece. Luke remained at Philippi to serve the new church. He spent six years there, from 50-57 A.D., gaining valuable pastoral experience.

Paul returned to Philippi around 57 A.D. during his third missionary journey, and this time Luke returned to Jerusalem with him, visiting the Christian communities at Troas, Miletus, Ephesus, Tyre, and Caesarea on the way (Acts 20:5-21:16). They were warmly welcomed in Jerusalem by James, the bishop of Jerusalem, and by the whole community, and Paul gave a complete report of their mission. It was not long before Paul found himself in trouble again, this time stirred up by Jews who accused him of defiling the Temple. Paul was arrested and imprisoned, first in Jerusalem and then (for two years) in Caesarea. It would seem that Luke stayed with Paul throughout all this time, helping him as much as he could (Acts 20:18-26:32).

After defending himself before King Agrippa, Paul was finally sent by Governor Felix to Rome, still as a prisoner. Luke went with Paul on what proved to be a very dangerous journey, sailing through a storm and eventually being shipwrecked near Malta. It was a great relief for them to reach Rome, where they were welcomed by the Roman Christians (Acts 26:1-28:16).

After his arrival in Rome, Paul was able to continue preaching, in spite of being a "private prisoner" (Acts 28: 16-30). We know that Luke helped him in this because Paul wrote to Philemon describing Like as one of his fellow workers (Phlm 24), and similarly to the Colossians (Col 4:14).

We do not know precisely what happened after Paul's release from prison. It is thought that Luke may have written his Gospel during this period, around 63 A.D., perhaps while revisiting the churches in Greece. Similarly, he may have written the Acts of the Apostles, as a continuation of his Gospel, at this time.

During Paul's second imprisonment, from 66-67 A.D., we find Luke once more at his side. In fact he seems to have been Paul's only companion at this time. Paul wrote to Timothy:

Do your best to come to me soon. Demas fell in love with this present world and has deserted me, going off to Thessalonica. Crescens went to Galatia, and Titus to Dalmatia. Only Luke is with me. (2 Tm 4:9-11)

Some scripture scholars think that Luke wrote his Gospel and the Acts of the Apostles during this period, or perhaps even after Paul's death. Nothing is known for certain about Luke's last years, and there are various different traditions. According to some sources he died as a martyr.

Luke's liturgical feast is celebrated on October 18.

The Composition of Luke's Gospel

If we study this Gospel carefully it would seem that Luke probably got the material for his book from three sources.

Some parts are very similar to parts of Mark and Matthew. This suggests the common catechetical teaching, source *M* (M from "original Mark").

Other parts are very similar to parts of Matthew, but not found in Mark. This suggests that Luke and Matthew shared a common collection of verbal traditions, source *Q* (Q from *Quelle*, the German for source).

Still other parts are peculiar to Luke and known as *L*.

We can reconstruct to some extent how Luke composed his Gospel. Luke followed the basic arrangement of *M*, so that he has many passages parallel to and in exactly the same order as Mark. To this basis, Luke added a series of passages derived from *Q* and *L*. The most important addition is the "journey to Jerusalem," which is almost entirely composed from *Q* and *L*. Luke omitted the smaller journeys which appear in Mark (Mk 6:45-8:26). Luke's Gospel can be schematized as follows:

Proper to Luke	*Parallel to Matthew and Mark*
1:1-4: Foreword	
1:5-2:52: Infancy	
	3:1-9:50: Ministry in Galilee
9:51-19:27: Journey to Jerusalem (Also draws on *Q*)	
	19:28-23:56: Ministry in Jerusalem
24:1-53: Resurrection	

Throughout his Gospel, Luke makes Jerusalem symbolic and gives it a special theological significance. It is in Jerusalem that Luke places the beginning of the Messianic era, with the promise of the birth of John the Baptist to Zechariah (1:5-25). Luke alone tells us that Jesus was taken as an infant to be presented in the Temple and again when he was twelve years old (2:22-38, 2:41-50). In his account of the Transfiguration only Luke adds an explicit allusion to dying in Jerusalem (9:31). Jesus' decision to go to Jerusalem is presented in a solemn way, and thereafter there are constant references to this decision (9:53, 13:22, 17:11, 19:11, 19:28). During this journey to Jerusalem Jesus mentions the city several times, foretelling its destruction (13:1-5, 19:41-44), and foretelling his own suffering there (18:31-34). It is Jesus' entrance into Jerusalem that marks the beginning of the end (19:28-40). While in the city, he again foretells its destruction (21:20-24, 23:27-31). After the Resurrection it is to Jerusalem that the disciples who were travelling to Emmaus return (24:13-35). Jesus appears to the disciples in Jerusalem and instructs them to preach to all nations beginning in Jerusalem (24:36-39). It is in Jerusalem that Luke draws his Gospel to a conclusion (24:52-53).

Some of the best-known parables of Jesus are preserved only in Luke's edition of the gospel.

1.	The parable of the Rich Fool	12:13-21
2.	The parable of the Unfruitful Fig Tree	13:6-9
3.	The parable of the Man Who Built a Tower	14:28-30
4.	The parable of the King Who Went to Battle 14:31-33	
5.	The parable of the Lost Coin	15:8-10
6.	The parable of the Prodigal Son	15:11-32
7.	The parable of the Unjust Steward	16:1-8
8.	The parable of the Rich Man and Lazarus	16:19-31

Luke places all these parables in the context of the journey up to Jerusalem.

Luke's Foreword

We should pay special attention to Luke's introduction to his Gospel (1:1-4):

Dear Theophilus! Many people have done their best to write a report of the things that have taken place among us. They wrote what we have been told by those who saw things from the beginning and proclaimed the message. And so, Your Excellency, because I have carefully studied all these matters from their beginning, I thought it would be good to write an orderly account for you. I do this so that you will know the full truth about everything which you have been taught.

Who was Theophilus? His Greek name literally means "lover of God." He is later referred to as "Your Excellency," so he was probably some distinguished official, who seems to have asked for information. The other people who have "done their best" are Matthew, Mark, and other (private) Gospel editors. Mark and Matthew present the preaching of the apostles who themselves were eyewitnesses. Luke admits that he is not an eyewitness but that he intends to present a systematic summary of the apostles' preaching, having investigated it very thoroughly. In other words, Luke intends his Gospel to expand and give further information about the apostles' preaching.

This foreword tells us two fundamental things about Luke's Gospel. Luke's Gospel presupposes the existence of cate-

chetical teaching. Its purpose is to provide further reading. In
this respect Luke's Gospel differs from those of Matthew and
Mark, which were intended for catechetical use (teaching about
the Christian faith) and for liturgical use (to be read aloud in the
Christian assembly). In contrast, Luke's Gospel is presented
for personal reading.

We also learn that Luke's Gospel is meant to explain the
teaching of the apostles to Greek converts. Mark and Matthew
present the basic preaching of the apostles principally in a
Jewish context. By addressing his Gospel to Theophilus, a
Greek, Luke is making it clear that while he is presenting the
teaching of Jesus and the preaching of the apostles, he is doing
so in a way that Gentiles would better understand. Luke,
himself a convert from a Gentile background, is ideally suited to
resolve the difficulties that Gentiles might meet. Luke is not
opposing the original teaching, but is confirming it and explaining it.

Characteristics of Luke's Gospel

Luke, the Gentile convert, stressed two themes in his Gospel:
salvation is for everyone, and the good news is truly *good*. We
should receive it with joy.

Salvation for All Mankind. Given Luke's purpose of
confirming the faith of the new Gentile converts it is not
surprising that he emphasizes those aspects of Jesus' teaching
which show him as the Savior of all men. Mark and Matthew
include the universality of Christ's salvation in their Gospels,
but Luke makes it the main theme of his. In so doing, Luke
re-echoes the preaching of Paul, the great apostle of the
Gentiles, with whom he had so much contact. These are some
features from Luke's Gospel which highlight this universality:

In Luke's genealogy of Jesus he traces Jesus' ancestors back
to Adam, the father of all mankind (3:23-38). Matthew, in
contrast, goes back only to Abraham (Mt 1:1).

Only Luke mentions that Jesus' birth coincided with the

census of the whole Roman Empire, that is to say, the whole of the known civilized world (2:1-7).

When the angels announce Jesus' birth they sing that it will mean "peace on earth to those with whom God is pleased," not only to the Jews, but to all (2:14).

When Jesus is presented in the Temple, Simeon speaks of the "salvation which you have prepared in the presence of all peoples: a light to reveal your will to the Gentiles" (2:25-35).

Luke dates the beginning of Jesus' public ministry by reference to the Jewish rulers but adds that it was "the fifteenth year of the rule of Emperor Tiberius" (3:1).

In his description of John the Baptist's preaching, Luke has him quote one more line from Isaiah than the other evangelists (Is 40:3-5), "All mankind will see God's salvation!" (3:6).

Luke quotes Jesus' last message to his disciples: the message about repentance and the forgiveness of sins must be "preached to all nations" (24:47).

Of the synoptics, Luke alone includes encounters of Jesus with Samaritans. In contrast to the contempt and hostility with which the Jews usually treated these people, Jesus is seen acting with kindness and concern: Jesus rebukes the disciples when they want to call down fire on a Samaritan village that had refused them accommodation (9:51-56); of the ten lepers healed by Jesus the only one who returns to give thanks is a Samaritan (17:11-19); Jesus illustrates his teaching on Christian love with the parable of the Good Samaritan (10:25-37).

Luke has also taken a particular interest in noting down the words and deeds of Jesus concerning women. It may be that in the common catechetical teaching the role of women in the church had not been sufficiently explained. What was Jesus' attitude towards women? Did they have a place in his affection? Did they have a part to play in Jesus' plan of salvation? Luke points out some women in a way that speaks for itself.

Mary occupies a prominent place in Luke's Gospel, and he underlines the uniqueness of her vocation (1:26-56, 2:5-7, 16-19, 21-22, 34-35, 48-52, 11:27-28). Elizabeth is mentioned with high esteem (1:5-6, 13, 24-25, 39-45, 57ff), as is the prophetess Anna (2:36-38). Jesus' heart is filled with pity for the widow of Nain (7:11-17) and he converts and consoles Mary Magdalene (7:36-50).

Luke explicitly mentions that as Jesus travels through the towns and villages preaching, he is accompanied by Mary Magdalene, Joanna, Susanna, and many other women (8:1-3). Martha and Mary welcome Jesus into their home (10:38-42). Jesus cures the crippled woman (13:10-13). On his way to die Jesus meets and speaks to the weeping women of Jerusalem (23:27-31). Luke also mentions the women we know from the Gospels of Matthew and Mark (4:38-39, 8:43-48, 21:1-4, 23:49, 24:1-12). No doubt Luke wanted to stress this aspect of Jesus' ministry for pastoral reasons. The part played by Mary and other women in Jesus' plan of salvation has been so vividly described by Luke that it is an inexhaustible source of meditation and inspiration to our own day.

Another particular aspect of Luke's Gospel is the way he notes special events in Jesus' life which characterize him as a loving Savior: the conversion of Mary Magdalene (7:36-50); the conversion of Zacchaeus (19:1-10); Jesus' weeping over Jerusalem (19:41-44; see also 13:34-35); his prayer for his executioners (23:34); his promise to the good thief (23:39-43); his conversation with the disciples on the way to Emmaus (24:13-35).

Jesus is the loving Savior of all Gentiles and women, the evil and the "good."

The Good News of Great Joy. We saw earlier how the Gospel message took its name from the Old English for good news and joyful tidings. Luke expresses in his Gospel the joy that is ours because Christ has liberated us. He tells us that the angels and God himself rejoice over a sinner's repentance:

> I tell you, there will be more joy in heaven over one sinner who repents than over ninety-nine respectable people who do not need to repent. (15:7)

I tell you, the angels of God rejoice over one sinner who repents. (15:10)

God's joy is described most movingly in the parable of the Prodigal Son:

He [the prodigal son] was still a long way from home when his father saw him; his heart was filled with pity, and he ran, threw his arms around his son, and kissed him. . . . he said, "Bring the best robe and put it on him. Put a ring on his finger and shoes on his feet. Then go and get the prize calf and kill it, and let us celebrate with a feast!" (15:20, 22-23)

Joy is the promise when the birth of John the Baptist is announced: "How glad and happy you will be, and how happy many others will be when he is born!" (1:14). The promise is fullfilled in the angels' announcement of Jesus' birth:

I am here with good news for you, which will bring great joy to all the people. This very day in David's town your Savior was born—Christ the Lord! (2:11)

The response to Jesus' message is always one of joy:

The seventy-two men came back in great joy. "Lord," they said, "even the demons obeyed us when we gave them command in your name!" (10:17)

The people rejoiced over all the wonderful things that he did. (13:17)

The large crowd of his disciples began to thank God and praise him in loud voices for all the great things that they had seen. (triumphant approach to Jerusalem, 19:37)

They worshipped him and went back into Jerusalem, filled with great joy, and spent all their time in the Temple giving thanks to God. (after Jesus' ascension, 24:52-53)

Luke's Gospel is also notable for its hymns of praise and joy:

> My heart praises the Lord;
>> my soul is glad because of God my savior.
> (Mary's song, 1:46-55)

> Let us praise the Lord, the God of Israel!
>> He has come to the help of his people and has set them
>> free.
> (Zechariah's song, 1:68-79)

> Glory to God in the highest heaven,
>> and peace on earth to those with whom he is pleased!
> (the angels' song, 2:24)

> Now, Lord, you have kept your promise,
>> and you may let your servant go in peace.
> (Simeon's song, 2:29-32)

Dante called Luke "the singer of Jesus' kindness." Certainly kindness is a keynote in Luke's Gospel: Jesus' kindness towards Jews and Gentiles; towards his disciples; towards women; towards Jerusalem; towards sinners. Our response, like the response described in the Gospel, ought to be one of joy and gratitude.

FIVE

The Gospel of John

IN THE EARLY CHURCH there were two prominent persons called John—John the elder and John the apostle. Unfortunately, John the apostle is sometimes referred to as John the elder, because of his seniority. Understandably, this has caused some confusion as to which of these was the author of the fourth Gospel.

In addition to internal evidence in the Gospel itself (21:24), tradition almost unanimously maintains that John the apostle wrote the Gospel. There is a foreword to a Latin translation of the Gospel (c. 150-200) which says:

> Here begins the writing according to John himself when he was still alive. Papias, called the Hierapolitan, who was a devoted disciple of John tells us this in his last five books of commentary on Scripture.

As one of the most ancient writers (130 A.D.), and a disciple of John the apostle, it is hardly likely that Papias would be mistaken. Furthermore, Irenaeus of Lyons explicitly says, "Last of all John, too, the disciple of the Lord who leaned against his breast, himself brought out a gospel while he was in Ephesus." Irenaeus was personally instructed by Polycarp, who was himself a contemporary of John the apostle. At about the same time Theophilus of Antioch (180), Clement of Alexandria (150-215), Origen (186-254), Tertullian (160-240), and the Muratorian

The John Rylands papyrus is the oldest known bit of New Testament writing. This fragment, containing scraps of four verses of John's Gospel, dates possibly as early as 94 A.D. and no later than 135 A.D.

Canon all expressly attribute the fourth Gospel to John the apostle. Eusebius (c. 265-340), Epiphanius (315-403), and Jerome (c. 342-419) all affirm this same tradition.

The fourth Gospel was well enough known before 150 A.D. to have been used by Ignatius of Antioch (c. 115), by Papias, by Justin, and probably by Clement of Rome. Archaeological evidence supports this. Papyrus fragments of John's Gospel, found in Egypt, have been dated as belonging to a period before 150 A.D.; this would not be possible if the Gospel had not been written quite some time before. It seems most likely that John's Gospel was written 95-100 A.D.

This does not mean that the complete Gospel as we have it

today came from the hand of John the apostle. The end of Chapter 20 (20:20-31) would make a very fitting conclusion. Chapter 21 is more like an appendix, and almost certainly added by John's disciples after his death. In a similar way, there are various passages throughout the Gospel which may have been amplified by the disciples. This is why scripture scholars say that John's Gospel, although it was certainly in existence at a very early date, was most probably edited and published later.

John's Life

John (in Hebrew, Jochanan, literally "God is gracious") was one of the sons of Zebedee, mentioned in the synoptic gospels, the younger brother of James (Mt 4:21; Mk 1:19; Lk 5:10). From comparing Matthew 27:56 and Mark 15:40, it seems most probable that Salome, who witnessed the crucifixion, was John's mother. His father, Zebedee, was a prosperous enough fisherman to be able to employ others (Mk 1:20), and both James and John followed the same occupation as their father.

It seems highly probable that John was a disciple of John the Baptist. From John the Baptist he would have learned about the need of preparing for the coming of the Messiah. The Gospel itself, after the prologue, begins with John the Baptist's preaching, and in fact it is John the Baptist who prompts John the evangelist to make contact with Jesus. John and Andrew eventually follow him back to his house (1:35-39). Subsequently, Andrew brings his brother Simon (Peter) to Jesus, and we may suppose that it is John who brings his brother (1:40-42). These preliminary contacts lead to John leaving his nets to become, with the other apostles, a "fisher of men."

During Christ's public ministry, John, together with Peter and James, enjoyed a special friendship with Jesus: John was chosen to witness the raising of Jairus' daughter (Mk 5:37); he witnessed the Transfiguration (Mk 9:2); he had the place of honor at Jesus' side at the Last Supper (Jn 13:23); he was present in Gethsemane (Mk 14:33-37). He and his brother were nicknamed by Jesus "men of thunder" (Mk 3:17), and there are a number of incidents which justify this nickname: wanting to call down fire on an inhospitable village (Lk 9:54); the squabble over places of honor in Jesus' kingdom (Mt 20:20-28); objecting to someone driving out demons in Jesus' name (Mk 9:38). John himself was very aware of this special friendship, and expresses it in his Gospel. John was a key witness to Jesus' passion and Resurrection (1 Jn 1:1): he was present at Jesus' death (19:26); he was the first apostle to reach the empty tomb (20:3-4); he was the first to recognize Jesus on the shore of Tiberias (21:7).

After Jesus' Ascension John was considered one of the prominent leaders of the community that Jesus left behind. It was John and Peter who cured the lame man in the Temple, and bore witness to Christ before the Sanhedrin and all the people (Acts 3-4). After Stephen's martyrdom, it was John who accompanied Peter to the new converts in Samaria (Acts 8:14). When Paul submitted his preaching, he sought approval from "the leaders, the pillars of the church, James, Peter, and John" (Gal 2:2, 9).

We do not know for certain when John left Jerusalem, but it is highly likely that it was just before the outbreak of the Jewish-Roman War in 68-70. According to tradition, John settled in Ephesus. His leadership may be gauged from his seven letters to the churches in Asia (Rv 1:4-3:22). About 95, John was exiled to Patmos, and it was from this period that we probably get the final text of the Book of Revelation. In subsequent years he wrote the Gospel and his first letter. Most scholars think that his second and third letters are earlier. At the beginning of Trajan's reign (c. 100) John died at Ephesus, the last of the apostles.

John's liturgical feast is celebrated on December 27.

The Organization of John's Gospel. In Jewish ritual, the number seven had a special place and importance: the Sabbath was kept as a "holy day" every seventh day; the period from Passover to Pentecost lasted seven times seven days; the major feasts and rites of purification were made to last seven days; in the Temple, it was customary to sprinkle the blood of sacrifice or the water of purification seven times; seven kinds of gifts were suitable for sacrifice (oxen, sheep, goats, pigeons, wheat, oil, and wine); the candlestick in the sanctuary had seven branches. Seven was a symbolic number used to express sacredness and prosperity or good fortune. In the composition of his Gospel, John seems to have used the number seven to help to get across the idea that Christ's life and his work of salvation are the source of holiness and happiness for all mankind. Underlying the Gospel we can detect a pattern of seven weeks. Similarly, John chooses seven of Jesus' miracles and records seven of Jesus' statements of self-revelation, all of which begin "I am . . ." Schematically, John's Gospel can be laid out as follows:

The Pattern of Weeks	*Miraculous Signs*	*The "I am . . ." statements*
	1:1-18	
	Foreword	
	1:19-2:12	
The week of the first encounters	Changing water into wine	
	2:13-4:54	
The week of the great conversions —Nicodemus —the Samaritan woman —the Galilean official	Curing the official's son	

The Pattern of Weeks	*Miraculous Signs*	*The "I am . . ." statements*
	5:1-6:71	
The week of the bread of life	Curing the lame man Multiplying the bread Walking on the water	"I am the bread of life." (6:35ff)
	7:1-9:41	
The week of light	Healing the man born blind	"I am the light of the world." (8:12ff)
	10:1-11:57	
The week of the good shepherd	Raising Lazarus from the dead	"I am the gate." (10:7ff) "I am the good shepherd." (10:11ff) "I am the resurrection and the life." (11:25ff)
	12:1-19:42	
The week of Christ's sacrificial death		"I am the way, the truth, and the life." (14:6ff) "I am the real vine." (15:1ff)
	20:1-29	
The week of the Resurrection		

20:30-31

John's conclusion

21:1-25

John's disciples'
conclusion

Characteristics of John's Gospel

John's Purpose. At the time when John's Gospel received its final shape (c. 95) the other editions by Matthew, Mark, and Luke were already widely used in the Christian communities. Why, then, should John have thought it necessary to provide a further edition? John's intention is to go further than the editions of Matthew, Mark, and Luke. They were writing for Christians who had only recently received the faith, for catechumens and converts. John is writing for mature Christians who are already familiar with the truths of the gospel. John provides a more profound insight into the personality of Christ and the purpose of his life, death, and Resurrection.

For this reason John does not think it necessary to repeat much of the teaching or all of the incidents found in the other three editions. He does not repeat the parables and moral instruction found in Matthew, Mark, and Luke. Christ's teaching on charity is the only moral teaching with which John's Gospel deals at length. In fact, Jesus' instruction to the disciples that they should serve one another (Mt 20:20-28; Mk 10:35-45) is expressed more urgently in John's Gospel, and highlighted by Jesus washing his disciples' feet (Jn 13:1-35).

Similarly, many of the events in Jesus' life are mentioned only in passing by John, because he presupposes we know of them from the other gospel editions: Jesus' baptism by John the Baptist (1:32); John the Baptist's imprisonment by Herod (3:24); Mary's anointing of Jesus' feet (11:2); Barabbas' history (18:40). John does no more than refer to these events.

When John selected miracles to highlight the purpose of his Gospel, he took some which had not yet been narrated in the other gospel editions (2:1ff, 5:1ff, 9:1ff, 11:1ff). Even cases where John does repeat an episode found in Matthew, Mark, or Luke, he does so only as an introduction to a theological elaboration. Each one of the seven miracles which John gives is specifically chosen to highlight the particular theme of the accompanying discussion: changing water into wine symbolizes the newness of life brought by Christ (2:1-12); curing the Gentile official's son shows Christ as the Savior of the world (4:43-54); restoring health to the lame man reveals him as the author of life (5:1-9a, 9b-47); the multiplication of the bread demonstrates that Christ is the bread of life (6:1-15, 25-71); walking on the water reveals Jesus as the only true guide (6:16-21); the cure of the man born blind symbolizes Christ as the light of the world (9:1-7, 8-41); the raising of Lazarus reveals Jesus as the resurrection and the life (11:1-44). John always insists on calling miracles "signs" (2:11, 3:2, 4:54, 6:2, etc.)

Jesus' teaching about the Kingdom of Heaven is recorded by Matthew, Mark, and Luke, but John passes over it as well-known to his reader. Instead, John elaborates Jesus' discourses about himself. In John's Gospel practically all the quoted words of Jesus concern his self-revelation, that is, they explain the mystery of his person. The key points, or climaxes, of his self-revelation are the seven "I am . . . " phrases. It is not accidental that these phrases increase in number and length as John proceeds.

Jesus' Identity. The key questions of John's Gospel revolve around Jesus' identity and origins. Who is he? Where did he come from? What is his relationship with the Father?

In the early part of John's Gospel, people ask questions about Jesus' earthly origin:

[Nathanael asked] "Can anything good come from Nazareth?" (1:46)

[Some of the people said] "When the Messiah comes, no one will know where he is from. And we all know where this man comes from." (7:27)

Others said, "The Messiah will not come from Galilee." (7:41)

"Study the Scriptures and you will learn that no prophet ever comes from Galilee." (7:52)

[The Pharisees said] "We know that God spoke to Moses; as for that fellow, however, we do not even know where he comes from!" (9:29)

Jesus responded to these questions by revealing his divine origins:

I have come with my Father's authority. (5:43)

[God's bread is] the one who comes down from heaven and gives life to the world. (6:33)

Do you really know me and know where I am from? I have not come on my own authority. He who sent me, however, is truthful. . . . I know him, because I come from him and he sent me. (7:28-29)

I know where I came from and where I am going. . . . I testify on my own behalf and the Father who sent me also testifies on my behalf. (8:14, 18)

I came from God and now I am here. I did not come on my own authority, but he sent me. (8:42)

Jesus knew that he had come from God and was going to God. (13:3)

Gradually it becomes clear that Jesus is God. He and the Father are one:

What the Father does, the Son also does. (5:19)

He who is from God is the only one who has seen the Father. (6:46)

If you knew me, you would know my Father also. (8:19)

When you lift up the Son of Man, you will know that I Am Who I Am. (8:28)

Whoever sees me also sees him who sent me. (12:45)

[To Philip] Whoever has seen me has seen the Father. Why, then, do you say, "Show us the Father?" (14:9)

The Father and I are one. (10:30)

Father! Give me glory in your presence now, the same glory I had with you before the world was made. (17:5)

I will ask the Father, and he will give you another Helper, who will stay with you forever. (14:16, 26)

John helps us to discover the mystery of Jesus' nature—his origin in the Father through the power of the Spirit, as well as his true humanity. For many of Jesus' Jewish contemporaries, his earthly origins were all too apparent, and his obvious humanity became an obstacle to faith in him as the Son of God. But, through his works and words, Jesus demonstrated his origin (5:36).

John's Personal Testimony. Matthew, Mark, and Luke recorded Jesus' words and deeds in the way in which they were being preached and handed on in the church. Because of this, their narratives about Jesus and their reports of his words are somewhat impersonal and formal, set into fixed patterns of expression. In Mark's Gospel there are some traces of Peter's own testimony, yet this edition, too, closely follows the pattern of the common instruction. By contrast, John's Gospel is very markedly a personal testimony. John presents not a memorized text, learned by heart and handed on from teacher to pupil in a fixed formulation, but rather the personal witness of a man who tells us about Jesus from his own living memory and from his meditation on it.

The fact that John was writing from personal memory helps to explain why, even though this Gospel was the last to be written and, as such, furthest in time from the places and events it records, its description at times is extremely accurate. Recent archaeological excavations have uncovered a pool with five porches near the Temple, corresponding to John's description of the pool called Bethzatha (5:2). In one of Jesus' disputes with the Pharisees John has them say that the Temple is in its forty-sixth year of construction (2:20). Modern calculations have verified this dating, which is all the more remarkable since John would have been writing about twenty-five years after the destruction of the Temple. When describing Jesus' ordeal in Pilate's palace, John mentions a stone pavement, in Hebrew *gabbatha* (19:13), which has been uncovered. There are many other particular references of this kind (3:23, 9:7, 10:22-23, etc.) which mark this Gospel as the account of a man drawing from his own memory.

Another feature of John's Gospel consistent with his writing from personal memory is that in recording Jesus' words he confuses Jesus' way of speaking with his own. This is something within our own experience. Often, when we are repeating what someone else has said we repeat the other person's message but unconsciously put it in our own manner of speaking. This is all the more true when the individual has absorbed the other person's words as completely as John made Jesus' words his own. Sometimes it is difficult to distinguish Jesus' words from John's commentary on them. For example, compare 3:16-21 (Jesus' words) with 3:31-36 (John's commentary). John quoted freely from his own memory, reporting Jesus' message as faithfully as he could.

We can be certain that John himself did not write down his Gospel, but that it is the work of disciples in the sense that what John taught and dictated, they wrote down. In the final edition

Traditional symbols of the evangelists from sixth-century mosaics in the Basilica of San Vitale, Ravenna, Italy. Shown are a lion (Mark) and the eagle (John).

of John's Gospel, we can see traces of their editing. We have already mentioned that the final chapter is a conclusion that they added. But there are other smaller instances:

One of the soldiers, however, plunged his spear into Jesus' side, and at once blood and water poured out. (The one who

saw this happen has spoken of it, so that you also may believe.
What he said is true, and he knows that he speaks the truth.)
(Jn 19:34-36)

The first part would be John's words; the second part added by
the disciples, who are trying to add weight to his words by
insisting that John was a witness to Jesus' death. Some versions
of the New Testament put such additions in brackets, to help
readers distinguish them.

A Special Note: The Evangelists in Art

In the Book of Revelation, which many scholars attribute to
John, there is a description of four strange heavenly beings who
stand before God's throne, singing God's praises unceasingly:

> The first one looked like a lion; the second looked like a bull;
> the third had a face like a man's face; and the fourth looked
> like an eagle in flight. (Rv 4:7)

The Fathers of the church saw in these four creatures symbolic
representations of the four evangelists. Jerome, for example,
explains it this way:

> The lion is Mark, since his Gospel begins in the desert, the
> habitat of lions; the bull is Luke, since he mentions sacrifice
> at the beginning of his Gospel, and bulls are sacrificial
> victims; the man is Matthew, because he opens his Gospel
> with a genealogy of Jesus' human descent; the eagle is John,
> since his gospel is full of soaring and lofty thoughts.

Of course, such an interpretation of the symbolic names is very
arbitrary, but you will find that these symbols have been widely
used in Christian art to characterize the four evangelists.

SIX

Facts of Everyday Life

THE GOSPELS bring us into the daily life of first-century Palestine. It will help our understanding of the Gospels to understand something of the facts of everyday life in Jesus' world. Here we will examine what people wore and ate, the tools they used, weights and measures, and what they used for money.

Clothing

Jesus' contemporaries seem to have used various types of clothing of different origins. Some ancient Hebrew customs remained but new ways of dressing had come in from the Greek and Roman world. There was a wide variety of usage.

The simplest garment was a linen cloth. This could be worn as a loincloth (fig. 1) or could be thrown around the body and slung over the shoulder by one end (fig. 2). Jesus put on such a cloth when washing the disciples' feet (Jn 13:4). The young man who fled from the guards was wearing this garment (Mk 14:51). We find it also used for keeping money (Lk 19:20) and for wrapping corpses (Jn 11:44, 20:6-7).

Many people wore a shirt or short tunic (fig. 3), which reached to the knees. It was the dress most suited for ordinary work. When anyone was dressed with only this shirt, he was considered naked (Jn 21:7). The phrase "I was naked and you have clothed me" (Mt 25:36) refers to a man who had only such a shirt.

Instead of this shirt many wore a long tunic. This was the most common everyday clothing. This tunic often had sleeves (fig. 4) and reached the ankles. The front was open and was held together by a girdle.

For travel or work the lower end of the tunic would be tucked under the girdle. When Jesus said, "Let your loins be girded" (Lk 12:35, 17:8), he meant "Be ready for action." Jesus foretold that someone else would gird Peter to say that Peter would be forced to go to the place of his martyrdom (Jn 21:18). The tunic was often pulled up at the girdle to make a pocket: this is what Jesus was referring to when he said that his disciples should not carry money "in their girdles" (Mt 10:9; Mk 6:8).

Rich people would, at times, wear two tunics, perhaps a long tunic with a short one underneath. John the Baptist said that those who have two tunics should give one to the person who has none (Lk 3:11). Jesus forbade his disciples to wear two tunics on their apostolic journeys (Mt 10:10; Mk 6:9; Lk 9:3). It may be that he was opposed to the taking along of an extra tunic in reserve.

The most important outer garment was the mantle or cloak, usually made of wool, camel hair, or sheepskin, for protection against the cold. The mantle was the official dress for occasions of social importance, and it expressed a man's social status. The madness of the demoniac is expressed by the statement that he went about without mantle (Lk 8:27). After his cure people find him properly dressed (Mk 5:15).

The mantle was a square piece of cloth that was normally a combination of two long strips sewn together (fig. 5). After the two strips had been sewn together the two extremities (left and right) would be folded over, the top ends being stitched together (fig. 6). After holes had been made at the sides, to allow the arms to come through, the mantle could be worn (fig. 7). The soldiers under the cross did not divide the Lord's mantle, when they saw that it was special, made of one piece of woven cloth without any seams in it (Jn 19:23).

The value and significance of the mantle is indicated in many Gospel passages. No one would spoil a good (old) mantle by

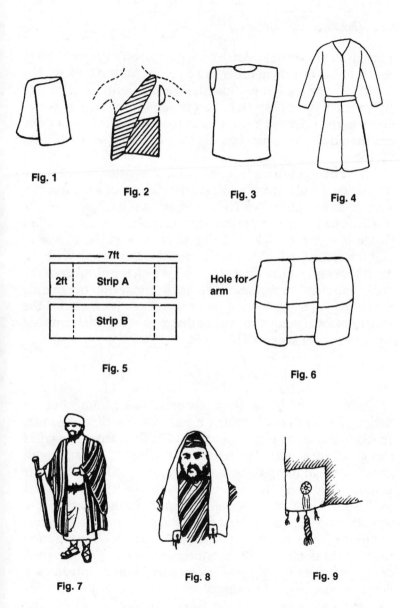

Fig. 1

Fig. 2

Fig. 3

Fig. 4

7ft

2ft | Strip A

Strip B

Fig. 5

Hole for arm

Fig. 6

Fig. 7

Fig. 8

Fig. 9

Clothing in the time of Jesus

putting an unshrunken patch on it (Mt 9:16ff). People tried to touch Jesus' mantle in order to be cured (Mt 9:20, 14:36; Mk 5:27ff). They laid their mantles before Jesus' feet at the triumphant entry (Mt 21:7). Regarding the fall of Jerusalem, Jesus warned that men working in the field, with only a tunic on, should flee without rescuing their mantles (Mt 24:18; Mk 13:16).

The Pharisees used special prayer mantles which were draped over the head (fig. 8). At the corners of such mantles they made special fringes (fig. 9)—a small square patch of silk was attached to the corners and through a hole in the middle a fringe of eight threads and five knots was made. *Fringe* in Hebrew is *sisith,* which has the numerical value of 600. With the eight threads and five knots the total is 613, the number of the commandments in the Law. Kissing the fringe thus became for the scribes an expression of love of the Law. Jesus chided the Pharisees for attaching so much value to such externals without a genuine inner sanctity (Mt 23:5).

Food

The main food of the Jews was bread made from wheat or barley. The process of making bread was so well-known that Jesus often refers to it in his teaching. The first step was to grind the grain in a mill. He refers to "women . . . at a mill grinding meal: one will be taken away, the other will be left behind" (Mt 24:41) to express the unexpectedness of the last judgment. The flour was then leavened. Jesus speaks of the woman who leavens a bushel of flour with a bit of yeast "until the whole batch of dough rises" (Mt 13:33) to describe the way his doctrine will transform the world. The leavened dough was then made into flat cakes which were spread on a heated stone. After the miraculous catch of fish, the apostles eat near such a stone by the Sea of Galilee (Jn 21:9). The bread was taken off as soon as it had been baked, and was preferably eaten warm.

Since bread formed the principal food the same word also

means *food*. Hence "Give us today our daily bread" (Mt 6:11), "Man cannot live on bread alone" (Mt 4:4), and similar phrases refer to all food. Jesus chose bread for the eucharistic meal because it was the normal food, expressing very clearly that Jesus becomes the ordinary, daily food of his followers.

The bread was not cut, but broken with the fingers (Mt 14:19, 15:36, 26:26). One took a piece with the right hand and dipped it in a sauce (Mt 26:23). Passing such a piece to someone else was considered a token of friendship (Jn 13:26).

The Jews ate only twice a day (both meals are mentioned in Lk 14:12). The first meal was taken between 10:00 and 12:00 o'clock. It consisted of bread, fruits, and milk. At this meal one did not normally eat meat or drink wine (see Acts 2:15). The second meal was taken in the evening and was comprised of bread, wine, and some heavier dishes, such as fish (Mt 7:10, 14:17), eggs (Lk 11:12), or meat (Lk 15:29-30).

Jesus' contemporaries prayed before and after meals (Mt 14:19, 15:36). The Jews were so particular about this point that the scribes used to discuss what one should do if one had forgotten to say grace before meals. Some maintained that one should then return to the place where one had eaten and make up for the omission by praying there.

Jewish parents looked after their children well. Jesus' words about prayer would, therefore, deeply impress them:

> Would any of you who are fathers give your son a stone when he asks for bread? Or would you give him a snake when he asks for a fish? As bad as you are, you know how to give good things to your children. How much more, then, will your Father in heaven give good things to those who ask him!
>
> (Mt 7:9-11)

The "good things" are things we need. Bread and fish are ordinary food. No father will refuse such food to his son.

At feasts, but also at other times, the Jews would have formal dinners to which a certain number of persons were invited. These formal meals were arranged according to a well-set

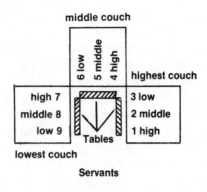

Fig. 10

pattern. The guests were not sitting but "lying at table" (Mt 9:10; Lk 7:36; Jn 13:23) on special couches on which they reclined with their feet away from the table. Resting on their left elbow, they took food with the right hand from a low table in front of the couch. We know from historians that there normally were three couches arranged in such a way that servants could approach the tables from the fourth side (fig. 10). On each couch three or four guests could take their places in a strict order of precedence: not only were the three couches different in standing, but on each couch the places were ranked as "high," "middle," or "low."

This arrangement at formal meals throws light on a number of Gospel passages. Jesus chides the Pharisees for seeking the "first places" (see fig. 10) at feasts (Mt 23:6). Jesus warns them not to take the first place on their own accord, lest the host suggest a "lower" place (Lk 14:7-11). Mary Magdalene could wash Jesus' feet and anoint them (Lk 7:36-50) by approaching from the far end of the couch. Two apostles are sent by Jesus to prepare a room for the Last Supper, to see to the arrangement of the three couches as well as the meal (Mk 14:15). From John's description of the conversation at the Last Supper (Jn 13-14) we can infer that they sat in the traditional arrangement of three tables.

Household Goods and Tools

Inside the house the Jews used oil lamps. This required four pieces of equipment (fig. 11): a jug of oil (D), a lamp stand (C), a little lamp (B), and in the lamp a cotton wick (A). The lamps for inside the house were flat and without a handle. These lamps did not give much light, and were most beneficial if they were put on the lampstand (Mt 5:15; Jn 5:35). Outside the house one carried torches—iron holders in which a burning piece of wood could be inserted. Such torches were used by the soldiers who arrested Jesus (Jn 18:3). Oil lamps could also be carried, if they had a handle. In Jesus' time the Roman lamp (fig. 12) was popular in Palestine, and when he says that we are to be ready like servants holding their lamps lit (Lk 12:35), he is thinking of such lamps. The lamps of the ten virgins who were invited for the marriage were also Roman lamps.

We are so accustomed to the luxury of matches that we never think of the trouble people had to take in order to light a fire. In Jesus' time this was done by rubbing wood, one piece against another. There was a little instrument for this (fig. 13). A piece of hardwood was fitted into the lower end of the main shape (E into D). With the left hand one held the knob (A) that slipped over the top of the shaft (B). The hardwood (E) underneath was put into a hole in a softwood plank (F); and by means of a stretched rope (C), which was held in the right hand, the shaft was made to turn (by moving the rope backwards and forwards). By the friction of the hardwood (E) in the softwood (F) the softwood would start to glow. This fire was then caught with reeds and transferred to where fire was needed. Firemaking was an elaborate job, often referred to in the Gospels (Lk 22:55). Jesus came to make a fire on the earth in a spiritual sense (Lk 12:49) and to bring "a baptism of fire" (Mt 3:11).

In the Lord's time locks were large and very clumsy, used only for very important closures, such as the main doors or gates of great buildings. The locks did not work by turning, but by sliding (fig. 14). Two halves of a crossbar (A and B) were nailed to the two parts or doors of the gate. Where the ends came together, the crossbars had been hollowed out, so that a smaller piece of iron or wood could slide across (C). When the piece (C) had been made to slide across (from B into A), it was held by nails (inside A) which fit into holes of the sliding piece. The key (D) could then be slipped underneath this piece to push the nails out and so unlock it. Jesus thinks of such keys when he promises the keys of the Kingdom to Peter (Mt 16:19) and when he accuses the Pharisees of having the keys to wisdom, but locking the doors to prevent people from entering (Lk 11:52).

The most important agricultural tool was the plow. The ordinary people used very simple models. The central beam could be attached to the yoke in front. At the other end the beam was bent into the share, which could be armed with different types of points. The plow was held from behind by a special handle. With such a loose plow it was absolutely necessary that the farmer pay constant attention to the work. A farmer who looked back after having put his hand to the plow could not produce good work (see Lk 9:62).

The yoke was really part of the plow. It was laid on the animals' necks so that the plow could be pulled by them. In Jesus' time yokes were of a simple design (fig. 15). There was a cross beam with ropes on the sides to tie the yoke to the animals' necks. The yoke became the symbol of burdens put on people. Jesus' yoke (Mt 11:29-30) visualizes a farmer who does not overtax his beasts of burden.

When the grain had been harvested with a sickle (which looked like our sickle), it was threshed. This could be done with sticks (if the grain amounted to only a small quantity) or by a threshing sledge (fig. 16). Such a sledge was a heavy piece of wood with iron pins underneath which, with the farmer standing on top, was pulled over the grain by oxen. The chaff was then separated from the grain in two stages. The threshed material was thrown up against the wind with winnowing shovels or forks (fig. 17). The grain would fall down straight, whereas most of the chaff would be blown aside. Whatever remained of the chaff could be eliminated by a process of

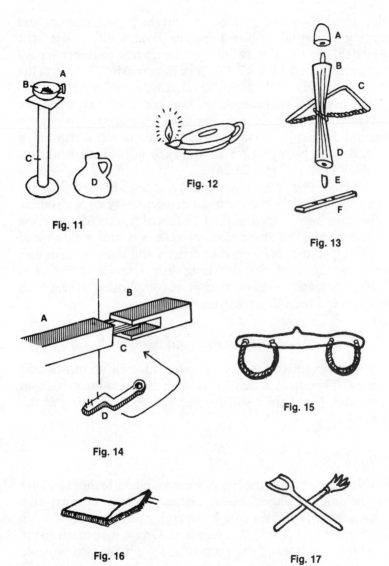

Fig. 11

Fig. 12

Fig. 13

Fig. 14

Fig. 15

Fig. 16

Fig. 17

Household tools

sieving. This whole process of threshing, winnowing, and sieving is implied when John the Baptist says, "He [the Messiah] has his winnowing shovel with him to thresh out all the grain" (Mt 3:12; Lk 3:17). As a farmer carefully selects the good grain, so the Messiah will select his own people.

For practical purposes in the home, a smaller type of sieve was used. Such a strainer or sieve helped to purify oil, wine, and various drinks. Jesus characterizes the unbalanced attitude of the Pharisees by saying, "You strain a fly out of your drink, but swallow a camel!" (Mt 23:24).

We know that Joseph (Mt 13:55) and Jesus himself (Mk 6:3) were carpenters in Nazareth. In extraordinary circumstances Jesus may have helped in the building of houses (doors, cross beams, etc.), but his ordinary work was the making and repairing of just such everyday articles and tools as plows and yokes, winnowing forks, threshing sledges, tables and couches, lampstands, and, perhaps, even more complicated articles such as locks and firemaking instruments.

Measurements and Money

The evangelists frequently refer to measurements and money. Therefore, a familiarity with the measurements and money of Jesus' time will further our understanding of the Gospels.

Length

Cubit. The *cubit* was the length from the elbow to the extremity of the middle finger, about eighteen inches or forty-five centimeters. Jesus asks who by worrying can add a *cubit* to his *helikia* (Mt 6:27; Lk 12:25), which, in Greek, may mean either "stature," "tallness," or "span of life." Of the two possible interpretations, "Who can add one *cubit* to his life's duration?" is the more likely one. Few are worried about becoming taller, but many are worried about living longer.

A Day's Journey. People reckoned distances by saying it was so many days' travelling. One day's journey would amount to ten to fifteen miles (sixteen to twenty-four kilometers).

Stadion. This was a Greek measure, derived from the length of the famous foot-race course at the Olympics—202 yards or 185 meters. Before Jesus came walking to them over the water, the apostles had rowed twenty-five to thirty *stadia* (Jn 6:19), that is, three or four miles (five or six kilometers). Bethany was about fifteen *stadia* (Jn 11:18) from Jerusalem, that is, about two miles (three kilometers).

Capacity

Cor or Homer. Amounted to 100 gallons or 450 liters. The "hundred *homer* of wheat" (Lk 16:7) in our calculation would amount to 1,250 bushels.

Bath. Amounted to ten gallons or forty-five liters. The "hundred *bath* of oil" (Lk 16:6) was the equivalent of 1,000 gallons.

Metrete. A Greek measure for liquids: 8.8 gallons or 39.4 liters. The six jars at Cana each held "two or three *metretes*" (Jn 2:6), approximately 600 liters in total.

Seah. A measure of grain equalling three and a half gallons or fifteen liters. The woman of the parable mixed leaven in "three *seahs* of meal" (Mt 13:33; Lk 13:21). This amounts to forty-five kilograms, and the little leaven permeates it all!

Modion. A very common measure for grain, containing about two gallons. Every farmer had a little basket in his house which corresponded to this measure. That is why Jesus says that no one lights a lamp to put it under this basket or under the couch, but on the lampstand (Mt 5:15; Mk 4:21; Lk 11:33).

Xestes or Log. A common measure for liquids, containing about two cups or half a liter. People would have a little bronze vessel of this size at home. The Pharisees washed such vessels before eating (Mk 7:4-8).

Weight and Money

Archaeologists have been able to determine quite accurately the weight in gold or silver of the coins used in Palestine during Jesus' time. We may approximately translate their value into dollar equivalents, not so much by the metal's value (i.e., at dollars per ounce) as by its purchasing power (one *drachma* a minimum daily wage, about $25).

Talent. Originally the *talent* was a weight of at most 900 ounces of gold. In Jesus' time the word *talent* was used for a value of money equivalent to about 630 ounces of silver. Its buying power would be nearly $150,000. The man in Matthew 25:14-30 gave considerable money to his servants to trade with—to one five *talents* ($650,000), to another two ($300,000), and to the third, one ($150,000).

Stater. Its silver value was less than one-half ounce. This is the equivalent of $100. Judas sold our Lord for thirty *staters*, that is, for $3,000 (Mt 26:15), the official price of a slave.

Didrachma. It equalled half a *stater*, $50. The Temple tax was a *didrachma* for each person (Mt 17:24). Through the miraculous catch Peter finds a *stater* in the fish's mouth, and can pay for Jesus and himself (Mt 17:27).

Drachma or Denarius. The silver value of this coin amounted to one-tenth of an ounce of silver. It was the ordinary daily wage of hired servants; the laborers in the vineyard had no reason to grumble (Mt 20:2). The unforgiving servant, who himself had a debt of one and one-half billion dollars, took his fellow servant by the throat as he owed him a hundred *denarii*, that is, $2,500

(Mt 18:28). It is obvious that the Lord wanted to contrast the great debt we owe to God and the smallness of the debt other people owe us.

Assarion. A small bronze coin with the buying power of $.50. Jesus said, "Aren't five sparrows sold for two *assaria* [$1.00]? Yet not one sparrow is forgotten by God! . . . You are worth much more than many sparrows!" (Lk 12:6-7; Mt 10:29).

Lepton. The smallest coin. It was square and made of bronze and its value approximates fifteen cents. The poor widow in the Temple threw two *lepta* (thirty cents) into the sacrificial box, and yet Christ said she had given more than all others "because she gave everything she had" (Mk 12:41-44).

Of course, the relative prices of things was different in the Lord's time, but these values will help us see the message Christ wanted to teach in examples taken from everyday experience.

SEVEN

Time

WE TAKE OUR UNIFORM measurements for time so much for granted that we are completely disoriented when we read the Gospels and find not dates of the month but references to seasons and feasts, not hours from a clock but watches in the night.

In Jesus' time in Palestine, three calendars were in effect: a Roman one and two overlapping Jewish ones—one civil, the other religious. Since the Jewish calendars predominated in the life of Jesus and the apostles, we will look at them first.

The Jewish Calendar

The Jews calculated the months strictly according to the phases of the moon, with every New Moon beginning a new month. If the sky was too cloudy to see the new moon appear, the new month would begin on the next day. In this way there could be months of twenty-nine or of thirty days.

The twelve months were arranged as follows:

Month Name	Time of Year	Main Feasts
1. Nisan	March-April	Passover
2. Iyyar	April—May	
3. Sivan	May—June	Pentecost
4. Tammuz	June—July	
5. Ab	July—August	

Month Name	*Time of Year*	*Main Feasts*
6. Elul	August—September	
7. Tishri	September—October	New Year (Trumpets), Atonement, Tabernacles
8. Marchesvan	October—November	
9. Chislev	November—December	Dedication
10. Tebeth	December—January	
11. Shebat	January—February	
12. Adar	February—March	Purim
(13.) Second Adar		

Since the yearly cycle of the sun has eleven days more than the 354 days required for twelve cycles of the moon, every now and then an extra month, called "Second Adar," was added to the year to make up for them. This extra month was not added on the strength of astronomical calculations; the determining factor was the condition of the harvest. If the harvest was not ripe enough, a central committee at Jerusalem would decide to add a month, thereby postponing the feast of Passover for four weeks.

The civil year began with the seventh month (Tishri). This had special advantages for business and for relations with other nations. The religious year was a cycle of feasts, beginning in Nisan.

Passover. Celebrated on the fifteenth of Nisan. A feast which, in biblical times, was to be celebrated at Jerusalem, this began on the full moon. It commemorated the Exodus and also inaugurated the barley harvest. A fuller explanation will come later.

Pentecost. Originally called "The Feast of Weeks," as it was celebrated seven weeks after Passover. Special sacrifices were offered, and also the first fruits of the wheat harvest. Going to Jerusalem was not obligaroty, but quite a few pilgrims did (Acts 2:5-11).

The Feast of Trumpets. On the seventh New Moon, the first day of Tishri, the civil New Year began and a day of rest was prescribed. The feast owes its name to the trumpets that were sounded at the opening of the celebrations in Jerusalem.

The Day of Atonement. A strict fast was observed on this day of penance, held on the tenth of Tishri. The high priest offered special sacrifices of atonement and brought the blood into the Holy of Holies (see Heb 9:6-15). In another ceremony the high priest would impose hands on a he-goat (placing all the sins of the people on it) and drive it into the desert.

The Feast of Tabernacles. This feast commemorated the stay in the desert and the giving of the Covenant. From the fifteenth to the twenty-first of Tishri, all Jews made little huts of branches (in the garden or in the house) and lived in them for seven days. Many went up to Jerusalem to partake in the celebrations there. Jesus was in Jerusalem during one such feast of Tabernacles (Jn 7:2, 10). During the week Jesus began to preach in the Temple (Jn 7:14). On the last day of the feast Jesus alluded to the ritual of mixing water and wine by calling himself the "spring of living water" (Jn 7:37-39), and to the ritual of lighting special candles, by calling himself the "light of the world" (Jn 8:12).

The Feast of Dedication. This festival, held on the twenty-fifth of Chislev, commemorated the solemn purification and rededication of the Temple in 165-164 B.C., after it had been desecrated by Antiochus Epiphanes. It is during this feast that Jesus had one of his discussions with the scribes in the Temple (Jn 10:22ff).

Purim. Purim, celebrated on the fourteenth and fifteenth of Adar, it commemorated the liberation from the Persians through Esther. The feast was of a secular nature. People enjoyed themselves, dancing and feasting. No special religious functions were prescribed.

Over and above these feasts, every New Moon was celebrated with special sacrifices. Many Jews considered it a day of rest, and it was generally observed as a religious feast.

A Closer Look at Passover

Passover was the most important feast and deserves special attention. There can be no doubt as to its ancient origin. In fact, two different celebrations were fused into it—the festival of the liberation from Egypt and the offering of the first fruits of the harvest. Because of this fusion, we find rites and ceremonies regarding both aspects.

On the first of the month of Nisan, usually around the end of March, Jews all over Palestine began to form bands and groups for the journey to Jerusalem. All men were obliged to take part in the pilgrimage. "Every year, Jesus' parents went to Jerusalem for the feast of Passover" (Lk 2:41-42). By the tenth of Nisan, hundreds of thousands of pilgrims had arrived in or near Jerusalem. Jesus' triumphant entry into Jerusalem took place among a crowd of such pilgrims (Mt 21:1-11; Jn 12:12-19).

Before noon on the fourteenth, all leavened bread was removed from the houses. From now on Jews would eat only unleavened bread. Because of this, Passover was also known as The Feast of the Unleavened Bread (Mt 26:17; Mk 14:1, 12; Lk 22:1, 7).

During the afternoon, preparations were made for the eating of the paschal meal. Between 2:30 and 5:00 P.M., the paschal lamb was taken to the Temple. There it was sacrificed and taken home for further preparation.

The feast would begin on the fifteenth of Nisan with the setting of the sun. People would eat the paschal lamb at home. No work was allowed on this day. On the sixteenth, the first fruits of the barley harvest were offered. The harvest could begin from this date. The solemn conclusion of the feast took place on the twenty-second of Nisan. Again a day of rest was prescribed.

The chronology of the Passover at Jesus' Passion and Resurrection raises some problems. This Passover seems to have fallen on a Sabbath (Jn 19:31), and on this basis can be identified with the eighth of April in the year 30 A.D. Jesus seems to have eaten the Passover one day before the actual feast, which was permitted in some cases. Assuming that he did, we come to the following chronology:

1. *Fourteenth Nisan* (evening)—Thursday, April 6, 30 A.D., Last Supper
2. *Fourteenth Nisan* (noon)—Friday, April 7, Crucifixion
3. *Fifteenth Nisan* (night, next day)—Saturday, April 8, Jesus in the tomb
4. *Sixteenth Nisan* (at dawn)—Sunday, April 9, Resurrection

Jesus' death was a Passover sacrifice; he died on the fourteenth of Nisan between noon and 3:00 P.M., precisely when the Jews were going up to the Temple to have their lambs slaughtered. The evangelists stress the time element to bring out this connection:

It was then *almost noon of the day before the Passover.* Pilate said to the people, "Here is your king!" They shouted back, "Kill him! Kill him!" . . . Then Pilate handed Jesus over to them to be crucified. (Jn 19:14-16)

At noon the old leaven had been thrown out. The paschal sacrifice could begin. Jesus was "the Lamb of God, who takes away the sins of the world" (Jn 1:29; 1 Cor 5:7). Jesus rose on the sixteenth of Nisan—the day of new beginnings, the first fruits, and the harvest. He was and is the "first fruits" from the dead (1 Cor 15:20, 23).

After their paschal lamb had been slaughtered in the Temple, people would take it home. They completed the sacrifice by sharing the sacrificial meal. Usually from ten to twenty people would gather in one house for this purpose. At each meal one person acted as the host, the "father" of the family. The ritual followed a set form.

The first cup was filled with wine and water. The host spoke these blessings:

> Blessed art Thou, Yahweh our God, King of the World, who hast created the fruit of the vine.
>
> Blessed art Thou, Yahweh our God, King of the World, who hast given to Thy people Israel feasts as a joy and as a commemoration.
>
> Blessed art Thou, Yahweh, who sanctifieth Israel and the times.

The first cup was then passed around and finished. The leader washed his hands, spoke a prayer of thanks, and distributed some unleavened bread and green herbs. The paschal lamb (roasted as one piece) was then brought in.

The second cup was filled with wine and water. The host explained the meaning of the feast, how it commemorated the liberation from slavery in Egypt. They sang the first part of the Hallel (Ps 113-114). The second cup was passed around. Again there was a washing of hands and a prayer of thanksgiving. Then followed the eating of the paschal lamb, together with the unleavened bread and bitter herbs, which were dipped into a sauce of various fruits (called *charosheth*).

The third cup was called the "cup of thanksgiving" (cf. 1 Cor 10:16), because of the thanksgiving that was spoken over the meal.

After the fourth cup the second part of the Hallel was sung (Ps 115-118), in which the hope of the Messianic restoration was expressed. The guests would then disperse to their homes.

The accounts of the Last Supper do not always indicate very precisely how the institution of the Eucharist fit into this pattern. People knew the paschal rite so well that it needed no description, and the evangelists were not interested in the old paschal meal and its rites but in the new things Jesus did. Some even say the Last Supper may not have been a paschal meal.

The following attempt at a reconstruction may be helpful:

A Word of Welcome. Jesus tells his disciples how he has desired to eat this Passover with them (Lk 22:14-15).

Initial Ablutions. Jesus himself washes the apostles' feet. This was not the custom, but he wanted to teach them about servanthood (Jn 13:14-17).

The Explanation. At the filling of the second cup Jesus may have explained how the paschal lamb symbolized his sacrifice. He may have spoken at length with his disciples, perhaps, as in John 14-16.

The Bread. This may have followed naturally after the prayer of thanksgiving at this point. Jesus indicated the new meaning of this bread, just as in the paschal rites it had been explained as the bread "eaten in a hurry" (Mt 26:26; Mk 14:22; Lk 22:17-19).

The Wine. In all likelihood this was the third cup, "the cup of thanksgiving." Luke carefully distinguishes this cup from the one that had gone before (Lk 22:17-20).

The Singing of the Hallel. This is clearly mentioned in Matthew 26:30 and Mark 14:26.

Jesus dipped some bread in a dish of *charosheth* and gave it to Judas (Jn 13:26), thereby foretelling Judas' betrayal. It cannot be precisely determined when in the meal this happened—whether before the bread was given (Mt 26:20-25, Mk 14:17-21, and Jn 13:21-30 imply this) or after (Lk 22:21-23).

Jesus' priestly prayer (Jn 17) could also be placed at various stages of the meal. Some commentators say that this was the prayer connected with Jesus' thanksgiving at the consecration. But it is more likely that it was the concluding prayer said at the end of the meal. John certainly seems to present it as such (Jn 18:1). It may also be that it is a reconstructed summary of prayers said by Jesus at various occasions.

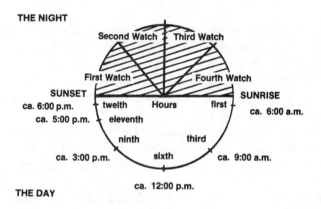

The Divisions of the Day

The Jews did not have clocks. All their calculations were made according to the rising and setting of the sun. In Palestine the times of sunrise and sunset vary less throughout the year than in areas further from the equator.

The day began with the setting of the sun. This means that the night belonged to the following day. The Sabbath, for instance, was reckoned as beginning with the setting of the sun and ending with the setting of the sun on the following day. When Jesus had preached on the Sabbath in Capernaum, people waited "until the sun had set" before they brought their sick, for then the Sabbath was over (Mk 1:32-33). Jesus was crucified on the day before the Sabbath. Since the Jews did not want corpses to remain on crosses during the Sabbath (Jn 19:31), Jesus and the others had to be buried before the setting of the sun. This explains the haste of the burial in the nearby tomb of Joseph of Arimathea (Jn 19:38-42).

The whole day was divided into twelve "hours of the day" and four "watches of the night," (see fig. 1). Jesus refers to this in his preaching (Mt 20:1-16; Jn 11:9-10).

We are able to determine to some extent the time indicated in some Gospel passages. I say "to some extent," because for the Jews the "hour" was not so much a precise unit as a period of time. The first hour could mean the period from 6:00 to 7:00 A.M. or even from 6:00 to 9:00 A.M. "The third hour," during which Jesus was crucified (Mk 15:25), could mean any time between 9:00 A.M. and 12:00 noon.

The four watches of the night had each received a special name: (1) "evening" (6:00-9:00 P.M.); (2) "midnight" (9:00-12:00 P.M.); (3) "cockcrow" (12:00-3:00 A.M.); and (4) "dawn" (3:00-6:00 A.M.). Jesus warns that he may come at any time to call us up for judgment—"evening, midnight, cockcrow, dawn" (Mk 13:35). While the apostles were toiling to cross the Sea of Galilee, Jesus had remained ashore to pray. "In the fourth watch of the night" he came towards them walking over the water (Mt 14:25; Mk 6:48), joining the apostles just before dawn.

The Sabbath and Sunday

Each seventh day was an obligatory day of prayer and rest. The meaning of the "rest" on the Sabbath centers around God's supremacy as creator of the universe (Gn 1:1-2:4a). Man should take time to set aside the everyday material world to worship God. That is why manual work was forbidden (Ex 20:8-11). In the course of time the rabbis and scribes had worked out thousands of prescriptions specifying what one was allowed or not allowed to do on the Sabbath. These traditional prescriptions tended to be legalistic and contrary to the real spirit of joy inherent in the Sabbath. Some of them are mentioned in the Gospels. No one was allowed to walk more than 2,000 steps, "a sabbath day's journey" (Acts 1:12). No one

was allowed to carry anything—the paralyzed man was criti-
cized for carrying his mat after he had been cured (Jn 5:10). No
one was allowed to harvest. The scribes had defined this as
taking as little as two ears of grain (Mt 12:2). No one was
allowed to take medicine or otherwise seek healing on the
Sabbath (Mt 12:9-13; Mk 3:1-5; Lk 6:6-10, 13:10-14, 14:1-6;
Jn 5:1-10, 9:14-16). Jesus says to such rabbinical conceptions
that the law of the Sabbath can be suspended because of a
higher law (Mt 12:5, 11; Lk 13:15, 14:5). But the most striking
thing Jesus said was "the Sabbath is meant for man, not man for
the Sabbath" (Mk 2:27). With this short phrase he introduced a
totally new understanding of the Law. God's Law was meant to
help man. Planning our day of rest should involve more than
simply avoiding external work. We must consider our total
circumstances and whether or not our plans fulfill God's
purpose.

Jesus' Resurrection achieved our redemption. Because of this
the church of Jesus celebrates each Sunday as a day to
commemorate the first Easter. For the Christians, Sunday took
the place of what the Sabbath had been for the Jews, but there
are great differences to be remembered. Every Sunday is a little
Easter and a day of joy. It should be hallowed by worship and by
rest, i.e., by being as free for God and as free from material work
as possible. In this abstaining from manual work it is the spirit
that counts, not external prescriptions. We sanctify Sunday by
making it a day of prayer, of joy, and of spiritual tranquility.
Our Christian feasts are in some way a continuation of the
Jewish feasts, but in another sense they mark a completely new
beginning, since they are centered on Christ and his life.

The Seasons of the Year

In Palestine the year is divided into two major seasons—the
dry summer from mid-June to mid-September and the rainy
season in the cooler part of the year. This rainy season is in itself
subdivided into the warmer rainy season and the colder season.

(See Sg 2:11, "The winter is over; the rains have stopped.") For our purposes we can say there are three periods, summer, rains, and cold season.

Cold Season (January, February, March). Frost is common at night upon the hills. Slight snowfalls occur occasionally in Jerusalem, and about once every five or ten years there is a heavy snowfall. On the eastern plateau, which is colder, snow is much more common and may occur every year. The average temperature in January is 40°F (5°C); in February, 35°F (2°C); in March, 45°F (8°C). This season is one of hardship—"Pray to God that you will not have to run away during the winter" (Mt 24:20). The Lord's death took place towards the end of this season (Lk 22:55; see also Jn 10:22).

Summer Season (April to September). No rain falls throughout this period, but winds bring moisture in the form of dew. This dew keeps the grapes growing during the drought. Dew is a symbol of blessing in the Bible (Gn 27:28). Gideon is able to wring out sufficient dew from the fleece to fill a bowl with water (Jgs 6:38).

The harvest is gathered during these months (early summer, especially in May) and the thanksgiving feast (Weeks or Pentecost) comes about seven weeks after Passover (cf. Jn 4:35). During these months a brisk sea-breeze blows inland daily towards the end of the afternoon. This breeze cools the land and is also used by the harvesters to sift the chaff from the grain of their crops (cf. Lk 3:17).

Mid-June is the time of great heat, and from then until mid-September there is prolonged drought. The temperature during these months varies according to location and altitude. It can easily reach 100°F (38°C) at the coast, but the nights are cool. The wind from the desert regions often prevails over the country. It is a hot, dry, uncomfortable wind—"And when you feel the south wind blowing, you say that it is going to get hot—and it does" (Lk 12:55). The withering of the grass which results from it is used by biblical writers as the symbol of the impermanence of riches (Is 40:6-8). However, this wind and others make this season the time for taking long sea voyages.

Rainy Season (October, November, December). In contrast to the regularity of the summer days, the rainy season is very unpredictable. During this season cyclonic storms seem to succeed each other quite regularly once a week, bringing heavy rain for about three days followed by four of fine weather. The rain-bearing storms come from the west (Mt 14:23-24). Before a storm the air is full of dust so when the westerly winds blow in, there are often wonderful sunsets and sunrises:

> When the sun is setting, you say, "We are going to have fine weather, because the sky is red." And early in the morning you say, "It is going to rain, because the sky is red and dark."
> (Mt 16:2)

The meeting of the cool sea air with the hot desert air can cause sudden thunderstorms, local but violent and abrupt (Mt 7:24ff). Because of the storms this is not the season for sailing voyages. It was towards the winter months that Paul was shipwrecked off the island of Malta. Acts 27 gives a good description of the storms that arise during this season.

To the people, rain means life and God's blessing. Even refugees today, shivering in sodden tents and caves, will repeat again and again, "Thank God for the rain! Thank God for the rain!" Life depends upon it, as people in desert countries know only too well. The average rainfall in Jerusalem is 22" (56 cm). Rainfall is more abundant in the north than in the south.

Christian Chronology

The Jews dated their calendar from the time of creation. The Romans dated events from the year in which Rome had been founded, for example, "in such and such a year *ab urbe condita*" (A.U.C.), or, after the founding of Rome.

It was natural that the first Christians should also use these generally accepted ways of dating events. As long as the church was persecuted, no new system of chronology (that is, of calculating time) could be introduced. But once Christian culture had spread widely and had found the support of the greater nations, it became natural to begin a new system of dating which took Christ's birth as the center. Christ's Incarnation was far more important than the founding of Rome, and it was the beginning of a new creation.

This mode of dating is expressed by the familiar abbreviations, B.C. and A.D. A.D. stands for *anno Domini,* "in the year of the Lord." All the years after Jesus' coming are thus called "years of the Lord." 1982 A.D. means "in the 1982nd year of the Lord's coming.

It stands to reason that it took some time to change over from the Roman way of calculating time to the Christian way. It is like changing from standard measures to the metric system. Moreover, some difficult dates had to be re-calculated. In what year had Jesus been born? What actual year was to be the first A.D.? One Scythian abbot, called Dennis the Little (who died in 540 A.D. in Rome), calculated the matter as well as he could and came to the conclusion that Jesus had been born in the year 754 A.U.C., or 754 years after the founding of Rome. Thus, the year 754 A.U.C. is the year 1 A.D., the first year after Christ's coming. This calculation was generally accepted and has been in use ever since. Abbot Dennis the Little deserves praise for the work he did, but he made a mistake. In fact, Christ was born four or five years before the year assigned by Dennis.

The actual date of Jesus' birth can be calculated as follows. Luke 2:14 says that Mary and Joseph went to Bethlehem for a general enrollment. This universal enrollment would seem to correspond with the decree issued by Augustus in the year 746 A.U.C. (8 B.C.). It would take at least one year for the decree to take effect in Palestine. Christ must, therefore, have been born after the year 747 A.U.C. (7 B.C.). King Herod the Great died in the year 750 A.U.C. (4 B.C.). This is known with certainty from the historical data of the beginning and length of his reign.

Historical writers also tell us a lunar eclipse took place just before Herod's death, and astronomers calculate that this eclipse took place on March 12-13, 750 A.U.C.—4 B.C. Since Herod was still alive when Christ was born (Mt 2), Christ must have been born *before* 750 A.U.C. (4 B.C.). Christ must then have been born in the period 747-750 A.U.C. (7-4 B.C.). Other considerations narrow this down to 749 or 750 A.U.C. (5 or 4 B.C.). For ordinary calculation of time, of course, we still hold to the officially accepted chronology originating with Dennis the Little.

EIGHT

The Lay of the Land

JESUS PREACHED his message of the Kingdom in a particular locality: Palestine, a land of considerable variety, not only in its landscape but also, to a certain extent, in its inhabitants. This chapter will survey the provinces of Jesus' time and pay particular attention to places mentioned in the Gospels and to Jesus' travels.

The Shape of the Landscape

The present form of the Palestinian landscape came about by a complicated process of mountain formation in very early times. Mountains are formed either by tensions in the earth or by layers of sand and stone deposited by the sea or the wind. During a very severe earthquake, the rocky platform underneath Palestine was broken open and the top layers sank into the hole, leaving a very long and deep trough—the Jordan Valley. The extent of this can be imagined if we remember that the crack is more than 300 miles long, and that the gap is in places more than thirty miles wide and 3,000 feet deep! This fault creates five regions in Palestine (see fig. 1).

1. The Plains. Mainly a narrow strip on the coast of the sea which sweeps inland around Mt. Tabor, forming a large valley called Esdraelon (or Jezreel).

2. The Hill Country. Hills and valleys of various types in the middle part of the land. The slopes of these hills can be cultivated.

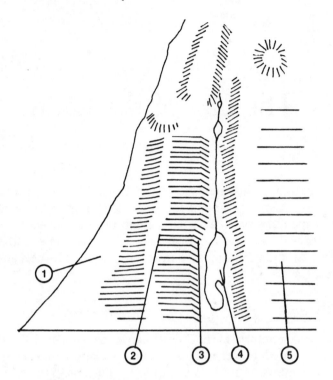

Fig. 1. Geographic regions of Palestine

3. The Desert. A barren and lifeless area, especially near the Dead Sea and further south.

4. The Jordan Valley. Holds the Sea of Galilee and the Dead Sea. Sinks deeper towards the south.

5. The Mountains of Trans-Jordan. This high plateau is partly fertile, partly desert.

The Provinces of Palestine in Jesus' Time

"Palestine" means "Land of the Philistines" (a nation occupying the coastal areas and dominating the land until King David defeated them). In the Gospels we read of the major provinces in Jesus' time: "Great crowds followed Jesus from Galilee and the Decapolis, from Jerusalem and Judea, and from the other side of the Jordan [Perea]" (Mt 4:25). As we look at each province, consult the map in Figure 2.

Judea. The inhabitants were mainly Jews who had returned from the Babylonian captivity. The leading religious classes had all settled here. Judea was the main seat of fanatical pro-Jewish nationalistic movements. The population was concentrated around Jerusalem, the capital, and around Jericho. The southern part of Judea and the region around the Dead Sea were desert. Jesus was tempted in the desert region south of Jericho (Mt 4:1).

Galilee. Galilee too had a Jewish population, but because of the many non-Jews who had settled in this province, society was more cosmopolitan. The Galileans had their own dialect. They were impetuous and zealous about religion. Their province was more prosperous than Judea, because of the greater fertility of the land, and more densely populated. The largest cities were Sephphoris (five miles north of Nazareth) and Tiberias, the capital.

Perea. This province lay on the other side of the Jordan and also had a large Jewish population. Its territory was larger than Galilee, but much less inhabitable. The people lived in small cities where valleys made agriculture possible, or in fortresses for the defense of Palestine.

Samaria. This province was reasonably prosperous. The inhabitants were descendants from the foreigners imported into Palestine by the Assyrian kings. In spite of earlier aberrations, they had gradually come to a full acceptance of monotheism and of the Law of Moses. Since the Jews did not permit them to come to Jerusalem for worship, they had erected their own shrine on Gerizim, a mountain near Sychar (Jn 4). There was a

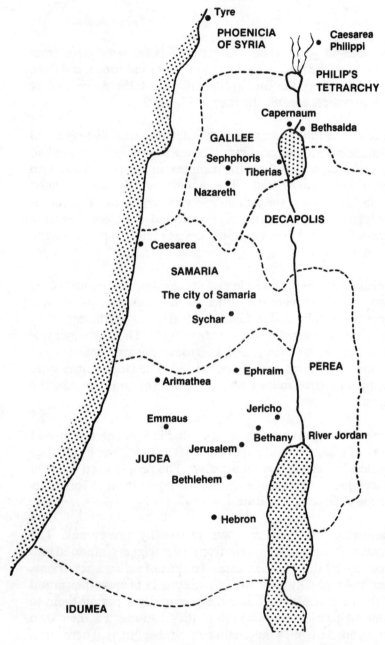

Fig. 2. Towns and provinces of Palestine

continuous state of fierce hostility between the Jews and the Samaritans. Samaria also had many Greek-speaking non-Jews. The city of Samaria, with its Greek and Roman temples, was completely pagan.

The Decapolis. This province arose from a confederation of ten cities which had received some measure of self-government from the Roman general Pompey in 64 B.C. Other cities joined later. The population was generally Gentile, and the cities flourished as centers of Greek (Hellenistic) culture. Leading among them were Scythopolis and Damascus.

Phoenicia of Syria. This was part of the Roman province of Syria. In the southernmost strip of this province there must have been a few Jewish villages, but the large majority of the inhabitants were non-Jews. Tyre and Sidon (north of Tyre) had gained a worldwide fame through their trade.

Philip's Tetrarchy. This comprised various regions that stretched to the north of Palestine—Gaulanitis (south of the Hermon), Ituraea, and Trachonitis (Lk 3:1). The inhabitants belonged to many non-Jewish nationalities. The main cities mentioned in the Gospels are Bethsaida (also called Iulias) and Caesarea Philippi (also called Paneas).

Idumea. This province was called after the Edomites who settled south of Judea after the first fall of Jerusalem. The population lived in small settlements in the desert wasteland. Herod the Great belonged to a leading Idumean family.

Jesus' Neighborhood: Northern Galilee

Some places in northern Galilee played a greater role in the Gospels and deserve more attention (see fig. 3).

Capernaum. Jesus went to live there (Mt 4:13). There he cured the officer's slave (Mt 8:5-12), the leper (Mt 8:2-3),

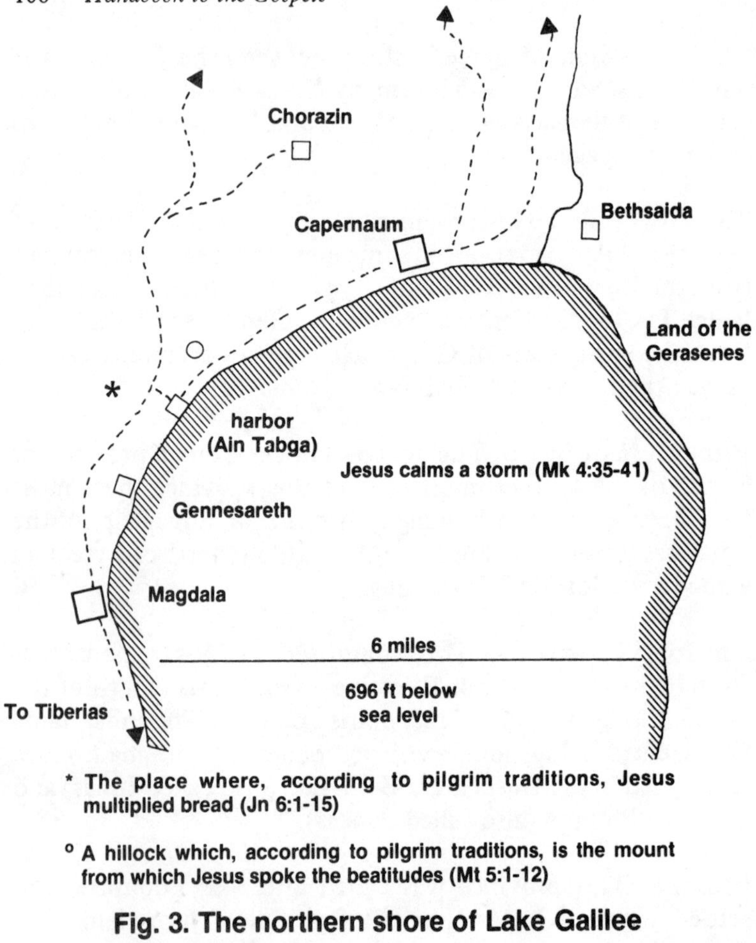

* The place where, according to pilgrim traditions, Jesus multiplied bread (Jn 6:1-15)

° A hillock which, according to pilgrim traditions, is the mount from which Jesus spoke the beatitudes (Mt 5:1-12)

Fig. 3. The northern shore of Lake Galilee

Peter's mother-in-law (Mt 8:14-15), the man with an evil spirit (Mk 1:21-26), the paralyzed man (Mk 2:1-12). In Capernaum's synagogue Jesus spoke of the eucharist (Jn 6:17, 24, 59). In this city Jesus called Matthew (Mt 9:9) and paid the Temple tax (Mt 17:24). Jesus denounced Capernaum for its lack of faith (Mt 11:23).

Chorazin. In spite of Jesus' miracles it was hardened in pride (Mt 11:21; Lk 10:13).

Bethsaida. Near this place Jesus walked on the water (Mk 6:45). Here he gave sight to a blind man (Mk 8:22), and withdrew with his disciples for some rest (Lk 9:10). It was also the birthplace of Philip (Jn 12:21).

Magdala. In this town Jesus was invited to have dinner with Simon the Pharisee. Mary Magdalene was converted on that occasion (Lk 7:36-8:2).

Ain Tabgha. A natural harbor and a good place for fishing on account of underwater wells there. This may have been the place where the risen Jesus appeared to the apostles and where he had breakfast with them (Jn 21).

Land of the Gerasenes. The precise whereabouts of this locality are not known, but it must have been on the east side of the lake. Jesus cured a man with evil spirits here (Mk 5:1-20). The lake itself had three names—Sea of Galilee, Lake of Gennesareth, Sea of Tiberias.

Jesus' Journeys

In many instances the Gospel accounts quite clearly describe Jesus' journeys. From archaeology we know the principal roads that existed in his time. With the help of such information we can reconstruct the exact routes he took. We will work out some examples here (see fig. 4).

Journey to Bethlehem. Joseph went from the town of Nazareth in Galilee to the town of Bethlehem in Judea (Lk 2:4). The most direct way would lead through Samaria. On the way to Bethlehem, Joseph and Mary had to pass through Jerusalem.

From Judea to Galilee. Jesus left Judea and went back to Galilee; on his way there he had to go through Samaria. "In Samaria he came to a town named Sychar. . . . Jacob's well was

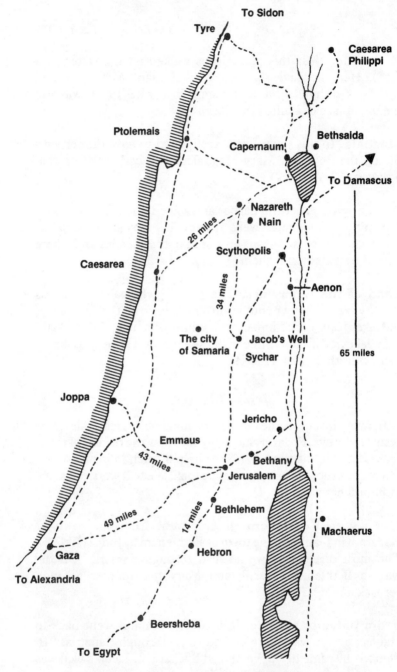

Fig. 4. Palestine: journeys and distances

there" (Jn 4:3). Sychar is just half-way between Jerusalem and Nazareth. Travellers would normally stop at the well.

A Trip to Tyre and Sidon

Then Jesus left and went away to the territory near the city of Tyre. . . . Jesus then left the neighborhood of Tyre and went on through Sidon to Lake Galilee, going by way of the territory of the Ten Towns (Mk 7:31).

Jesus makes a round trip. From Capernaum he goes north to Tyre and Sidon. Then he turns right and, making a large circle, returns to the Sea of Galilee.

The Road of the Good Samaritan (Lk 10:30). The road from Jerusalem to Jericho was well-known to all Jews. It was only fourteen miles long. Practically the whole road is one continuous descent into the Jordan Valley, from 2,100 feet above sea level to 1,000 feet below sea level. The second half of the road passes through the Desert of Judea, a place infested with robbers at the time of Jesus.

The Trip to Caesarea Philippi. Jesus crossed from the side of Capernaum to Bethsaida, and then proceeded north to Caesarea Philippi (the first part of this route not being an important road).

He left them, got back into the boat, and started across to the other side of the lake. . . . They came to Bethsaida. . . .Then Jesus and his disciples went away to the villages near Caesarea Philippi. (Mk 8:13, 22, 27)

Final Journey to Jerusalem. When Jesus left Galilee to go back to Judea, he sometimes crossed the River Jordan (Mt 19:1; Mk 10:1), not going through Samaria but by way of Perea. This road on the other side of the Jordan recrossed the river to go to

Jerusalem by way of Jericho (Mk 10:46), Bethphage, and
Bethany (Mk 11:1).

The Walk to Emmaus. "On that same day two of Jesus'
followers were going to a village named Emmaus, about eleven
kilometers from Jerusalem" (Lk 24:13). The location of
Emmaus is not altogether certain, nor the distance very definite
(the original Greek says "sixty *stadia*" but there are many
traditional explanations of this). In any case, it must have been
the road to Joppe which was followed by the disciples.

NINE

The Temple and the Synagogue

TWO BUILDINGS were important in the Judaism of Jesus' day—though their origins and their functions were very different. These were the Temple and the synagogue. The heart of Judaism was the Temple, and we look first to that.

History of the Temple

David Begins Preparations (998 B.C.). When King David had unified the Israelite tribes under his rule, he made Jerusalem his capital. He erected the sacred tent in this city, brought the Ark into it and thus made Jerusalem the religious center of Israel (2 Sm 6). David also conceived the idea of building a Temple for God (and the Ark). He himself could not fulfill this task, but he prepared the way by amassing materials and money (1 Chr 22:2-5) and selecting a beautiful spot just outside the city, Arauna's threshing floor, on top of the hill Moriah (2 Sm 24:18-25).

Solomon Completes the Building (960 B.C.). King Solomon put David's plan into operation. With the help of Phoenician artists he built a sanctuary so beautiful that it was considered one of the seven wonders of the world. The central shrine was a masterpiece of carved white limestone, cyprus and cedar woodwork, gold and silver decorations, and various kinds of the very top of the hill. In order to make spacious courts around the sanctuary, Solomon filled up the valley on one side of the hill, covering it with rubble and earth until a wide platform for the whole Temple area had been created. The Temple was dedicated with great solemnity (1 Kgs 5-8).

Babylonians Destroy the Temple (587 B.C.). The obstinate infidelity of the Jews made God withdraw his favor from the Temple. In punishment for Israel's sins the Temple was completely destroyed by Nebuchadnezzar, the king of the Babylonians (2 Kgs 25:1-17). All the treasure and precious furniture were carried off to Babylon. The ark was hidden and never found again. Only the empty Temple courtyard remained, filled with ashes and ruins.

Zerubbabel Rebuilds the Temple (515 B.C.). Some Jews who returned from the exile started rebuilding the Temple. Zerubbabel, a descendant of David and governor of Judah, had an important share in this work, so that the Temple was named after him (Neh 12:47). The work was begun in 537 B.C., but frequently had to be interrupted because of the hostility of the surrounding nations. The final product (515 B.C.) covered the same area as Solomon's Temple, but was much poorer in execution and decoration.

Herod the Great's Temple (20 B.C.). When Herod the Great became King of Palestine, he offered to restore this Temple of Zerubbabel. The central building was dilapidated. The sides of the courts had crumbled away in the course of the years. Herod offered to make this Temple one of the greatest structures in the Roman Empire, and after a good deal of hesitation the Pharisees and priests agreed to it. They put down many conditions. The building should not start until all the materials had been assembled. The inner sanctuary would be rebuilt by the priests themselves, who were to use materials prepared by workmen outside. The old building should only be taken down part by part, with the new parts immediately substituting for the old, so that sacrifices need never be interrupted. Herod agreed to all this. The sanctuary buildings were thus restored in the course of two years' hard labor. Herod also extended the size of the Temple courts by filling up the adjacent valleys and building a huge wall (Herod's Wall) around the whole square. The porches, fortresses, entrances, and gates were all very beautiful, and the whole complex did become one of the most outstanding structures of Herod's time (see fig. 1).

The construction was completed in 64 A.D., putting 18,000 men out of work. Six years later it was destroyed in the Roman War (68-70 A.D.).

Herod's Temple

Herod's Temple stood on the hill overlooking the Kedron Valley. Coming from the Mount of Olives one had more or less the view in Figure 1. The eye was caught immediately by two outstanding buildings: the central sanctuary and the Fortress of Antonia (where, possibly, Jesus was tried by Pilate). The traveller who approached the Temple from this side could not but be impressed by the sight. On one occasion Jesus and the apostles looked at the Temple buildings from the Mount of Olives (Mt 24:3; Mk 13:3). The disciples were taken with the beauty of the Temple (Mk 13:1), and Jesus foretold its destruction and the coming of the Last Judgment (Mt 24; Mk 13; Lk 21). Jesus wept over Jerusalem as he was coming down the same Mount of Olives (Lk 19:41-44). This magnificent building represented to Jesus the center, the core, of his own Jewish nation. Like any Jew, Jesus was proud of the Temple and loved it.

Coming from the Mount of Olives one would enter the Temple through the eastern gate. This is the gate used by Jesus on Palm Sunday (Mt 21:12; Mk 11:11; Lk 19:45), and by this gate he would leave again for Bethany (Mt 21:17; Mk 11:19).

If one entered the southern gate one came onto the Court of the Gentiles. This great square received its name from the fact

Fig. 1. The Temple of Herod as seen from the Mount of Olives

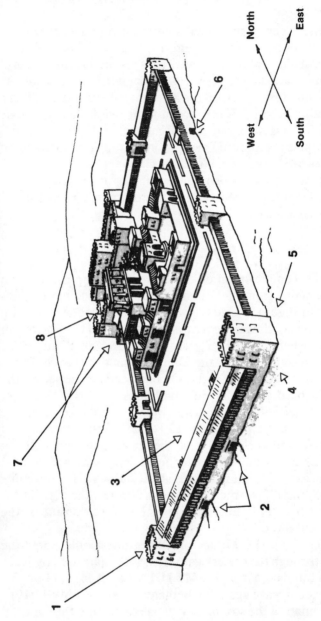

North
East
West
South

1. Southern Colonnades (called "The Royal Porch")
2. The Southern Gates
3. Court of the Gentiles
4. The Pinnacles
5. Eastern Colonnades (called "Solomon's Porch")
6. Eastern Gate
7. Central Sanctuary
8. Fortress of Antonia

Fig. 2. Temple of Herod: ground plan

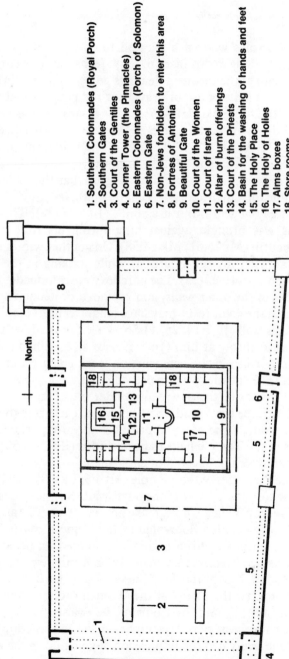

1. Southern Colonnades (Royal Porch)
2. Southern Gates
3. Court of the Gentiles
4. Corner Tower (the Pinnacles)
5. Eastern Colonnades (Porch of Solomon)
6. Eastern Gate
7. Non-Jews forbidden to enter this area
8. Fortress of Antonia
9. Beautiful Gate
10. Court of the Women
11. Court of Israel
12. Altar of burnt offerings
13. Court of the Priests
14. Basin for the washing of hands and feet
15. The Holy Place
16. The Holy of Holies
17. Alms boxes
18. Store rooms

that Gentiles were also allowed to enter it. No doubt many Gentiles came to this place to pray. Jesus was, therefore, highly indignant at the business dealings going on there: "My temple will be called a house of prayer for the people of all nations!" (Mt 21:12-13; Mk 11:15-17; Lk 19:45-46). In this same court Jesus disputed with the priests. During one such discussion (Mt 21:23-27; Mk 11:27-33; Lk 20:1-8), in which the priests were asking for a proof of his authority, Jesus pointed to his Resurrection, a far greater building-up than the building of the Temple then in progress: "Tear down this house of God and in three days I will build it again!" (Jn 2:18-22). This claim of Jesus was brought against him during his trial before the Sanhedrin (Mt 26:61; Mk 14:58). On another winter day Jesus was accosted by the Pharisees while walking in the Porch of Solomon (Jn 10:22-23). The porches were colonnades lining the insides of the outer walls, and provided protection against the sun and the cold. Jesus may have taught in the Temple at other times as well (Jn 7:14, 28, 11:56). One day the Jews picked up stones to throw at him (Jn 8:59). In all likelihood they were stones for use in the construction work going on in the outer court. The apostles were to preach in this same place (Acts 3:11, 5:12). It may be that it was also under one of these porches that the boy Jesus was found with the Jewish teachers in the Temple. At any rate, since Mary approaches the group, the innermost parts of the Temple have to be excluded (Lk 2:41-50), because women were not allowed to enter them.

The Pinnacles of the Temple (Mt 4:5; Lk 4:9) may have been on the southeast tower of the outer wall. The steep descent into the Kedron Valley would make any fall from it fatal.

A more detailed floor-plan of the Temple courts is in Figure 2. Gentiles could enter the Court of the Gentiles (no. 3), but a railing had been erected beyond which only Jews were allowed to pass (no. 7). Approaching the sanctuary one had to pass three inner courts: the Court of the Women (no. 10), the Court of Israel (no. 11), and the Court of the Priests (no. 13). Each of these courts was five steps higher than the preceding court so that one really had the impression of going up to the mountain of God. This would especially be true for those who entered the court from the side of the city through the Southern Gate (no. 2). These gates were actually tunnels underneath the Royal Porch (no. 1) which opened out into the Court of the Gentiles. (Compare: "Two men *went up* to the Temple to pray," [Lk 15:10]).

One could enter the Court of the Women (no. 10) through the Beautiful Gate (no. 9). It was at this gate that Peter cured the lame man who used to beg there (Acts 3:1-10). The Court of the Women owed its name to the fact that women were allowed to enter it but not go beyond it. In the corners of the court there were storerooms (no. 18) for keeping the wood, wine, oil, and other materials necessary for sacrifice. The other rooms seem to have been used for the ritual of declaring lepers clean (Mt 8:4; Lk 17:14) and for the rite of cutting one's hair at the end of a vow (Acts 21:23-24, 26).

The Court of the Women also contained thirteen alms boxes (no. 17), in which obligatory and voluntary contributions for the Temple were deposited.

> As Jesus sat near the temple treasury, he watched the people as they dropped in their money. Many rich men dropped in a lot of money; then a poor widow came along and dropped in two little copper coins, worth about a penny.
>
> (Mk 12:41-44; see also Lk 21:1-4)

Jesus used the occasion to teach his disciples about the way in which God values gifts. Jesus' teaching about himself as the "Light of the World" also took place "in the room where the offering boxes were placed" (Jn 8:20). In this court too the prophetess Anna worshipped God day and night (Lk 2:36-38).

When Mary and Joseph brought Jesus to the Temple for the ceremony of purification (Lk 2:22-24), Mary would have stayed behind in the Court of the Women while Joseph proceeded into the Court of Israel (no. 11), which only men could enter. This court was small, and was like a porch looking out on one side into the Court of the Priests (no. 13). The priest would have taken Joseph's offering of turtle doves up to the altar (no. 12) and performed the rite (Lv 12:1-8). Christ was thinking of this place when he said that the man who remembered his brother had something against him should leave his gift before the altar (Mt 5:23-24).

The Court of Israel is the place where Jewish men went to pray, facing the sanctuary (Lk 18:10-13) in the morning and the evening to join in the common prayers and in the sacrifice of incense. While the priest would enter the sanctuary, the crowd would wait for his return and his blessing (Lk 1:8-10, 21-22). Jesus must often have prayed here. Here the disciples gathered after his ascension to "give thanks to God" (Lk 24:53) and to say common prayers with all Christians, probably at three o'clock in the afternoon (Acts 2:46, 3:1). Here Paul had his vision regarding his special task (Acts 22:17). Here we have to imagine the scene of the parable: the Pharisee standing apart so that all can see him, the publican at the back in a corner (Lk 18:10-13).

The most sacred part of the Temple was undoubtedly the sanctuary. It was an impressively high building, built with white stones, some of which were of very great size—36 feet long, 18 feet broad, and 12 feet high! The building had two rooms (see fig. 3). The first room was called the Holy Place, and normally only priests could enter it. There were three objects in the room: the altar on which incense was burned (no. 1), the table with showbread offerings (no. 2), and the candlestick with seven branches (no. 3). The showbread consisted of twelve loaves, representing the twelve tribes of Israel, and stood continually before God as an oblation (Lv 24:5-9). Periodically it had to be renewed. Priests, and only priests, had then to eat the old loaves. Jesus reminds the Pharisees that David ate of these loaves when no other bread could be found, and did not sin in doing so, because in special circumstances laws do not bind (Mt 12:3-4; Mk 2:25-26; 1 Sm 21:5-7).

The priests were divided into twelve priestly orders. Each of these orders did service for one month out of a year. Zechariah belonged to the priestly order of Abijah (Lk 1:5), and left his

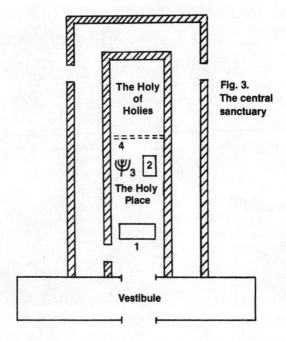

Fig. 3.
The central
sanctuary

The Holy
of
Holies

The Holy
Place

Vestibule

home to serve his month in Jerusalem (Lk 1:23). It was the custom of the priests to determine by lot who was to perform the oblation of incense; once when it fell to Zechariah, he entered the Holy Place alone (Lk 1:8-9) and there saw a vision "at the right side of the altar where the incense was burned" (Lk 1:11). When Zechariah came out into the Court of Priests, facing the people in the Court of Israel who were waiting for him, he could not speak (Lk 1:21-22).

Beyond the Holy Place was a smaller room called the Holy of Holies. This room should have contained the Ark of the Covenant, but, as the Ark was not found after the exile, it was empty. There were no windows or doors to let in light. As far as we know there was nothing inside except a flat, black stone on which the high priest put a thurible during the one occasion of

Modern view of the Temple area showing the Dome of the Rock

the year when he, and he alone, was allowed to enter the room: on the Day of Atonement. The Holy of Holies was separated from the Holy Place by a curtain of precious materials, the veil (no. 4). It is this veil that was split in two at Jesus' death (Mt 27:51; Mk 15:38; Lk 23:45). We must understand the symbolic meaning of this. In the structure of the Temple, God was not approachable: non-Jews and women could not enter, the men could not enter the Court of the Priests, and only the high priest could enter the Holy of Holies. By Jesus' sacrifice all have direct access to God.

It is abundantly clear from Jesus' words and actions that he greatly respected the Temple of Jerusalem. Jesus always gave honorific titles to the Temple, calling it "the house of God" (Mt 12:4; Lk 6:4), "my Father's house" (Jn 2:16), and "a house of prayer for all the nations" (Mk 11:17; see also Mt 21:13; Lk 19:46). Out of this respect he undertook the difficult task of driving out the merchants. In a dispute with the Pharisees he said that God, who lived in the Temple, sanctified everything in it (Mt 23:16-22). When asked to pay the Temple tax, he explained that as God's Son he was exempted, but he paid the tax so not to offend (Mt 17:24-27). Jesus participated in the prayers and sacrifices in the Temple. He often preached and taught in it.

Though Jesus proved his respect in deeds, he at the same time taught that his coming would mean the end of the Temple.

For Jews, sacrifice could only be offered in the Temple. On Sabbath days they could gather for prayer in synagogues (prayer-halls), but they could not offer sacrifice. Now Jesus taught that the Temple was to lose its position.

He himself is the Temple built by the Resurrection. Arguing with the Pharisees, Jesus said that as the priests are allowed to work on the Sabbath, because they work for the Temple, his disciples too are allowed to work on the Sabbath, for "something greater than the temple is here" (Mt 12:5-6). To the Samaritan woman, Jesus announced a completely new way of sacrifice, in which the place is not important and which does not consist of burnt offerings (Jn 4:20-24). Jesus announced the destruction of the Temple (Mt 24:2; Mk 13:2; Lk 21:6) as the sign that God had forsaken his former home (Mt 23:37-39; Lk 13:34-35). For Christians, therefore, it is no longer the Temple of Jerusalem, but Jesus himself, that forms the center of worship. We ourselves are the church, the new Temple (1 Cor 3:9, 16-17; 2 Cor 6:16; Eph 2:19-22). Our Temple is Christ himself, and we are living temples insofar as we are united to him. Our new sacrifice is the eucharist, which can be celebrated anywhere in his memory (Lk 22:19-20).

The Synagogue

When we think of Jesus going about preaching and teaching, we often think of him doing this out-of-doors, perhaps sitting

LEFT: A modern synagogue in Jerusalem

BELOW: Heichal Shlomo Synagogue in Jerusalem. The ark is shown.

on a hill with the people gathered all around him. This may be true of some occasions, but he usually taught people in their synagogues.

> Jesus went all over Galilee, teaching in the synagogues, preaching the Good News about the Kingdom. (Mt 4:23)

> Jesus and his disciples came to the town of Capernaum, and on the next Sabbath Jesus went to the synagogue and began to teach. . . . So he traveled all over Galilee, preaching in the synagogues and driving out demons. (Mk 1:21, 39)

> Then Jesus went to Nazareth . . . and on the Sabbath he went as usual to the synagogue. (Lk 4:15-16)

Paul and the other apostles also used to preach in the synagogues wherever they went. This was the other great focal point of Jewish life.

When the first Temple was destroyed in 587 B.C. and the majority of the Jews were taken into exile, they began to have prayer assemblies in other places, especially on Sabbaths and New Moons. These places of assembly for prayer were called synagogues and continued even after the Temple was restored. The word *synagogue* refers both to the people assembled and to the place of assembly. Every village had its own synagogue, and each town had several. In Jerusalem there seem to have been between 300 and 400 synagogues. Any Jew might build one or even turn his own house into one. In Luke 7:5 we find that a Roman officer built one. Any group of ten men could assemble, hence those of the same trade or profession would have their own, thus the synagogues of the Freedmen, of the Cyreneans, and Alexandrians (Acts 6:9).

The synagogue served three purposes: it was a house of prayer and worship; it was the place where community affairs were discussed and disputes were judged and settled; it was the local school and catechism class combined, where the Mosaic Law was studied and children learned the rudiments of education. Children were taken there at the age of five, rich and

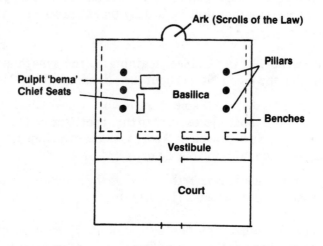

Fig. 4. The plan of an ancient synagogue

poor alike. The Lord surely went to the synagogue at Nazareth for his early education. There he would have learned part of the Law by heart, i.e., the first five books of the Old Testament.

In all probability the synagogues were modelled after the Temple in Jerusalem, with a court, vestibule, and an inner room called the *basilica* (see fig. 4). The most important feature was the *tebhah* or ark in which were kept the scrolls of the Law and the Prophets, preserved in a leather case and covered with linen. The ark was set in the apse of the building and shut by a door or curtain. A lamp continually burned before it. In the apse were also kept the trumpets used to proclaim the holy days. In the body of the basilica was the pulpit (*bema*) from which the Law and Prophets were read out loud each Sabbath, and from where the sermon was given, sitting down (Lk 4:16-20); sitting was the normal posture for teaching (Mt 5:1-2). The men would sit around on benches or stools, but there were special places of honor near the pulpit (Mt 23:6). Women could attend but had to sit in the gallery that ran around the sides of the building. If there were no gallery they would still sit separate from the men.

There was no altar in the synagogue. The only decoration might be a seven-branched candlestick, or the five- or six-pointed Star of David. Outside the building there was usually water available for ablutions. The people prayed standing, turned towards Jerusalem, as did the reader of the Law and the preacher.

The synagogue was opened three times a day for those who wished to pray, but the most important day of prayer was the Sabbath. The service on the Sabbath was fixed, and in no way resembled the Temple service. It had nothing sacrificial about it. No priest was necessary, and if there was a priest in the community, he did not lead the whole service. The normal Sabbath service ran as follows:

1. Opening prayers: *Shema* (Dt 6:4-9) and The Eighteen Benedictions.

2. Reading of the Law (by seven readers) from the pulpit. All readers of the Law were allowed to comment on the text they had just read. This commentary was called *midrash*. The whole Law (five books) was read over a three-year period.

3. A lesson was read from one of the Prophets by one person according to his own choice.

4. Sermon or Instruction.

5. Blessing from Numbers 6:24-26, given by a priest if present. At the end of the service each person gave alms to the collectors as he left the synagogue. The whole service, which took place in the morning, lasted about an hour. This custom of reading scripture and instruction was maintained in the early church.

The management of the meeting-house was in the hands of the community. There was no special priest or minister. The "ruler" of the synagogue was appointed by the people. He saw to public order, maintenance, etc. (Lk 8:41, 13:14; Acts 13:15). Besides the ruler there was also the attendant (Lk 4:20), who was the general factotum: servant, sacristan, caretaker, and even sometimes schoolmaster, if there were no more qualified person available. This person handed Jesus the scroll of Isaiah in Nazareth (Lk 4:17, 20).

The importance of the synagogue cannot be overestimated in

the lives of the Jews at the time of Christ. Everyone, without exception, went to the synagogue not only for worship, but also for administrative and judicial business. The synagogue settled court cases among the Jewish community. It had the power to excommunicate anyone from its assemblies (Mt 23:13; Lk 21:12; Jn 9:22, 35) and to whip offenders and criminals (Mt 10:17, 23:34). Outside Palestine it was the synagogue that ensured the unity of the Jews and prevented believers from being swallowed up in the morass of paganism.

TEN

The Religious Life of the Day

THE REQUIREMENTS and observances of Judaism are more than simply important background to the Gospels. Jesus' whole mission was to complete for all men and women the work God began among the Jews. Thus, to understand Jesus' mission, we must have a good understanding of what the Jews believed, how they worshipped, and how their religious leadership functioned.

The Requirements of the Law

In the Sermon on the Mount, Jesus referred to "the Law of Moses and the teachings of the Prophets" (Mt 5:17). To a practicing Jew the term "Law and Prophets" stood for the sum total of God's revelation. Each Sabbath he heard the reading from the Law (the first five books of the Bible) and the Prophets. The books of wisdom (Wisdom, Tobias, Job, Proverbs, Ecclesiastes, Song of Songs, etc.) and the historical books (Joshua, Judges, Samuel, Kings, Chronicles, Maccabees, etc.) were not normally read in the regular Sabbath service. The pious Jew would know the Law by heart or at least very well. It was the foundation of his education. That is why the Lord and the apostles could refer to passages without complex citations or explanation (Mt 12:5, 12:7; Mk 7:6, 10). In fact, since Matthew was writing for Jews, his references to them are many (Mt 1:23, 2:18, 23, 4:15-16, 8:17, 12:18-21, 13:35, 21:5, 27:9-10); his whole theme is that Jesus came to fulfill the Law and the

Prophets. At the transfiguration, when Peter, James, and John see Jesus talking with Moses and Elijah (Mt 17:1-13; Mk 9:2-13; Lk 9:28-36), Moses is the personification of the Law and Elijah of the Prophets—making the event suggestive of the Messiahship of Jesus.

A Jewish boy would begin to learn the Law at the age of five. At ten he would begin to study the tradition explaining the Law. At thirteen he would be required to know the whole of the Law of Moses (Pentateuch or Torah) and follow its prescriptions. The first five books of the Bible were used to teach a child the ABCs, language, grammar, history, geography. It was said, "A child ought to be fattened with the Torah as an ox is fattened in the stall." And, "The maxims of the Law go in by the blood and come out at the lips." Girls too learned the Law. The Talmud says, "Every man is required to teach his daughter the Torah."

Let us look at some of the elements of Jewish life in Jesus' day.

Prayer, Fasting, and Almsgiving. These were the chief works of piety imposed by the Law on Jews; Jesus also prescribed them for his followers.

Prayer. Beside the official prayers in the Temple and the synagogue, Jews were expected to pray three times daily, at the third, sixth, and ninth hours (morning, afternoon, and evening). This was a duty of all males over thirteen years of age. We find the apostles going to pray in the Temple at the ninth hour (Acts 3:1) and Peter praying at noon (Acts 10:9).

In praying, a Jew would wrap himself in his *tallith* (prayer shawl) and wrap the *tephillin* (phylacteries) on his arms and forehead. These *tephillin* are small containers in which passages from Exodus and Deuteronomy written on parchment were kept.

They do everything so that people will see them. Look at the straps with scripture verses on them which they wear on their foreheads and arms, and notice how large they are! Notice also how long are the tassels on their cloaks! (Mt 23:5)

Prayers were usually said standing (Mk 11:25; Lk 18:11, 13), but kneeling, prostrations, touching the face to the floor, and other postures were also used. Hands were usually held uplifted (Ps 28:2, 63:4; 1 Tm 2:8). Many prayers were used, especially the psalms, but the two most common prayers said every day were the *Shema* and the *Shemoneh Esreh* (Eighteen Benedictions). These two prayers also were used every Sabbath in the synagogue service.

The *Shema* (Listen!) is a profession of faith which every Jew knew by heart:

> Israel, remember this! The Lord—and the Lord alone—is our God. Love the Lord your God with all your heart, with all your soul, and with all your strength. Never forget these commands that I am giving you today. Teach them to your children. Repeat them when you are at home and when you are away, when you are resting and when you are working. Tie them to your arms and wear them on your foreheads as a reminder. Write them on the doorposts of your houses and on your gates. (Dt 6:4-9; see also 11:13-21)

The prayer continues for two paragraphs more. When Jesus is questioned as to the greatest commandment he replies with this prayer (Mt 22:34-40; Mk 12:28-34; Lk 10:25-28).

The *Shemoneh Esreh* is a longer prayer containing requests for daily bread, spiritual grace, the forgiveness of sins, the restoration of Jerusalem, the reuniting of the tribes, and the advent of the Kingdom of God. When Jesus taught the disciples to pray, his prayer is a kind of simplified *Shemoneh Esreh*. Many of the expressions, including the first two words, "Our Father," are taken from that prayer. In the Lord's teaching on prayer (Mt 6:5-15, 7:7-12; Lk 11:1-13) he only condemns the abuses which can render prayer useless as true communication with God and worship of him, not formulated prayer itself.

Fasting. There was one public day of fasting obligatory for all, the Day of Atonement, but private voluntary fasting was commonly done in sorrow for sins (David, Job, Paul in Acts

9:9). Some Pharisees fasted every Monday and Thursday (Lk 18:12) and Anna fasted often (Lk 2:37). The Lord himself fasted for forty days before his public ministry began, just as Moses and Elijah did (Mt 4:1-4; Ex 34:28; 1 Kgs 19:8). Jesus' teaching on fasting, just as his teaching on prayer, was nothing new; he wanted to remove the external show, to purify it from the abuses that had crept in, and to renew the inner spirit and motivation of fasting (Mt 6:16-18). He said that his followers would fast after the bridegroom had left (Mt 9:14-15; Mk 2:18-20; Lk 5:33-34). Of course, fasting then meant total abstention from all food and drink. Our commonest way of fasting, with one full meal per day being permitted, is mild indeed in comparison.

Almsgiving. In the Gospels, the Lord speaks out against abuses in almsgiving (Mt 6:1-4). He also preaches on the blessings of almsgiving (Mt 25:34-35). In the early church the needs of the poor were effectively met; Jesus' teaching on temporal goods was put into practice.

> No one said that any of his belongings was his own, but they all shared with one another everything they had. . . . There was no one in the group who was in need. (Acts 4:32, 34)

But Jesus really taught nothing basically new in regard to almsgiving. In this matter he stressed the existing obligation to give alms (Dt 15:11) and raised it from legalism to the ideal. To refuse alms, say Jewish writers, is "even graver than idolatry" (Rabbi Joshua ben Gorba). Hence when the publican (tax-collector) Zacchaeus said he would give half of what he had to the poor (Lk 19:8), he was merely fulfilling his long neglected duty, imposed by the Law: "You shall open wide your hand to your brother, to the needy and to the poor in the land" (Dt 15:11).

Matthew intentionally sets out the good news in the context of these three duties (Mt 6:1-6, 16-18) to show that Jesus came not to do away with the Law and the Prophets, "but to make their teachings come true" (Mt 5:17).

Clean and Unclean: Purification and Ablution. Among the Jews, physical cleanliness rendered a man ready to approach God if his motives were proper. "Cleanliness," says Rabbi A. Cohen, "is not merely a near neighbor to piety; it is an integral part of it."

It is not clear why the Jews thought certain things make a man unclean. Partly it was due to a fear of the unknown (e.g., leprosy). Partly it was for hygienic reasons. Partly it was out of reverence for God and his holy places. The Law of Moses clearly distinguished between the clean and the unclean, the holy and the unholy (Lv 10:10). Uncleanliness was primarily *ceremonial* defilement, not *moral,* unless done willfully. For example, touching a dead body rendered a man ceremonially unclean, but he would do a morally good action in burying the body of a friend or relative. Moral defilement separates a man from God. Ceremonial defilement would only keep a Jew from service in the Temple or synagogue and from fellowship with other Jews. In Jesus' time there were some teachers of the Law who elevated the ritual of cleanliness over the moral and ethical. The Lord denounced these teachers:

> It is not what goes into a person's mouth that makes him ritually unclean . . . from his heart come the evil ideas which lead him to kill, commit adultery, . . . to rob, lie, and slander others. These are the things that make a person unclean.
> (Mt 15:1, 19-20; see also Mk 7:1-23)

Ceremonial (external) uncleanliness was contracted in several ways, and many of them are mentioned in the Gospels.

Contact with a dead body made a man unclean for seven days (Nm 19:11f).

Leprosy, whether in a person, clothing, or a house, was unclean (Lv 13:14). In Mark 1:40 Jesus met a leper who said, "You can make me clean." Jesus responded, "Be clean," then sent the man away to offer the purification rite as found in Leviticus 14 (sacrifice of one bird and release of another, washing of clothes, shaving of hair, and bathing of body).

Certain foods made the person who ate them unclean. There were unclean fish, birds, and animals (Lv 11; Dt 14). Jesus spoke of this type of uncleanness (Mt 15:1-20; Mk 7:1-23).

All sexual functions or those connected with the organs of reproduction were unclean (Lv 12, 15). Childbirth made the mother unclean for forty days if the child were a boy, eighty days if a girl. The rite of purification is mentioned in Leviticus 12 and Luke 2:24.

Any contact with blood was feared. Any animal that was eaten (even though a clean animal) without the blood being drained from it made the eater unclean (Ez 4:14; Ex 22:31; Lv 17:15, 22:8). Menstruation made a woman unclean for seven days, and her impurity was contagious (Lv 15:19-24). When the woman who suffered from severe bleeding for twelve years secretly touched Jesus' cloak she knew that, by the Law, anything or anyone she touched would be rendered unclean. That is why when Jesus asked, "Who touched me?" she came "trembling" and threw herself at his feet (Lk 8:43).

We find this background of ceremonial cleanliness in many places in the Gospels: the washing of hands before eating (Mt 15:2), the ritual of entering houses (Jn 2:6), the purification necessary to eat the Passover meal (Jn 11:55, 18:28). Jesus came frequently into conflict with the lawyers and Pharisees on the point of cleanliness. He insisted solely upon moral purity. The rules of cleanliness were made to lead the people to consider their inner (moral) state, but that was often forgotten. What matters is internal cleanness before God who looks not at the face but into the heart. The laws of ceremonial cleanliness were, therefore, abolished by Jesus (Mt 15:1-20; Acts 15).

Circumcision. The Law stated with finality that every male child was to be circumcised. This was done eight days after birth (Lk 1:59, 2:21). Circumcision was a rite practiced among many nations surrounding the Jews—Egyptians, Midianites, Edomites, Canaanites—but to the Jews this was a special religious rite, for in it they saw the mark of their membership in the people of God. God's plan for the salvation of the world was at work through the family and offspring of Abraham. God ratified this choice by sealing in it a covenant or treaty or testament: "You and your descendants must all agree to circumcise every male among you" (Gn 17:10). Circumcision showed that the person was a descendant of Abraham (either physically or spiritually). By the ceremony he was consecrated to God. A person who was not circumcised was unclean, and to call a Jew "uncircumcised" was the greatest of insults. At the time of the Maccabees, Jewish mothers chose death rather than give up circumcising their sons (1 Mc 1:60; 2 Mc 6:10). At his circumcision a male child would be named.

Circumcision was only the sign of an internal faith. It was through faith in God's promises that Abraham was justified by God. This was to set the example of finding favor (justification) for all his descendants. Those who were only outwardly circumcised but who did not have faith in God were an abomination in God's sight. Circumcision without faith made no one holy. John the Baptist warned:

> Do those things that will show that you have turned from your sins. And don't start saying among yourselves that Abraham is your ancestor. I tell you that God can take these stones and make descendants for Abraham.
>
> (Lk 3:8; see also Mt 3:9)

When Christians believe in Christ, they are baptized. Baptism is our circumcision—a circumcision of the heart, not of the flesh. Paul explains:

> After all, who is a real Jew, truly circumcised? It is not the man who is a Jew on the outside, whose circumcision is a physical thing. Rather, the real Jew is the person who is a Jew on the inside, that is, whose heart has been circumcised, and this is the work of God's Spirit, not of the written Law.
>
> (Rom 2:28-29)

As a result [of baptism], there is no longer any distinction between Gentiles and Jews, circumcised and uncircumcised, barbarians, savages, slaves, and free men, but Christ is all, Christ is in all. (Col 3:11)

Believers are the true children of Abraham—he is our father in faith.

Blasphemy. The person, and therefore the name, of God is to be honored and revered. Cursing and reviling it instead constitutes blasphemy. Not only God himself, but also his holy places and especially the Temple were objects against which a person could blaspheme. On hearing a blasphemy the pious Jew tore the hem of his cloak as a sign of horror (Mt 26:65; Mk 14:63). The penalty for blasphemy was death by stoning (Lv 24:10-23). Stephen the deacon was stoned to death for imputed blasphemy (Acts 6:13, 7:58).

The Jews accused Jesus chiefly of blasphemy, as when he forgave the sins of the crippled man (Mt 9:3; Mk 2:7), and on several occasions they tried to stone him to death for it (Jn 8:59, 10:33). They accused him of blasphemy again before the high priest (Mk 14:57-59), and finally sentenced him to death because he claimed to be God's son, which they considered blasphemous.

Diaspora. *Diaspora* is the Greek word for "dispersion." In biblical times the word was used of those Jews whose home was beyond the borders of Israel. At the time of the exile (587 B.C.) many Jews were taken away from their land. After the exile many did not return. They founded their communities (with their own synagogues) and numbered about seven or eight million within the confines of the Roman Empire. The chief centers of settlement were Rome and Alexandria, but there were colonies of Jews everywhere. Paul came from Tarsus; Simon who carried the cross of Jesus came from Cyrene (North Africa); Barnabas came from Cyprus, etc. It was among these scattered communities that Paul preached. At one time the Jews thought Jesus too would go there (Jn 7:35). At the Passover many of these Diaspora Jews came on pilgrimage to Jerusalem (Acts 2:9-11).

Proselytes. The word proselyte means "new arrival." It came to refer to those Gentiles (by birth) who had been converted to Judaism and who shared in Jewish beliefs, practices, and hopes.

In the period from about the third century B.C. onwards there seems to have been much missionary activity on the part of the Jews, especially by the Jews of the Diaspora (Mt 23:15). Converts were numerous despite the abhorrence of circumcision, the Sabbath, and abstention from pork (the pig was an unclean animal, Lv 11:7). Jewish morality and the doctrine of the one God appealed to many.

On entering Judaism, a proselyte would be received in three stages: circumcision, purification (or baptism), sacrifice. There were many sympathizers who did not go through the whole ritual (especially the rite of circumcision). We see from Acts (2:11, 6:5, 13:43) that many of the converts to the message of Christ in the early church were from this section of sympathizers and believers. Those deterred by circumcision were not put off by the cross. Moreover, these people had none of the national/racial prejudices that would be so strongly ingrained in a born Jew (Acts 13:16, 43, 16:14ff).

After the destruction of Jerusalem and the Temple (70 A.D.) the Jews abandoned their interest in the conversion of the world. In God's plan this task now rests upon us, the followers of his Son.

The Religious Leaders of the Jews

At the time of Jesus, Palestine was politically under the dominion of Herod's dynasty and of the Romans. The culture of the Greeks and the Romans—with their arts, their sports, their democratic institutions, and their literature—had made an impact on Palestine. Certain cities, such as Sebaste (Samaria), Sephphoris, Scythopolis, Caesarea, and Tiberias were constructed as Greek cities. Such towns even possessed Greek and Roman temples where gods from all parts of the Roman Empire were worshipped. Many Jews who studied at famous schools of learning felt attracted to this Greek and Roman culture and, obviously, some sought to imitate it.

In the preceding centuries, the Jewish people had suffered cruel persecutions under the Syrian kings who wanted to force them to accept Greek culture and Greek polytheism. Antiochus Epiphanes (175-164 B.C.), in particular, condemned and executed many orthodox Jews. The Books of the Maccabees tell us of their heroic martyrdom and of the liberation wars that arose as a result of the persecutions. It was through this tremendous spiritual as well as political struggle that a group of zealous orthodox Jews came to the fore—the Pharisees. Much of the leadership that had until then been enjoyed by the priestly classes now passed to the Pharisees. In Jesus' time there was no external persecution, but the pressure from Hellenism (Greek culture) could still be felt. In fact, another influential group of Jews was inclined to attempt a compromise with Greek culture—the Sadducees. Religious leadership in the Jewish community resided with the three groups represented in Figure 1.

The Sadducees counted quite a few priests and high priests among their ranks. Yet they have to be considered a separate group since they also included outstanding lay people.

The Priestly Classes. Among the twelve tribes of Israel one tribe, the tribe of Levi, had been chosen to perform priestly functions in the Temple. This did not mean that all Levites could offer sacrifices; only the family of Aaron could (Lv 8-9). As time went on, even within the family of Aaron only one particular branch was entrusted with the most sacred rites, the clan of Zadok (1 Kgs 1:26-27, 4:2). When the Jews returned from their Babylonian exile only those descendants from Zadok who could prove their genealogy were recognized as priests (see Neh 7, especially 7:63-65). Those who could so prove their descent were subdivided into twelve classes.

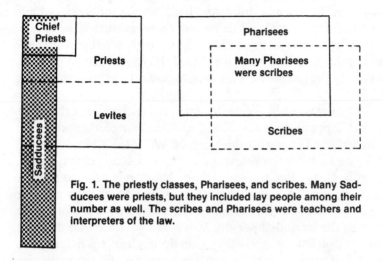

Fig. 1. The priestly classes, Pharisees, and scribes. Many Sadducees were priests, but they included lay people among their number as well. The scribes and Pharisees were teachers and interpreters of the law.

But it was not enough to be descended from the priestly line. At the time of Jesus, only certain men were selected for the sacrificial functions. A special commission investigated each applicant and accepted only those members of Zadokite families who had reached a definite social and intellectual standard. These young men were usually taken from a small number of favorite families. Only they would be ordained. This ordination was an impressive ceremony. The candidates purified themselves in a ritual bath and were then dressed in white linen and anointed with oil. They offered three sacrifices—one bull and two rams. The consecrating priest took some of the blood of the last animal sacrificed, mixed it with oil, and anointed the candidate with it on the right ear, the right thumb, and the right foot. He then made the candidate sit down and put into his hands and on his knees some of the ram's fat, some unleavened bread, and a cake of flour and oil. This cake was then taken and burnt upon the altar.

Once a priest had been ordained, he shared in the duties and privileges of the priestly class. When his group's turn came, he would go to Jerusalem and help in the priestly ministry of sacrifice. Zechariah, John the Baptist's father, received his vision in the Temple while he was there on duty (Lk 1:5-23). The priests were allowed to eat the showbreads that were kept on the table in the holy place (Mt 12:4). On the day of rest, the Sabbath, the priests were allowed to do work in the Temple (Mt 12:5).

The priests could declare lepers cured and could perform for them the purification sacrifice. Jesus sent some lepers who were cured to the Temple for this purpose (Mt 8:4; Lk 17:14). Before offering sacrifice the priests had to be absolutely clean, that is, ritually clean. For instance, they should not have touched a dead person. In the parable of the Good Samaritan we hear Jesus say that a priest and a Levite passed by without giving help to the wounded person. It is quite possible that they did this out of fear of becoming ritually unclean by helping the wounded man. But, of course, they made a great mistake, for charity is more important than the rules of ritual cleanliness before sacrifice (Lk 10:31-32).

Some priests lived in or near the Temple buildings. They were overseers who had fixed duties in organizing the labor done by the Levites, such as the cleaning of the Temple buildings, the transport of the required materials, the guarding of the precincts, and so on. One priest was in charge of the Temple guards (Acts 4:1). It may have been this officer who was sent with his guards to arrest Jesus in the Garden of Gethsemane (Mt 26:47; Jn 18:3).

Strictly speaking, there was only one high priest who was responsible for the total supervision of the Temple services and who performed certain exclusive functions (such as entering the Holy of Holies on the Day of Atonement), but in the Gospels we often find the high priests mentioned as a group. This is because the Romans were very much aware of the influence the high priest had among the people, and appointed to that office only such men as suited them. High priests who failed to please them were deposed. In this way quite a few men had been high priests at some point, and afterwards retained a certain standing and considerable influence. Moreover, they were usually taken from the same families, so that they really formed an influential group.

The most prominent family during Jesus' lifetime was the family of Annas. After having been high priest himself for some years (7-11 A.D.), Annas saw five of his sons become high priests. (See fig. 2). Caiaphas, appointed high priest by the Roman procurator Valerius Gratus (18 A.D.) and deposed by Vitellius (36 A.D.), was Annas' son-in-law. Caiaphas, also known as Joseph Caiaphas, was high priest for all these nineteen years with only brief interruptions. Although Annas had been deposed in 11 A.D. he still maintained an unrivalled position as the head of this high-priestly family.

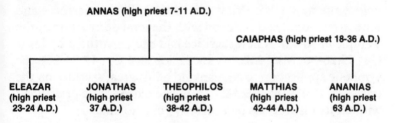

ANNAS (high priest 7-11 A.D.)

CAIAPHAS (high priest 18-36 A.D.)

ELEAZAR (high priest 23-24 A.D.)	JONATHAS (high priest 37 A.D.)	THEOPHILOS (high priest 38-42 A.D.)	MATTHIAS (high priest 42-44 A.D.)	ANANIAS (high priest 63 A.D.)

This explains why Luke can say that John the Baptist began to preach while Annas and Caiaphas were high priests (Lk 3:2). Caiaphas actually was the high priest but his father-in-law had maintained active control in the situation. After Jesus' arrest, Annas was the first to interrogate Jesus. Only after this inquiry did Annas send Jesus to Caiaphas (Jn 18:1-24). Acts describes Annas as the main figure in the proceedings against Peter and John:

The next day the Jewish leaders, the elders, and the teachers of the Law gathered in Jerusalem. They met with the High Priest Annas and with Caiaphas, John, Alexander, and the others who belonged to the High Priest's family. (Acts 4:5-6)

Annas was Jesus' leading adversary in the high-priestly group, but Caiaphas too had a personal share in the persecution of the Lord. John tells us that it was Caiaphas who suggested that Jesus should be killed to forestall political difficulties (Jn 11:48-50). This fits very well with Caiaphas' pro-Roman sympathies. He was not kept as high priest for so long without reason. Caiaphas also showed himself a capable diplomat during Jesus' trial. He desperately wanted a juridically valid reason for condemning him to death. When the accusations of the false witnesses failed, he tried to make Jesus utter a compromising statement. Jesus declared himself equal to God. Caiaphas, who as high priest should have been the first to accept and welcome Jesus, used this statement as grounds for condemning him to death (Mt 26:59-66).

Little did Annas and Caiaphas realize that they were standing before the new High Priest for all time. Their sacrifices and ministries would end for good with the total destruction of the Temple in 70 A.D. A new sacrifice had been instituted by Jesus (Mt 25:26-30; Mk 14:22-26; Lk 22:15-20; 1 Cor 11:23-26), the symbolic application to all mankind of his great sacrifice on the cross (Jn 10:17-18, 12:23-24, 32). The old Aaronic priesthood with all its institutions had thereby come to an end.

The Sadducees. Among the rich and the noble families, quite a few persons tried to be modern and up-to-date by encouraging Greek customs and art. After some time these groups became known as "Sadducees" (from Zadok), since a considerable number belonged to the priestly families. Sadducees enjoyed Greek sports, gladly frequented Greek buildings, and took pride in studying Greek literature. In general, they wanted to be broad-minded and not nationalistic with regard to art, poetry, and culture.

The Sadducees also restricted their faith to the doctrines contained in the Pentateuch. They considered many later teachings (on the resurrection of the body, on angels) and some later moral practices as superfluous to the basic Jewish religion. The Sadducees taught that we must not rely one-sidedly on

God's providence. Man himself should try to solve his difficulties and not put the blame for everything on lack of prayer.

The Sadducees commonly acquiesced in Roman rule. They thought cooperation with the Romans the best policy. Caiaphas was a Sadducee and tried to keep peace with the Romans. The exclamation "The only king we have is the Emperor" (Jn 19:15) could only be made by Sadducees.

The Sadducees were a small group of independent thinkers. In some cases they went too far and fell into indifferentism and skepticism. They were not liked by the people and were positively hated by the scribes and Pharisees. On one occasion Jesus argues with the Sadducees about the resurrection of the dead (Mt 22:23-33). This convincing argument, taken from the Pentateuch, totally silenced them.

The Scribes: Teachers of the Law. In reaction to the persecution of the Syrian kings, the study of the Law—which had already begun to flourish after the exile—became almost a passion. Every letter of the old Law (the Torah) was considered of the greatest importance. The teaching and the rules contained in the Law needed to be ever more faithfully explained and taught to others. It was natural that in this movement some outstanding men should rise as teachers. After some time this grew into an intricate system of instruction. Some learned men were recognized as "teachers of the Law" or "scribes." They received the title Rabbi or Rabboni. Such teachers attracted disciples and taught them in a "house of instruction." The instruction usually followed a set procedure.

The rabbi would take one line from the Law, e.g., "You shall do no work on the Sabbath day, neither you, nor your servant, nor your maid servant" (Ex 29:10ff).

He would then explain that there are thousand of applications that follow from this law. Take, for example, carrying burdens on the Sabbath. This is obviously forbidden because it means work. Now what about a woman wearing ornaments on the Sabbath? Would that be allowed? The rabbi would explain that certain ornaments of bigger size would be considered a "burden" in the opinion of the old teachers. Other ornaments could be worn. In some cases the teachers of old disagreed among themselves.

After this explanation the rabbi would sum up the conclusion in the words of tradition. This summary was repeated so often that the disciples could recite it by heart. Here is an example of such a summary (from the Mishnah, Sabbath treatise, VI, I, 3, 5):

With what on her person may a woman go out on the Sabbath? And with what may she not go out? A woman must not go out with linen or woolen laces, nor with straps on her head, because she cannot bathe with them on, but must first unfasten them; nor with a frontlet and pendants thereto (unless they are sewn to her cap); nor with the lining of the frontlet; nor with a golden ornament in the shape of a town; nor with a tight gold chain; nor with nose-rings; nor with finger-rings on which there is no seal; nor with a needle without any eye; (but if she has gone out with one of these last two things she is not too guilty; she need not bring the sin-offerings). . . . A woman must not go out with a needle that has an eye; nor with a finger-ring that has a seal on it; nor with a turban-type headdress; nor with a smelling bottle, or balm-flask. (Rabbi Meir says that if she went out with any of these things, with any of them, she is guilty and bound to bring the sin-offering. But other teachers of old said that she would be allowed to take the smelling-bottle or balm-flask.) A woman may go out with plaits of hair, whether of her own, or of another woman, or of an animal; with frontlets and pendants if they are sewn to her cap; with the lining of her frontlet or with false curls; with soft wool in her ear or soft wool in her shoe; with a grain of pepper or of salt or with whatever she is accustomed to put into her mouth (provided she does not put it into her mouth especially on the Sabbath; and if she drop it from her mouth she may not pick it up again).

Rabbi Meir allows her to wear a false tooth or a gilt tooth. Other teachers of old forbid it.

Notice to what detailed prescriptions these laws were extended. We may admire the zeal displayed in it, but we shall also recognize the danger of legalism inherent in such prescriptions. Characteristic of rabbinical teaching is also the appeal to the teachings of certain rabbis (such as Rabbi Meir) and teachers of former times.

The Pharisees. Pharisees were people who had separated themselves from the ordinary folk to live more saintly lives ("Pharisee" is derived from the word for *the separated one*). In a certain sense Pharisees were like monks, persons who had made up their mind to serve God very strictly according to the Law, and who had taken up some especially severe practices (extra fasts, long prayers, etc.). The Pharisees were very much on the front line during the Hellenistic persecutions. They proved fanatical in their loyalty to the ancient practices and were extremely nationalistic. The Pharisees accepted the resurrection of the body, the existence of angels, and God's direct providence in this world as doctrines of faith.

Not every scribe was automatically a Pharisee, nor was every Pharisee a scribe. But most Pharisees were scribes and most scribes were Pharisees. For this reason the two groups are considered practically identical in the Gospels.

The Pharisees were the fiercest opponents of the Sadducees. The following chart highlights the differences between these two groups:

Sadducees	*Pharisees*
Belonged mostly to the priestly and the upper classes.	Belonged mostly to the non-priestly classes. Anyone could become a Pharisee.
They occupied important posts, especially in the	Most of the Pharisees were teachers of the Law, with a

Temple. Most of the high priests were Sadducees.	place in the synagogues as well as the Temple precincts.
In spite of their power and prestige they were despised by the people.	They had great influence with the ordinary people, who considered them saints and listened to their teachings.
Only the Torah was accepted as the source of moral obligations.	The Pharisees accepted all the instructions and traditions as binding.
They rejected later doctrines such as the resurrection of the dead, angels and devils, and God's direct providence.	They accepted the resurrection of the dead and the final judgment, the existence of angels and devils, God's direct providence, Messianism.
They were inclined to be sympathetic to Roman rule.	They were looking forward to the liberation from Roman rule and would go to any length to achieve their end.
They were in danger of becoming skeptics, with little interest in religious truth or in objective justice.	They were in danger of falling into extreme fanaticism and legalism.

The Sanhedrin. The Sanhedrin was the supreme religious council of the Jews at the time of Jesus. It surely also had some political power, but it functioned mainly as the highest tribunal and as the advisory board of the high priest in religious matters.

Three different groups made up the membership of the Sanhedrin:

1. *The high priests.* The ruling high priest presided. Other members of the influential high-priestly families had a vote in the deliberations.

2. *The elders.* These were various prominent persons, perhaps appointed because of their social position, merit, etc. (e.g., Joseph of Arimathea).

3. *The scribes.* The legal experts. Whereas high priests and elders could normally be reckoned to be Sadducees, the scribes were practically all Pharisees.

We meet the Sanhedrin in the Gospels as the official body through whose ruling Jesus' opponents had him killed. At one session they formally decided to kill Jesus (Jn 11:47-53), and after his triumphant entry into Jerusalem they decided to do it quickly (Mt 26:3-5). After they had arrested him they condemned him to death, probably in two sessions (Mt 26:57-66; Lk 22:54-55, 63-71). Jesus is handed over to Pilate by the official mandate of the Sanhedrin (Mt 27:1-2; Jn 18:30).

Jesus' Attitudes Towards the Religious Leaders

Jesus appreciated the good intentions and the valuable work of many scribes and Pharisees. A glance at the Gospels will suffice to convince us of this:

Jesus admitted their authority. He acknowledged the teaching authority of the scribes, saying that people should follow their prescriptions, since "they are sitting on the seat of Moses" (Mt 23:2).

Jesus also dealt with them in a friendly manner. One scribe wanted to become Jesus' disciple (Mt 8:19). Another scribe praised him for having defeated the Sadducees on the question of the immortality of the soul (Lk 20:38). Jesus also praised a scribe for having very aptly answered the question concerning the principal law (Lk 10:28). One Pharisee invited Jesus to dinner, and Jesus taught quite a few lessons there (Lk 14:1-24). Perhaps the best example of friendship is the fact that some Pharisees warned Jesus against the wicked plans of Herod (Lk 13:31-33).

Jesus had some particular friends among the religious leaders. Some Pharisees with whom Jesus had contact are known to us by name. Nicodemus went to Jesus by night and listened to him for a long time (Jn 3). On a later occasion he defended Jesus against the accusations made by other Pharisees (Jn 7:45-52), and after Jesus' death he assisted in giving him a worthy burial (Jn 19:39). Jesus was in the house of a Pharisee called Simon when Mary Magdalene came in to confess her sins (Lk 7:36-50). Gamaliel, who defended the apostles in the court case against Peter and John (Acts 5:34), must have known and listened to Jesus. This is all the more likely as Stephen and Paul, both disciples of Gamaliel, seem to be deeply involved in the controversy about Jesus.

Jesus also often taught like a scribe and conducted himself like a scribe. He gathered disciples around himself, and taught them more or less as scribes would. He was called "Rabbi" by everyone, and he did not forbid this (Mt 26:25; Mk 10:51; Jn 20:16). Even Jesus' apostles were in a certain sense scribes, for Jesus said that he would send them as "scribes" (Mt 23:34) and compared a "scribe well versed in the Kingdom of Heaven" to the head of a family who brings new things and old ones from his storeroom (Mt 13:52).

Yet there is a great difference between Jesus and the scribes. First of all, Jesus acted and spoke with power:

> When Jesus finished saying these things, the crowd was amazed at the way he taught. He wasn't like the teachers of the Law; instead, he taught with authority. (Mt 7:28-29)

> [The people said] "What is this? Is it some kind of new teaching? This man has authority to give orders to the evil spirits and they obey him!" (Mk 1:27)

In the Sermon on the Mount, Jesus perfected the old commandments by his new law of charity (Mt 5). He also drastically changed some existing regulations. Whereas other rabbis discussed the various reasons for which divorce could be granted (as permitted in the Law), Jesus declared all divorce forbidden (Mt 19:3-9). He also abolished the prescriptions of ritual cleanliness (Mk 7:1-2, especially 19). Furthermore, Jesus acted with authority in performing all his miracles, and he gave this authority to his disciples.

Jesus also had to correct the scribes and Pharisees in many respects. They had deviated far from the true ideal of sanctity as God wanted to see it practiced. The Pharisees for their part accused Jesus of these "faults": not keeping the traditional customs such as the ritual washing of hands before meals (Mt 15:1ff; Mk 7:1ff; Lk 11:37ff); eating with sinners (Mt 9:11, 14; Mk 2:16; Lk 5:33); driving out devils through Beelzebub (Mt 9:34, 12:2; Mk 2:24); performing miracles on the Sabbath (Mt 12:9-13; Lk 13:10-17, 14:1ff; Jn 5:1-18, 9:1-17); and claiming special authority, and even equality with God the Father (Jn 5:19-47, 8:13). They sought to compromise Jesus by initiating discussions on difficult subjects: tax to be paid to the emperor (Mt 22:15), divorce (Mt 19:3), and divine signs (Mt 16:1-4). Eventually the discussions centered around Jesus' mission and his person ("Son of David," Mt 22:42; "the Son," Jn 5:19-47; the "Bread of Life," Jn 6:25-59).

Jesus vigorously condemned the Pharisaic attitude. He warned his disciples against these mistakes (Mt 16:1-6; Mk 8:11ff). Well known is Jesus' long sermon against the hypocrisy, legalism, formalism, and pride of many scribes (Mt 23:1-36; Lk 11:39-44). But notice how even this sermon ends in the passionate desire of the Lord to bring these scribes too to conversion (Mt 23:37-39). The fanaticism of the Pharisees could not endure such opposition. In their blindness they imagined Jesus to be the chief obstacle to the faithful observance of the Law. So they decided to kill him. The Gospels mention Jesus' discourse on the Sabbath as the first occasion for this plot to remove Jesus for the good of religion (Mt 12:14; Mk 3:6).

ELEVEN

The Political Situation

THE TIME OF JESUS was a time of complex political upheaval. During Jesus' earthly life, the political structure of Palestine changed drastically, as the Romans assumed direct control from local kings. Jesus' path crossed those of political rulers frequently. Indeed, they had him executed. Let us examine the shifting political scene of Jesus' time, and his attitude toward it.

The Family of Herod the Great

To understand the political situation in Palestine during Jesus' life, we have to make the acquaintance of Herod the Great and his family, the local rulers (fig. 1).

Herod the Great (37-4 B.C.). Not a Jew himself, Herod came from Idumea and was in culture and religious belief totally Hellenistic. By great personal talents and a ruthless policy of exterminating all his adversaries, he had managed to secure the kingship over the whole of Palestine. He was known for his cruelty; he killed even many of his relatives, including his eldest sons Antipater, Alexander, and Aristobulus. The least suspicion of insurrection sufficed for bloodshed. The murder of the innocent children in Matthew 2:16-18 is typical of Herod.

Herod was extremely unpopular. The Jews hated him as a foreign ruler and also because of his pagan practices. To compensate for this Herod promised to rebuild the Temple of

149

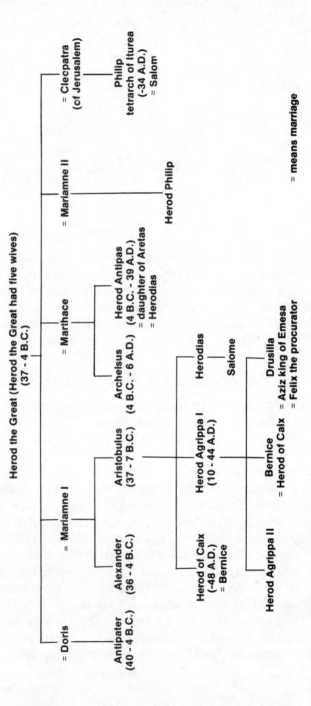

Fig. 1. The family of Herod the Great

Jerusalem. This was a gigantic job, with 1,000 priests as overseers and 10,000 workmen. The work began in the year 20 B.C. and continued for more than eighty years.

Herod Antipas (4 B.C.-39 A.D.). Herod the Great's fifth son, he is the person best known to us from the Gospels. When Herod died, Palestine was divided between Archelaus, Herod Antipas, and Philip. As ruler (ethnarch) of Galilee and Perea, Herod Antipas was destined to meet Christ. Like his father, Herod Antipas did not adhere to the Jewish religion. He was a Greek in heart and soul, but for diplomatic reasons he tried to avoid religious clashes with the people. He lived a life of luxury and comfort. Two main incidents recounted in the Gospels illustrate his attitude.

Philip, son of Mariamne II and Herod the Great, had married Herodias, his niece. They had a child, Salome. After Philip had divorced Herodias, Herod Antipas took her as his wife. John the Baptist reproached him for this. Fearing John's influence with the people Herod imprisoned him and finally had him beheaded at the request of Herodias and Salome (Mk 6:16-29; Mt 14:1-12).

Herod had heard about Jesus' ministry and was interested in it for political reasons (Lk 13:31) and out of curiosity (Lk 9:7-9). During Jesus' trial he shows a complete disregard for justice and a typically Hellenistic search for novelties. Jesus proves the stronger personality. Herod covers up his defeat by mocking Jesus (Lk 23:6-12).

Herod Agrippa I (10-44 A.D.). Grandson of Herod the Great, Agrippa unleashed a persecution against the early Christian community at Jerusalem. He did this to please the Jews, not out of religious conviction. This Herod was a friend of Claudius, the Roman emperor, and thus very powerful. His death was seen as God's punishment for his pride (Acts 12:1-23). Paul was later to defend his preaching before Herod Agrippa I's children, King Agrippa II and Bernice (Acts 25:13-27). They seem to have been well disposed towards Paul (Acts 26).

It is essential to keep these three Herods distinct: Herod the Great, king when Jesus was born; Herod Antipas, king when Jesus preached; Herod Agrippa I, king after Jesus' death.

Politics During Jesus' Earthly Life

Herod's dynasty rose and fell during Jesus' earthly life. The main forces at work in the many political changes of this time were the ambitions of Herod the Great's family, the gradual increase of Roman control, and an ever-growing Jewish nationalism. We should try to see these events alongside the events of the Gospels (see fig. 3).

5 B.C.: Jesus' Birth; Herod the Great in Control. Herod the Great was subject to the emperor, but possessed a good deal of independent power. Against this background, we understand the story of the Magi. Herod resided in Jerusalem as his capital city (Mt 2:1), and if Joseph was to flee from Herod's power, he had to take his family to Egypt, since all Palestine was under Herod's control (Mt 2:13-15).

4 B.C.: The Division of Palestine. Herod the Great died while Jesus and his family were in Egypt. Herod's sons disputed over the inheritance left by their father. Emperor Augustus stepped in and divided the territory. Archelaus received Idumea, Judea, and Samaria (capital at Jerusalem). Herod Antipas, who was destined to meet Jesus, received Galilee and Perea (capital at Tiberias). Philip, son of Cleopatra, received Iturea and some other regions (see fig. 2).

Archelaus was just as unpredictable and cruel as his father. When Joseph was told to return to Palestine after Herod's death, he heard that Archelaus had succeeded his father, and went to Galilee instead of Judea (Mt 2:19-22).

6 A.D.: The Beginning of the Roman Procuratorship. Archelaus had all the bad qualities of his father and few of his good ones. In the first months of his rule he executed more than

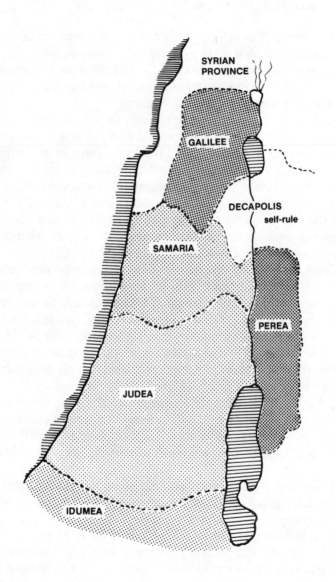

Fig. 2. Political divisions of Palestine

3,000 people. The influential families plotted against him, and more than once sent messengers to the Roman emperor with the request to depose him. Eventually Augustus took action. He exiled Archelaus to Gaul and appointed a Roman procurator to look after Idumea, Judea, and Samaria.

Jesus must have been ten or eleven years old at this time. We read how he went up to the Temple when he was twelve, soon after this great political change. We do not know what questions he asked the teachers in the Temple, or what answers he gave. We may speculate, perhaps, whether Jesus was asking them if, in the light of the recent Roman occupation of Judea, the time for the Messiah had not come, if they were so sure that the Messiah would bring political freedom, if the Messiah did not have a mission for the whole empire (Lk 2:41-50).

Jesus later related the parable of a nobleman who went to a far country to be made king. During his absence his countrymen sent messengers after him to say, "We don't want this man to be our king" (Lk 19:12-27). Jesus then described how this man, on his return, judged his countrymen severely on their fidelity or infidelity. It may be that this image of the Last Judgment reflected Archaelaus' severe court trials after his return from Rome as king.

John the Baptist began to preach in the fifteenth year of Emperor Tiberius (Lk 3:1). We know from secular history that Tiberius became co-ruler with Augustus in the year 765 A.U.C. (12 A.D.). His fifteenth year was thus the year 780 A.U.C., that is, 27 A.D.

Jesus was about thirty years old when he was baptized by John (Lk 3:23). Since Jesus was born in 5 or 4 B.C., he would be about thirty in 26 or 27 A.D.

The Roman procurator at the time of Jesus' public life was Pontius Pilate (26-36 A.D.). He was normally stationed at Caesarea (on the coast), where he kept an army of five cohorts (1,000 men each).

The procurator's main task was to collect (procure) taxes, to ensure the internal peace, to confirm all death sentences of the Jewish courts, and to report all developments to Rome.

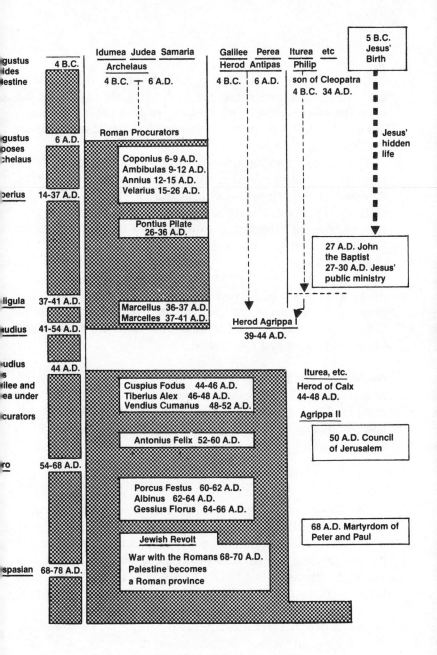

Fig. 3. Roman rule in Palestine

Pontius Pilate was a tough governor. He despised the Jews but tried to avoid conflicts. He was constantly improving his own status—financially too. Pilate used to go to Jerusalem during the Passover, in case disturbances should arise during the feast.

When Jesus' trial was taken to Pilate for confirmation, Pilate tried to evade it by pointing out that Jesus belonged to Herod Antipas' jurisdiction, since Jesus came from Galilee (Lk 23:6-7). Herod could have saved Jesus by summoning him to his own court in Tiberias. Instead, to please the high priests, he waived his right and sent Jesus back to Pilate as a compliment (Lk 23:8-12).

39-44 A.D.: Rule of Herod Agrippa I. Herod Agrippa I, a personal friend of the emperor, succeeded Antipas as ruler of Galilee and Perea. For a short time he recovered all the land that Herod the Great had possessed.

68-70 A.D.: The Jewish Revolt. The Jewish revolt of 68 A.D. led to a great war. The Romans conquered the whole of Palestine and killed most of the Jews. Jerusalem was besieged, captured, and completely destroyed, as Jesus had foretold (Mk 13:14-23; Lk 21:20-24).

Jesus' Attitude Toward Political Rulers

The Gospels show that Jesus acknowledged political authority. When the Roman officer compared Jesus' authority over disease with his own military authority, Jesus praised him for his insight into the parallel workings of God (Mt 8:10, 13). When the Pharisees tried to trap Jesus over the issue of paying taxes to the emperor, Jesus recognized that since the emperor was responsible for the welfare of the people, he had the right to authority over them (Mt 22:15-22; Mk 12:13-17; Lk 20:20-26). When brought before Pilate, Jesus never denied Pilate's authority to judge him (Jn 19:10-11). It is clear, therefore, that

Jesus acknowledged political power as something good, to be respected and esteemed.

Jesus took many examples in his teaching from politics. In one parable a king prepares a wedding feast (Mt 22:1-14; Lk 14:15-24), and in another a king settles accounts with his governors (Mt 18:23-35). When instructing his disciples on the need to calculate the sacrifices for God's Kingdom, Jesus gave the examples of the man (probably a king) who wants to build a tower (Lk 14:28-30) and the king who is going to war with an army (Lk 14:31-33). Such parables illustrate that Jesus took the political order, with kings who collect taxes, hear court cases, wage war, who build, etc., as a normal part of human society.

At the same time, Jesus taught the limitations of political power and the duties of political rulers. John the Baptist had taught tax collectors and military personnel how to do their duty (Lk 3:12-14). Jesus disapproved of the life of dissipation, such as that led by Herod Antipas (Mt 11:8; Lk 7:25, 9:32, 23:9). He reminded Pilate of the fact that he received his authority from God (Jn 19:11) and, therefore, it was something of which he would have to give an account (Mt 25:14-30). His code of sanctity is demanded from all men without any exception (Mt 25:31-46). He himself is the supreme king who will judge all men.

Jesus and Jewish Nationalism

The nationalistic uprisings of the Jews that finally led to the Jewish War of 68-70 A.D. had their beginnings during Jesus' own time. Some examples are seen in the Gospels.

The revolt of Judas the Galilean probably took place during Jesus' early years (Acts 5:37). From historians we learn that this nationalistic hero had thousands of followers and that he captured the city of Sephphoris (five miles north of Nazareth). Jesus may have witnessed the whole event himself. If not, he would have at least heard about it from those who had been personally involved.

In the year 30 A.D., a group of Galileans began a revolt in Jerusalem by starting riots in three places—in the Temple, near Pilate's residence, and near the pool of Siloam (Lk 13:1-5 speaks of this). Pilate successfully suppressed this revolt, killing many of the Galileans. Jesus used the occasion to warn all of the need to be ready to die (by proper repentance).

When Pilate tried to liberate Jesus by proposing him as the prisoner to be set free during the Passover, the Pharisees started clamoring for Barabbas. Barabbas had taken part in a riot, and, in spite of being a murderer, he would easily win the people's support as a national hero (Mt 27:16; Mk 15:6-11; Lk 23:18-19; Jn 18:40).

The people expected the Messiah to be their political leader, who would redeem them from the family of Herod the Great (the Idumeans) and from the rule of the Romans. From the beginning there was the serious danger that Jesus' mission would be misunderstood as a political revolt. Jesus took special measures to prevent this.

In the first period of his ministry he deliberately avoided the title Messiah. He tried to avoid all popular commotions by performing miracles in secret and forbidding popular outbursts of enthusiasm. Only after he had sufficiently demonstrated the true nature of his spiritual mission did he proclaim himself the Messiah with the carefully selected term "Son of Man."

Jesus refused to be made king by the people after the multiplication of the loaves (Jn 6:15). He forced the disciples to leave that area so that they would not get involved (Mt 14:22-23).

When he entered Jerusalem he came not as a military conqueror sitting on horseback, but on an ass (Mt 21:1-5).

When the disciples misunderstood Jesus' words about taking swords with them (Lk 22:35-38—meant symbolically as a mark of their being left alone), he told them to put the swords back, for "all who take the sword will die by the sword!" (Mt 26:51-54; Lk 22:49-51). Jesus has all authority in heaven and on earth (Mt 28:18) and, therefore all political authority. But he deliberately gave up this political authority in order to fulfill his spiritual mission. This is expressed in the story of the temptations (especially Mt 4:8-11; Lk 4:5-8).

Jesus foresaw the persecutions which his followers are sure to undergo, and he prepared his disciples for it. His followers should not oppose such persecutions with armed resistance, but should use the occasion to witness to him and his message (Mt 10:16-31; Mk 13:9-13; Lk 12:11-12). To all opposition they must show kindness and meekness (Mt 5:38-48) and rejoice because of God's reward (Mt 5:10-12). In all tribulation they will have his inner peace (Jn 14:27). In this way Christ initiated a spiritual conquest of the world which does not depend on political power (Mt 28:18-20; Mk 16:15; Lk 24:45-47; Acts 1:8).

TWELVE

The Manner of Speaking

LANGUAGE AND THOUGHT are very much related to each other. We cannot think without expressing our thought in words. The language we speak has an influence on our thought as well as on the expression of it. Of course, thoughts can be translated from one language into another. Yet, if we want to understand a person very well, it is often a help to go back to the original words which he spoke in his own language. In the same way it is useful for us to know something of the language which Jesus spoke.

Jesus spoke the Aramaic language of the common man of his time. Aramaic, Hebrew, Arabic, and Syriac belong to the group of Semitic languages. These languages have one outstanding characteristic—practically all their words are built on roots of three consonants. The same roots can acquire new meanings by the addition of vowels inside the roots or by the addition of other consonants.

Let us take an example from Aramaic—the root *Sh-B-Q*, which indicates "leaving." With these three root consonants many derived words can be obtained by the addition of vowels or other consonants.

sbq	he left	*sabq*	a deserter
sbiq	he was left	*misbq*	neglect
sebuq	leave it!	*sbiq*	a foundling
sbbq	he left completely	*mthsbbq*	outcast
hsbq	he made (him) leave	*husbq*	evacuated

In the conjugation of the verb (which has only two tenses, perfect and imperfect) the pronouns of the subject *and* of the object are added on.

sbq	he left	*sbqthni*	you left me
sbqth	she left	*sbqtheh*	you left him
sbqtha	you (sing.) left	*sbqthah*	you left her
sbqeth	I left	*sbqthenah*	you left us
sbqu	they left (masc.)	*sbquni*	you left me
sbqa	they left (fem.)	*sbquk*	they left you
sbqthun	you (plur.) left	*sbquhi*	they left him
sbqna	we left	*sbqukon*	they left you (plur.)

In this way almost a complete sentence can be expressed in one word. Many subtle differences in meaning can be implied by the variations of form. Of course, between these semantic consonants and vowels, short "filler" vowels are added for the pronunciation. "You left me" thus becomes "Shebaqthani" (Mt 27:46).

Aramaic (like other Semitic languages) has a terse structure that is difficult to translate into other languages. It also abounds in rich melodious sounds so that rhyme and alliteration come without any effort.

Forms of Speech

Semitic languages, like all languages, employ characteristic forms of speech to express meaning. Many forms of Semitic speech cannot be translated into English without losing some of their impact. However, our reading of the Gospels will be greatly enriched if we appreciate the way Semites expressed themselves.

Parallel Statements. One feature of Semitic poetry is that it tends to express a thought twice in slightly different forms. This parallelism is often used to express completeness.

Give to him who begs from you,
and do not refuse him who would borrow from you.
(Mt 5:42)

Lay up for yourselves treasures in heaven,
where neither moth nor rust consumes them
and where thieves do not break in and steal. (Mt 6:20)

And at that time two men will be working in the field:
one will be taken away, the other will be left behind.
Two women will be at a mill grinding meal:
one will be taken away, the other will be left behind.
(Mt 24:40ff)

In such cases we should not look for a different meaning in each half of the parallelism. Both really express one truth. The repetition in the parallelism has the function of embellishing the statement (making it more beautiful), of clarifying the statement, and of further imprinting it on the hearer's memory.

Negative and Positive. In one form of parallelism the same truth is put first in the positive and then in the negative form. To the Semitic mind this expresses that one wants to exclude all other possibilities. Suppose that one wants to announce, "Only adults may see this film." In a Semitic language this could be expressed, "Adults may see the film; non-adults may not." Jesus employed this form of speaking quite often.

Statement	*Meaning*
If you forgive people's sins, they are forgiven; If you do not forgive them, they are not forgiven. (Jn 20:23)	You will have universal power to forgive sins.
Do not condemn others, and God will not condemn you;	God will forgive you to the same degree in which you forgive others.

Forgive others, and God
will forgive you. (Lk 6:37)

Do not be afraid of those who kill the body but cannot kill the soul; Rather be afraid of God, who can destroy both body and soul in hell. (Mt 10:28)	Fear only God and no one else!

What you prohibit on earth will be prohibited in heaven, And what you permit on earth will be permitted in heaven. (Mt 18:18)	You have God's authority for all the laws which you will impose.

There are also examples in which this principle of exclusion has been applied in a more extensive way. In the parable of the Last Judgment (Mt 25:31-46), Jesus first praises the blessed "for all that you have done to the least of mine you have done to me" (the positive statement), then curses the wicked "for what you have not done for the least of mine, you have not done for me" (the negative statement). The parable thus expresses that all men without exception will be judged regarding their fraternal charity.

Inclusion, or Ring Construction. The Jews also had the custom of beginning and ending a passage with the same thought. It was a natural way of bringing out the unity of an idea in their statement. This form of speech has received the official name inclusion, since one particular thought or statement includes, grasps, or embraces the intermediate phrases. It is also known as ring construction. We find numerous examples in the Gospels. Consider this one from Matthew:

You will know them [false prophets] by what they do.

Thorn bushes do not bear grapes,
and briars do not bear figs.
A healthy tree bears good fruit,
but a poor tree bears bad fruit.
A healthy tree cannot bear bad fruit,
and a poor tree cannot bear good fruit.
And any tree that does not bear good fruit
is cut down and thrown into the fire.

So then, you will know the false prophets by the way they act.
(Mt 7:16-20)

The thought that we will know the false prophets by the way they act brackets the passage. Notice that this sentence is also the most important one—it accurately summarizes what Christ wants to say by the examples. Other instances of such inclusive phrases abound in the Gospels. Here are a few familiar phrases that are repeated at the beginning and the end of passages:

The Kingdom of heaven belongs to them! (Mt 5:3, 10)

The evil people of this day. . . . (Mt 12:39, 45)

By what right do you do these things? (Mk 11:28, 33)

Listen. . . . (Mk 4:3, 9)

You reject God's law. . . . (Mk 7:9, 13)

Nothing from the outside makes a man unclean. . . .
(Mk 7:18, 23)

Unless you give up all you cannot be my disciple. . . .
(Lk 14:26, 33)

The Son does nothing of his own. . . . (Jn 5:19, 30)

This is my commandment: love one another! (Jn 15:12, 17)

The Hebrew Genitive. On the whole Semitic languages do not use many adjectives. This gives rise to some very peculiar constructions in which a noun is made to substitute for an adjective. Instead of speaking of a "fat pig," one would say, "a pig of fatness." "Beautiful ring" becomes "ring of beauty." A "courageous hero" would be a "hero of courage." In this construction we should particularly notice that it is the second noun which substitutes for the adjective: "the God of mercy" means "the merciful God."

In good translations this noun construction, commonly known as the Hebrew genitive, is simply translated by the appropriate adjective. However, we will meet cases where the noun construction has not been translated. Consider Matthew 12:4, 15:9, 24:15, and John 14:17.

The Hebrew Superlative. With the exception of Arabic, Semitic languages do not possess a special form for the superlative or the comparative. The superlative and comparative degrees have therefore to be expressed in other ways. At times we simply find a positive statement which is meant as a superlative.

Statement	*Meaning*
Blessed are you among women. (Lk 1:42)	You are the most fortunate woman that ever lived.
Which is the great commandment in the law? (Mt 22:36)	Which is the greatest commandment in the Law?
Mary has chosen the good portion. . . . (Lk 10:42)	Mary has chosen the better (the best) portion.

At other times a comparison between two things is expressed simply by affirming the one and denying the other:

I desire mercy, and not sacrifice. (Mt 9:13; 12:7)	I prefer mercy to sacrifice.

For the words you will speak will not be yours; they will come from the Spirit of your Father speaking through you.　(Mt 10:20)	It will be more the Spirit of my Father speaking in you than you speaking yourselves!
He who believes in me, believes not in me but in him who sent me.　(Jn 12:44)	Faith in me rests more on him who sent me than on me.
Rejoice not in this, that spirits are subject to you; but rejoice in this that your names are written in heaven! (Lk 10:20)	You should be more happy about the prospect of heaven than in having power over devils.

Notice in these examples that the denial is only partial. Matthew 9:13 does not say that God does not want sacrifice. It only says that God (who wants sacrifice, prefers mercy. In other words, he thinks mercy more important.

These Hebrew constructions may sometimes be badly misunderstood. A typical case of use of denial for the comparative form may be seen in the word *to hate*. This word often means "to love less than." The two passages below are parallel, but seem to say different things in English.

If anyone comes to me and does not hate his own father and mother and wife and children and brothers and sisters, he cannot be my disciple.	He who loves father and mother more than me is not worthy of me; and he who loves son or daughter more than me is not worthy of me. (Mt 10:37)

Jesus does not demand that we hate our parents, but that we love them less than God. In this way we also have to understand the phrase "You shall love your neighbor and hate your enemy" (Mt 5:43) to mean "Love your neighbor more than your enemy." The Old Testament did not command the Jews to hate their enemies, but it allowed them to love their friends more. Jesus taught that we have to love our enemies just as much!

Hyperbole, or Exaggeration. Quite a few Jewish statements are phrased in such strong terms that they cannot be taken literally. We call these statements hyperboles. We meet this form of speech in every language ("It's raining cats and dogs," "So-and-so is snowed under with work"), but for Jews it was not a matter of repeating fixed expressions—they would employ hyperbole whenever the occasion offered itself, even in new situations. Jesus used this form of speech often:

> How dare you say to your brother, "Please, let me take that speck out of your eye," when you have a log in your own eye?
> (Mt 7:4)

> It is much harder for a rich person to enter the Kingdom of God than for a camel to go through the eye of a needle.
> (Mk 10:25)

> You strain a fly out of your drink, but swallow a camel!
> (Mt 23:24)

Such expressions are obviously not to be taken literally. They are very strong statements intended to bring the truth home in a way that we will never forget. Consider Jesus' real advice in these lines.

If your right eye causes you to sin, take it out and throw it away! It is much better for you to lose a part of your body than to have your whole body thrown into hell! (Mt 5:29)

Jesus does not want us to mutilate ourselves, but is instead teaching the gravity of sin.

I tell you: do not use any vow. . . . Just say "Yes" or

Jesus does not forbid oaths altogether, but we should

"No"—anything else you say comes from the Evil One. (Mt 5:34ff) only use them on very grave occasions (as when Jesus spoke under oath before the Sanhedrin, Mt 26:63).

In some of the Lord's theological utterances, we have to remember this hyperbolic way of speaking lest we seriously misunderstand his words.

> No one knows, however, when that day and hour [of the Last Judgment] will come—neither the angels in heaven nor the Son; the Father alone knows. (Mt 24:36)

Jesus did not mean that he actually does not know the date of the Judgment. For he knows all the Father knows (Jn 5:19-20ff; Mt 11:27; Jn 10:14-15), and he is himself the Judge (Mt 16:27, 25:31-46). Moreover, many angels may know through God's revelation to them (why should he hide it from them?). Jesus meant that neither he nor the angels will reveal the date of the Last Judgment. It will be revealed only by the event itself, which the Father will bring about. In this sense only the Father knows that date.

If we understand this hyperbolic aspect of Jewish speaking, we will be able to solve some apparent conflicts in the texts. For example, the apparent conflict between these two passages has troubled many readers:

> Anyone who is not for me is really against me; anyone who does not help me gather is really scattering. (Mt 12:30)

> Whoever is not against us is for us. (Mk 9:40)

Seen out of context, these would seem to contradict one another. But the first was spoken when Jesus was accused of being helped by the devil. He replied that only those who actually support him by constructive action can be reckoned to be his helpers. The second was spoken in the context of the man who drove out devils in Jesus' name. Jesus said that such a person should not be reckoned an enemy. There is no contradiction, but in both cases Jesus expressed one aspect of the same truth very strongly: only really constructive support makes us helpers of Jesus, yet we should allow for certain people who support him at least to some extent.

Idiomatic Expressions. Many fairly common phrases in the Gospels have rather specialized meanings. Let us look at several important ones:

Adulterous Generation (Mt 12:39, 16:4; Mk 8:38). "Generation" stands for the average period between the time a man becomes an adult himself until his son becomes an adult, i.e., about thirty years. When Jesus said "this generation," he meant his contemporaries.

In the Old Testament, "adultery" is often the name given to Israel's fall into idolatry. Israel was "married" to God; therefore her turning to other gods was called adultery. Jesus used the term in this Old Testament sense. It has nothing to do with physical adultery. "This adulterous generation" means "the faithless, unreliable people of my time."

Amen, Amen, I Say to You (Mt 5:18, 6:2). The introduction to a solemn declaration. The Jews employed "Amen" as a solemn affirmation of one's obligation ("I agree"). However, they never used the expression in the way in which Jesus used it—that is, to emphasize that he pronounced the statement on his own authority (see Mk 1:22).

To Be Called. "To be called" this or that means, in Hebrew idiomatic usage, that one "is" this or that; see Matthew 5:9, 19, 21:13; Luke 1:32, 15:19.

Brother and Sister. For Jews all relatives were "brothers" and "sisters" (Mt 5:22ff). The Gospels speak of Jesus' sisters (Mk 6:3) and brothers (Mt 13:55) in this sense (see also Mt 12:46ff; Jn 2:12). The early Christians always addressed one another as "brother" and "sister," because all Christians are brothers and sisters of the Lord.

Eating and Drinking. It is rather difficult to describe what is meant by the idiom "eating and drinking." Perhaps we might define it as "living a full human life." Study its meaning in these examples:

In the days before the flood people ate and drank, men and women married, up to the very day Noah went into the boat. (Mt 24:38)	Until the very last day people remained engrossed in their ordinary human affairs.
When John came, he fasted. . . .When the Son of Man came, he ate and drank. (Mt 11:18-19)	John did extraordinary penance and Jesus lived an ordinary human life, yet both were criticized.

See also how the expression is used in Matthew 6:25-31 (the worries of ordinary human life) and in Luke 22:16-18 (Jesus' ordinary human life is completed).

Eating and Drinking with. In Hebrew idiom, "eating and drinking with" someone means "having friendly relations with" that person. The wicked servant "eats and drinks with drunkards" (Mt 24:49). Jesus was accused of eating and drinking with sinners (Mt 9:11). The damned will complain at the Last Judgment, "We ate and drank with you" (Lk 13:26). The symbolism of the Last Supper (and of the eucharist) expresses the same idea: by eating and drinking with Jesus we have true friendship with him. That is why Jesus longs to eat this supper with us (Lk 22:15) and why he promises we will eat and drink at his table in heaven (Lk 22:30).

Eunuch (Mt 19:11-12). Oriental princes usually had many wives. They were in constant fear that their servants would have relations with these women. For this reason certain slaves were (by operation) made physically incapable of having normal sexual relations. These slaves were known as "eunuchs," and they were usually put in charge of household affairs. In Jesus' time the word *eunuch* meant "a man who cannot marry." In

Matthew 19:11-12 Jesus recommends celibacy for God's sake.

Flesh and Blood. This expression stands for "a human person."

[The sons of God are] born not of blood nor the will of the flesh nor of the will of man, but of God. (Jn 1:13)	We become God's children not by a human birth (a birth from human beings) but by a divine birth (from God our Father).
Flesh and blood has not revealed this to you, but my Father who is in heaven. (Mt 16:17)	No human person has revealed this, but God the Father himself.

In the eucharist, Jesus gives us himself as a complete person (Jn 6:54ff). Sometimes the word *flesh* carries a similar meaning even when it stands by itself, as if "flesh and blood" were implied (Mt 19:5, 24:22, 26:41).

House of Israel. A prophetic title of the Jewish people. Jesus will reign over the House of Jacob (Lk 1:33). He sent his apostles first to the lost sheep of the House of Israel (Mt 10:6, 15:24).

Iota, or dot. The *iota* (letter *i*) was the smallest Greek letter. Jesus said that not even a iota or a dot (small writing mark) will pass away from the Law (Mt 5:18).

Son of. . . . This phrase may express any type of relationship in Hebrew. One has to examine the word for its exact meaning in practically each case.

sons of the bridechamber (Mt 9:15)	wedding guests
sons of thunder (Mk 3:17)	impetuous men (the men of thunder)
son of peace (Lk 10:6)	a peaceful person
sons of this world (Lk 16:8)	worldly people

son of perdition (Jn 17:12)	the man who risks damnation
sons of the evil one (Mt 13:38)	devilish, wicked people
sons of light (Lk 16:8)	those who received light
sons of the resurrection (Lk 20:36)	people who have been raised
sons of God (Lk 20:36)	people who live in and through God

You have said it. An affirmation, meaning yes. Jesus replied to Caiaphas' question about his divinity with this expression (Mt 26:63-64). He gave a similar reply to Pilate (Mt 27:11; Mk 15:2; Jn 18:37).

Visiting. According to Semitic mentality one does not visit another person without giving help, advice, consolation, and so on. The word can acquire various meanings of this sort in different contexts.

God has visited his people. (Lk 1:68, 7:16)	God has helped, redeemed his people.
I was in prison and you visited me. (Mt 25:36, 43)	I was in prison and you looked after me.

What have you to do with us? The words express a refusal, or a withdrawal. The evil spirits spoke these words to Jesus to make him leave them in peace (Mt 8:29; Mk 1:24; Lk 4:34). Jesus spoke the same words to Mary (Jn 2:4) to indicate that he had not intended to perform a miracle, though, at her request he does it anyway (Jn 2:5-11).

Literary Forms

It is a fundamental law of learning that we understand unknown things from a comparison with known things. If we are told that horses were rather small fifty million years ago, this makes little impression on us. But if someone tells us, "Horses at that time were as small as our cats," then we suddenly realize what is meant. Jesus uses this fundamental law of our mind to convey his message. From well-known and easy examples he leads his audience to a grasp of more difficult and unknown subjects. Before we can discuss the precise nature of these parables, we need to distinguish them from related forms of speech, such as the comparison, the metaphor, and the allegory.

Comparisons. In a comparison we make an explicit statement that one or another object (person, event) is *like* another object (person, event).

Statement	*Meaning*
"Every teacher of the Law who becomes a disciple in in the Kingdom of heaven is like a homeowner who takes new and old things out of his storage room." (Mt 13:52)	The master of the house always kept useful objects in his storeroom; whenever required he would produce them. Jesus says that a Christian scribe will in the same way produce useful teachings from the store of revelation.
"The Son of Man will come like the lightning which flashes across the whole sky from the east to the west." (Mt 24:27)	People know how fast lightning travels. The coming of the Son of Man will be just as rapid.

Sometimes the comparison is elaborate:

"You are like salt for all mankind. But if salt loses its saltiness, there is no way to make it salty again. It has	Here we have to complete the comparison: You are like salt. Unsalty salt is good for nothing. So you

| become worthless, so it is thrown out and people trample on it." (Mt 5:13) | will also be good for nothing if you lose your quality and your virtue. |

Metaphors. We often do not say in so many words that one object (person, event) "is like" another object (person, event)— we simply apply the one term directly to the object. For instance, if we think a person is as large as an elephant, we will simply say, "That elephant is coming again!" Everyone knows that we are not speaking of a real elephant but that we are comparing somebody to such an animal. In this case we call the word *elephant* a metaphor. It is used not in its original sense but in a transferred sense.

"You snakes!" (John the Baptist to the Pharisees, Mt 3:7; cf., Lk 3:7). The Pharisees were, of course, not real snakes, but the figure of speech communicates the point.

"Take care . . . and be on your guard against the yeast of the Pharisees and the yeast of Herod" (Mk 8:15). Yeast has the power of slowly infiltrating and permeating the dough into which it is put. The influence of the Pharisees (their legalism) and of Herod Antipas (materialism and religious indifference) might also affect the apostles. So Jesus warned them against this influence as if it were yeast.

"He will not break a bruised reed or quench a smoldering wick" (Mt 12:20). The bent reed and the flickering lamp are images of a person who is very weak and on the point of (spiritual) collapse. Jesus will give such a person an extra chance. Other metaphors in the Gospels are Jesus' yoke and burden (Mt 11:30), drinking the chalice (accepting suffering: Mt 20:23; Mk 10:38), the keys of the kingdom (authority: Mt 16:19), to carry one's cross (Lk 9:23, 14:27), the crops ripe for the harvest (promising ministry: Jn 4:35), to be a slave of sin (Jn 8:34ff); taking care of Jesus' sheep (Jn 21:16ff).

Allegories. If we work out a metaphor into a longer story it may become an allegory, i.e., a story in which all the elements (or practically all the elements) are metaphors. Study the following allegory from an Indian weekly newspaper. Through this story, the editor says what we find in the second column.

Two sisters, called Lalee and Fatimah lived in the same house. They were happy and content, until one day a stranger, Mr. Chou, rented a house next to one of the sisters. Chou became a great friend of Fatimah. He gave her presents. But he did not like Lalee and he plotted with Fatimah against Lalee. Since then Lalee and Fatimah have become enemies. . . ."

India and Pakistan used to be one nation. There was great friendship between them. But China conquered Tibet and so became their neighbor. China began a policy of friendship with Pakistan. It supplied arms. This Chinese diplomacy has resulted in a misunderstanding between India and Pakistan.

Characteristic of such an allegory is that all elements of the story have a separate meaning, e.g., "renting a house," "becoming friends," "giving presents," etc. In reality the whole story is a sustained metaphor, because it is all the time speaking of one term (Mr. Chou) but meaning something else (China).

The Gospels contain very few allegories. Compare the following:

"I am the real vine, and my Father is the gardener. He breaks off every branch in me that does not bear fruit, and he prunes every branch that does bear fruit so that it will be clean and bear more fruit." (Jn 15:1-2)

Through me all receive grace. My Father fosters this life of grace. Christians can cut themselves off from this grace. But Christians who live holy lives are perfected so that they grow in sanctity.

"I am the gate for the sheep. All others who came

All those looking for salvation find it through me.

before me are thieves and robbers, but the sheep did not listen to them. I am the gate. Whoever comes in by me will be saved; he will come in and go out and find pasture." (Jn 10:7-9)

Other so-called Messiahs who came earlier only had military or political aims. People did not follow them. He who becomes my disciple will be saved. He will find security and spiritual food.

Such allegories we find most frequently in the Gospel of John. Usually, it is not a question of a real allegory in the fullest sense of the word (there is no story), but of a very elaborate metaphor. In the other Gospels there is one parable which approaches the form of an allegory.

"Once there was man who went out to sow grain. As he scattered the seed in the field, some of it fell along the path, and the birds came and ate it up. Some of it fell on rocky ground, where there was little soil. . . . Some of the seed fell among thorn bushes, which grew up and choked the plants. . . . But some seeds fell in good soil, and the plants sprouted, grew, and bore grain."
(Mk 4:3-5, 7-8)

Apostles are sent by God to preach. When they preach God's message, their words are heard by some people, but only—as it were—in passing. The devil does not give them a chance to listen to it properly. Other people listen, but their faith has no roots. . . . In others it is materialism that chokes faith. . . . In others faith produces sanctity.
(See Mk 4:13-20)

Parables

Parables are stories which illustrate some truth. They differ from allegories mainly in the fact that parables should be interpreted as one unit. The various elements are not meant to convey separate meanings.

Perhaps we might explain a parable in this way. Suppose I want to explain that true virtue can also exist in a man who looks insignificant. I might say, "Under the dress of a beggar there may be a prince." I may also tell a parable.

> A very rich king lived in a beautiful palace. He had a son whom he loved and on whom he spent all possible care. He provided him with magnificent clothes, with the most costly foods, and the most competent servants. The prince, one day, wanted to test his father's love and put on a beggar's dress to sit by the side of a road where he knew his father was going to pass. His father came driving past in a golden chariot. Seeing his son, he stopped the chariot, ran to his son, embraced him and said, "How are you, my child?" The son replied, "Don't you feel repulsion for me since I am dressed as a beggar?" The king said, "You are my son and a prince whatever your dress may be."

Notice in the parable the many elements which do not have a separate meaning: the palace of the king, the costly foods and competent servants of the prince, the son sitting by the side of the road, the king going in a chariot, etc. The point is that the son remained a true son and a prince in spite of the beggar's clothes he was wearing. The details in the parable are only there to make the parable more lively, more beautiful, more interesting. Parables only seek to teach one central truth.

Jesus frequently taught in parables. Quite a few parables have been handed on in an abbreviated form. Some examples of these are the copious harvest with few workers (Mt 9:37-38), the bridegroom and his guests (Mt 9:14-15), the old and the new wine (Lk 5:39), the uprooted plants and blind leaders of the blind (Mt 15:13-14), the corpse and the vultures (Lk 17:37), the doctor called to cure the sick (Mt 9:12-13). Jesus may sometimes have told them as long parables, and at other times spoken them in the shortened form in which we find them in the Gospels now. Others are full parables.

Parables of The Kingdom	Matthew	Mark	Luke
1. The sower	13:3-9, 18-23	4:3-9, 13-21	8:5-8, 11-15
2. The growing seed		4:26-29	
3. The weeds	13:24-30 36-43		
4. The mustard seed	13:31-32	4:30-32	13:18-19
5. The leaven	13:33		13:20-21
6. The pearl	13:45-46		
7. The hidden treasure	13:44		
8. The fishing net	13:47-50		
9. The unwilling children	11:16-19		12:31-35
10. The unfruitful fig tree			13:6-9
11. The workers in the vineyard	20:1-16		
12. The two brothers	21:28-32		
13. The royal marriage feast	22:1-14		
14. The great dinner			14:16-24
15. The wicked workers	21:33-46	12:1-2	20:9-19
16. The lost sheep	18:12-14		15:3-7
17. The lost drachma			15:8-10
18. The prodigal son		15:11-32	
19. The two creditors			7:41-47
20. The Pharisee and the tax collector			18:9-14
21. Lazarus and the rich man			16:19-31
22. The vigilant servants	13:33-37		12:35-38
23. The ten girls	25:1-13		
24. The unreliable servant	24:45-51		12:41-46
25. The five talents	25:14-30		
26. The ten gold coins			19:11-27
27. The rich fool			12:16-21
28. The good Samaritan			10:30-37
29. The unforgiving servant	18:23-35		

Parables of The Kingdom	Matthew	Mark	Luke
30. The troublesome friend			11:5-8
31. The unjust judge			16:1-13
32. The dishonest manager			18:1-8

Rules of Interpretation for Parables. Parables contain depths of meaning and can be difficult to understand. Follow these simple rules when interpreting them.

1. *In order to understand the parable we have first to grasp its meaning in the ordinary sense of the story.*

Jesus spoke in parables in order to make his point clear. His stories were taken from the everyday experiences of the Jews of his own time. They knew immediately what he was talking about in the parable, but for us it is sometimes more difficult since we live in a different country, so many centuries later. We should, therefore, first of all try to grasp what the story meant to the Jews of Jesus' own time. The parable of the Good Samaritan will mean far more to us if we know how much the Samaritans were despised by the Jews (Lk 10:30-37). The full meaning of the parable of the woman mixing yeast in the dough (Mt 13:33) will escape us if we do not know what "three measures of meal" means. When we hear that this is seventy-five pounds, we realize that Jesus wanted to emphasize how large an amount can be permeated by a little yeast. When reading the parables or explaining them to others we should, therefore, begin by looking at the story as a story. The story in its immediate and ordinary meaning should first be clear.

2. *Every parable illustrates one principal truth. This truth can be known from the obvious intention of the parable, from the context, or from the explanation added by Jesus or by the evangelist.*

The main thing to remember is that the parable illustrates only one truth. Normally it is not difficult to find out what the truth is. Often the context leaves no doubt about the meaning of the parable. The parable of the Good Samaritan was given in reply to the question "Who is my neighbor?" (Lk 10:29). Jesus spoke of the two creditors in relation to Mary Magdalene's conversion (Lk 7:44-47), and he added the explanation then and there. The murmuring of the Pharisees against Jesus' friendship with the tax collectors (Lk 15:1-2) prompted Jesus to speak of the Lost Sheep, the Lost Drachma, and the Prodigal Son. The obvious intention of the parable itself is frequently enough to guide us. We realize that when Jesus spoke of the Unfruitful Fig Tree (Lk 13:6-9), he was speaking of the Jewish people which had so far not shown any fruits, i.e., results in response to all God's teaching and care for them. The servants who receive five, three, and one talents (Mt 25:14-30) obviously represent different sorts of people who will be judged according to the graces received.

The explanation of a parable is added in many instances. The parables of the Sower and of the Weeds were explained at length by Jesus himself (Mt 13:18-23, 36-43). At times the evangelist added an explanation, as when Luke states that Jesus told the parable of the Pharisee and the Publican for those "who were sure of their own goodness and despised everybody else" (Lk 18:9). The parable of the Unforgiving Servant ends with the Lord warning, "That is how my Father in heaven will treat every one of you unless you forgive your brother from your heart!" (Mt 18:35).

3. *The details of the parable confirm and underline the general truth of the parable, but do not contain a separate spiritual meaning.*

The details of the parable have the function of bringing the principal truth into sharper relief. They are secondary to this principal truth. They do not carry a distinct meaning. If due attention is not given to this rule, the parables could easily be misunderstood. In the parable of the Lost Drachma (Lk 15:8-10), the "lighting the lamp" and "sweeping the house" do not have a separate meaning. They underline the principal truth of the parable—that God will do everything possible to bring back a sinner. The man who finds the hidden treasure (Mt 13:44) hides it in the soil where he found it and buys that field. His honesty is not the issue; even if he is dishonest, the parable teaches us the total commitment that we should imitate on the spiritual plane. In the parable of the Unjust Judge (Lk 18:1-8), the principal truth is that perseverance will win us a hearing. The detail about the lack of honesty in the judge only underlines the point that if even an unjust judge will eventually listen, how much more God.

The Purpose of Teaching in Parables. Parables are used by Jewish writers to make difficult and profound truths easy to understand. Jesus spoke in parables for precisely the same reason. Even a brief study of the parables suffices to make this clear, but a certain passage in the Gospels has frequently disturbed people. This passage reads (in an outdated translation):

> "To you it is given to know the mystery of the kingdom of God; but to them that are without, all things are done in parables; That seeing they may see and not perceive; and hearing they may hear and not understand; lest at any time they should be converted and their sins should be forgiven them!" (Mk 4:11-12)

In this translation it sounds as if Jesus spoke in parables to prevent people from understanding his message properly, as if God does not want the people to be converted and have their sins forgiven. Obviously, this cannot be the meaning. It would go counter to everything else that Jesus taught.

What then is the meaning of this passage? Jesus quoted from Isaiah 6:9-10, in which God complains about his people, using a form of speech which we might call "exasperated anxiety." Imagine a mother who is terribly upset by her son's plan to join the army. Neither tears nor arguments succeed in making him change his mind. In the end the mother might address him as follows:

> "All right, then, go! Don't listen to your mother! Forget your parents who looked after you! Give yourself to a life of

cleaning guns and shooting people! Throw away all the money we have spent on your education!"

The mother means just the opposite of what she says. By speaking like this she hopes to move her son's heart. By it she expresses her exasperated anxiety. In the text quoted by Jesus, God speaks precisely in the same manner.

Examine the longer text of Matthew 13:13-16, which is parallel to Mark 4:11-12. There Jesus says he uses parables because people understand things with great difficulty. In Isaiah's prophecy God complains that the Jews are slow in understanding; God would so gladly forgive their sins (heal them), if they only converted. Fortunately, Jesus says, his disciples have a better understanding. With them he does not always need to speak in parables. He said:

> I have used figures of speech to tell you these things. But the time will come when I will not use figures of speech, but will speak to you plainly about the Father. (Jn 16:25)

An example of this point is the phrase "The Kingdom of Heaven is like . . . ," used to introduce eleven parables. In all these cases, Jesus does not mean that the Kingdom is like the owner of the field (Mt 13:24), or like the ten girls (Mt 25:1), or like the buyer (Mt 13:45). He means "You can learn something about the Kingdom of Heaven from the following story. There was a man who sowed good seed. . . ." The Kingdom of Heaven has a similarity to what is contained in the whole parable, not a similarity to the first person or object mentioned.

Deeper Meanings. Through the parables Jesus illustrates certain truths which everyone must know. But could it be that, apart from the first, obvious meaning of the parable, another more profound meaning may be found in the same parable? The parable of the Good Samaritan teaches us the virtue of fraternal charity. But could it be Jesus' intention to imply also another meaning—that the Jewish, levitical priesthood had failed, and that his own priesthood will replace it? Can we see the whole of mankind in the man who fell into the hands of robbers? Is Jesus the "Good Samaritan" who saves us by his loving care? The parable of the Prodigal Son teaches God's love for the sinner who repents. But can we see in the elder son the Jewish people (who did not want to be converted) and in the younger son the non-Jews (who first strayed from home, but then were reconciled)?

It is quite certain that some parables do contain some deeper meaning. And since they were spoken quite often, by Jesus himself and by the apostles, the lessons to be drawn from the parables could also vary according to the circumstances. So we see that from the one parable of the Lost Sheep two different lessons are drawn:

> If a man has a hundred sheep and one of them gets lost, he will leave the ninety-nine and look for the lost one until he finds it.

Matthew draws one lesson from the parable:

> In just the same way your Father in heaven does not want any of these little ones to be lost. (Mt 18:14)

Luke draws a somewhat different lesson:

> In the same way, I tell you, there will be more joy in heaven over one sinner who repents than over ninety-nine respectable people. . . . (Lk 15:7)

For a deeper meaning of individual parables one should consult a good commentary.

THIRTEEN

Getting To Know Jesus

NOW THAT WE have a better understanding of the world in which Jesus was born and in which he lived, we are prepared for a study of the person of Jesus himself. Jesus Christ, true Son of God by his divine nature, was at the same time the greatest man who ever lived. In this chapter, we shall try to understand something of his unsurpassed human character. We shall try to get to know him better as a man so that, through his humanity, we will better realize how he was the full revelation of God's love for us. Character does not depend on a person's external appearance. It has nothing to do with the color of one's skin, with one's stature, muscular build, bodily health, the soundness of one's teeth, or the beauty of one's fingers! Neither should we confuse character with the natural talents and gifts we have received, such as intelligence, a sense of humor, artistic talent, the gift of dealing spontaneously with people, and so on. Moreover, character simply cannot be identified with what we call a man's temperament—his energy, his moods, his quickness or slowness of feeling. In judging a man's character, we should also distinguish it from the circumstances of his life. These may be poverty, certain family backgrounds, events that influenced his life, such as war, sickness, and so on. Character is something more than all these things. It presupposes them all. It builds on them, but it cannot be identified with them.

Character is a man or woman's basic disposition, acquired by a person's free and conscious acts. Character is the way in which we have made use of our external appearance, our natural talents, our temperament, and the circumstances of our life. Character is the sum total of good habits, attitudes, and virtues acquired by our own conscious effort.

Jesus called Herod Antipas "a fox" (Lk 13:32), certainly referring to Herod's character. In Jesus' time, foxes were regarded more or less the same way we regard hyenas. They did a lot of damage to the crops, sneaking in under cover of darkness. They were not strong or courageous enough to attack other animals, but loved to gorge on half-finished carcasses. Herod Antipas was quite a talented person, but in the course of time he had acquired some low-to-the-ground habits and attitudes. He lived for his own comfort. He had become dishonest and cunning in his dealings with the Jews and the Romans. He had no scruples about having people murdered if this suited his purpose. All these qualities reveal Herod's character, i.e., the personality he had become by his own free and conscious acts. With the same natural dispositions and talents, and under the same circumstances, he could have made himself into a different personality—an honest, just, and conscientious ruler.

Getting to Know Jesus' Character

In daily life we meet dozens of persons whom we get to know well. We understand their character. We know their habits, attitudes, and virtues. We know what they are worth. But have we ever thought about the ways in which we acquired this knowledge? For, after all, a person's inner character is not something we can see with our eyes or measure with a yardstick. How, then, will we get to know Jesus' character?

Behavior and Attitude. We get to know someone's character by his behavior and his attitude. We should not simply judge by his external appearance, for appearances are deceptive. Two persons may both look very smart, but one may be lazy, the other hardworking. By behavior and attitude we mean the way in which a person reacts to certain circumstances, the emotions he displays, the expression of his personality in his general bearing and so on.

The Pharisees were angry when Jesus cured the man with the crippled hand on the Sabbath. Then "Jesus was angry as he looked around at them, but at the same time he felt sorry for them, because they were so stubborn and wrong" (Mk 3:5). Jesus did not say anything just then, but the expression on his face revealed his anger, his disappointment, and his sorrow. From this attitude we (just like the people present then) learn about his character.

While the apostles crossed the Sea of Galilee a storm arose. The boat was tossed up and down as huge waves crashed against the sides, splashing water all around and gradually filling the boat. But "Jesus was in the back of the boat, sleeping with his head on a pillow" (Mk 4:38). In spite of all that happens Jesus remained completely unperturbed. Nothing could so clearly demonstrate the calmness and serenity of his character.

Jesus went to Bethany where his friend Lazarus had died. After meeting Martha, he went to the tomb where Mary was mourning.

> Jesus saw her weeping, and he saw how the people who were with her were weeping also; his heart was touched, and he was deeply moved. . . . Jesus wept. "See how much he loved him!" the people said. (Jn 11:33, 35-36)

Jesus responded to the human sorrow of his friends with a very genuine expression of his own sympathy—he wept.

Jesus had been sent to Herod. Standing before Herod's throne he was made to undergo much humiliation. Herod interrogated him and invited him to perform miracles. The Pharisees accused him. The courtiers mocked him. All around Jesus there was shouting, laughter, jeering. But "Jesus made no answer" (Lk 23:9). He did not try to save his life by saying pleasant things to Herod. He did not think it any use to defend himself. His attitude of dignified silence proves the inner strength of his character.

The Gospels do not record the details of Jesus' external appearance. Obviously, these details are not considered important for the biblical message or for our understanding of Jesus' character. But the Gospels do present Jesus' behavior and attitude. When we read the episodes recorded in the Gospels, we should pay attention to his way of reacting to events, his emotions, the expressions on his face, his gestures, and so on. They will help us to know his character.

Speech and Conversation. We learn much about a man's character from what he says, not so much from what he says about himself, but from his *way* of speaking—his refinement, his emotions, his way of treating others, the things he values, and so on. Jesus' words and his conversations throw much light on his character.

In the parable of the Prodigal Son, Jesus describes the father's welcome: "He was still a long way from home when his father saw him . . . ran, threw his arms around his son, and kissed him" (Lk 15:20). From the very way in which Jesus described such touching scenes, from the whole atmosphere of the parable, we somehow understand Jesus' own kindness, mercy, and forgiveness. Jesus' own character is reflected in such parables.

The scribes wanted to trap Jesus with a question about taxes. They hoped that he would either forbid the paying of taxes to Rome (and incur the censure of the Romans) or allow these taxes (and incur the indignation of the Jewish nationalists). Jesus made them produce the tax coin, with the emperor's image on it, and said, "Pay to the Emperor what belongs to the Emperor, and pay to God what belongs to God!" (Mt 22:21). In the discussion, Jesus showed himself to be a master of men, and also a man of principle and a true leader.

When a certain disciple wanted to delay following Jesus in order to look after the affairs of his family (expressed by the words "to bury his father"), Jesus retorted, "Let the dead bury their own dead. You go and proclaim the Kingdom of God!" (Lk 9:60). Jesus' words were a demand expressing his conviction and revealing the depth of his own commitment.

At the Last Supper Jesus talked familiarly with his disciples. He said to Philip:

> For a long time I have been with you all; yet you do not know me, Philip? Whoever has seen me has seen the Father. Why, then, do you say, 'Show us the Father?' (Jn 14:9)

In such familiar discourses Jesus frequently allows us to obtain direct knowledge of his most cherished thoughts and desires.

Jesus' indignation sometimes rings out:

> How terrible for you, teachers of the Law and Pharisees! You hypocrites! You are like whitewashed tombs, which look fine on the outside but are full of bones and decaying corpses on the inside. (Mt 23:27)

These warnings and threats show how deeply Jesus detests hypocrisy and insincerity.

We should examine Jesus' words and see what they tell us of his character. To a certain extent we can hide our true character under words, if we wish to do so. But we cannot hide it altogether. Jesus did not want to hide his character from us. He spoke simple and straightforward language. He expressed himself without fear or inhibition. He taught the things that naturally flow from his rich inner convictions. It is, therefore, relatively easy to study Jesus' character from what he said.

Actions and Deeds. We are all familiar with proverbs such as "A friend in need is a friend indeed." Actions prove a man's character more than words ever can, for it is easy to say things and to make statements, but it requires real inner strength (character) to live up to these statements. It is by what we do that we demonstrate to what values we have committed ourselves. We learn much about Jesus from his deeds.

The first mission of the twelve apostles meant a great development for the Kingdom Jesus was preaching. We read how Jesus prepared himself for it, spending the whole night praying (Lk 6:12). This prayer of preparation convincingly illustrates the profound motivations with which Jesus fulfills his mission!

Tax collectors were considered traitors, since they worked for the Romans, and public sinners, since they often took unjust gains. When Zacchaeus wanted to see Jesus, he responded by saying, "I must stay in your house today" (Lk 19:5). Jesus' friendship with such "public sinners" frequently brought objections (see also Mt 9:9-13; Mk 2:13-17), but by it Jesus demonstrated the genuine kindness and mercy of a man who does not seek his own glory.

After the multiplication of the bread, the mob decided to make Jesus king. Jesus took resolute action by dispersing the crowd and by forcing his disciples to cross the lake at once (Mt 14:22; Jn 6:15). He did not allow the situation to get out of hand. A better demonstration of leadership could hardly be found.

Meeting a funeral procession outside Nain, Jesus was moved to compassion for the mother of the deceased person. He stopped the men who were carrying the dead body, raised the dead man, and "gave him back to his mother" (Lk 7:14, 15). In all Jesus' cures, his action resulted from sympathy and compassion. These miracles reveal not only his divine power, but also his great kindness.

At the Last Supper Jesus washed the feet of his disciples. It was not a mere symbol or an empty performance. By doing this work Jesus humiliated himself, thereby teaching us that he lived by the principles of selfless service and charity (Mt 20:24-28; Jn 13:3-15).

The greatest expression of Jesus' character must be seen in his voluntary death, a death he underwent as a sacrificial reconciliation for mankind. His own words were thereby realized: "The greatest love a person can have for his friends is to give his life for them" (Jn 15:13). All through his Passion, Jesus showed the dignity, loftiness, strength, and profundity of his character.

The Gospels record Jesus' actions. Let us reflect on these

actions from the angle of Jesus' character. We will be surprised to see how deep an insight they give us into his personality. Often Jesus' actions are unexpected and vigorous; often they are at the same time manifestations of his divine power; often they are meant to underline his message. Yet in and through all of them Jesus also revealed his true, inner character.

Reactions of Others. Frequently we learn to appreciate a person because of the attraction he or she exercises on others. Students may tell us about the teacher whom they respect. Even before we meet this teacher we ourselves will have a good idea of what his or her character is. The very fact that other people like or dislike a certain person, the fact that they fear him or despise him, the way in which they speak about him or act towards him—all these things help us to get to know a person's character. Of course, people can be mistaken and can be unjust in their judgment. Yet, to some extent, from the way others respond to him the character of a person can be known. This also applies to Jesus.

One day Jesus walked along the coast and saw Matthew in his custom house (Mt 9:9). "He said to him, 'Follow me.' Matthew got up and followed him." Matthew's reaction to Jesus' call must have been caused by the extraordinary impact Jesus had made on his life! From this, and from similar vocation narratives, we can deduce the impression Jesus made on his contemporaries.

After Jesus had calmed the storm, the disciples were overwhelmed with awe. "They were terribly afraid and began to say to one another, "Who is this man?"" (Mk 4:41). Their fear proves how Jesus' power went beyond their ordinary experience.

Parents brought their children to Jesus (Mk 10:16), and he "took the children in his arms, placed his hands on each of them, and blessed them." People are normally shrewd observers, and the fact that they want their children blessed by Jesus proves their trust in him.

While Jesus was attending an official dinner in the home of a

Pharisee, a repentant sinner entered the house, "stood behind Jesus, by his feet, crying and wetting his feet with her tears" (Lk 7:38). No doubt she had heard Jesus preaching and now wanted to live a better life. The confidence she had in Jesus, the affectionate way in which she washed his feet, show how much Jesus inspired people to trust in him.

Perhaps the greatest tribute to Jesus' intelligence and conviction is the following: "No one was able to give Jesus any answer, and from that day on no one dared to ask him any more questions" (Mt 22:46). The scribes thrived on their daily discussions. It was the thing they reveled in, the thing in which they had become thoroughly expert. Yet in Jesus they acknowledged their superior.

Pilate was deeply impressed by Jesus' character. From his conversations with Jesus we can see that he recognized Jesus' moral integrity. That is why he, while consenting to put Jesus to death for political reasons, had the notice "Jesus of Nazareth, the King of the Jews" put on the cross (Jn 19:19-22). The priests objected, but Pilate replied by saying that he really considered Jesus to be the King of the Jews—"What I have written stays written."

The reactions of Jesus' contemporaries teach us much about Jesus' character. His disciples were drawn by his great love and by the beauty of his ideals. The crowds admired him and followed him wherever he went. Sinners went to him to obtain forgiveness. Parents brought their children. Even Gentiles sought his help. The scribes and Pharisees respected and feared him in spite of their unbelief. In the reactions of all these people we see different aspects of Jesus' character reflected as in so many mirrors.

The Existential Approach to Jesus

Jesus is the mediator between God and man (1 Tm 2:5). Jesus' humanity was in itself a revelation of God. Seeing it, the apostles were actually "seeing" the Father (Jn 14:9), since in his humanity Jesus was the "exact likeness of God's own being"

(Heb 1:3). This means that getting to know Jesus' human character is one way of understanding God's revelation. It is the way in which the apostles first got to know Jesus as the revelation of the Father. Through a human understanding of Jesus they slowly came to appreciate his true, divine personality. We may call this the "psychological" approach to Jesus. Thus far, we have followed this psychological approach by trying to show how we too can to some extent learn to know Jesus' character from the Gospels. We have tried to demonstrate that careful meditation on the Gospel passages will reveal various aspects of Jesus' character. Such meditations are to be highly recommended. We can never know Jesus' humanity well enough. However, this psychological approach to Jesus is not the only one, and not even the most important one.

While admitting that the Gospel passages do reveal to us Jesus' character, we should at the same time recognize that they are far more concerned to teach us the *existential* function of his character. If the Gospels were intending a description of Jesus' human character as their first purpose, they would surely have added a precise description of Jesus' physical appearance and would have given far more details about Jesus' daily manner of life. They would also have retained some psychological analyses of all Jesus said or thought on particular occasions. Instead of this we find that the greater part of the Gospels are made up of Jesus' teachings or of small incidents from Jesus' life, recorded in a very brief and succinct fashion.

The main purpose of the Gospels in all passages is to show that Jesus is the promised Redeemer, that he is the Savior, the Son of God, the Lord, the Way, the Truth, and the Life. He is the Shepherd leading us to life, the source of living water, the light of the world, the one who will judge the living and the dead. All these truths express aspects of Jesus' existential role, and the Gospels invite us to accept Jesus as having this role to play in our *own* existence. Accepting Jesus in this way, we approach him in an existential manner. Reflect on these passages:

Whoever loves his father or mother more than me is not fit to be my disciple. . . . Whoever does not take up his cross and follow in my steps is not fit to be my disciple. . . . Whoever loses his life for my sake will gain it. (Mt 10:37-39)

Reflection: Loving Jesus above all means accepting his existential role as sole model and mediator.

I am the gate. Whoever comes in by me will be saved.
(Jn 10:9)
I am the vine and you are the branches. . . . remain in me.
(Jn 15:5)
I am the bread of life. . . . He who comes to me will never be hungry. (Jn 6:35)

Reflection: Being "saved" by Jesus means receiving our supernatural existence from him. It is an existential dependence.

It may be useful to work out in some detail how to meditate on the Gospels, making use of both the existential and psychological approaches. Take the incident of Jesus' conflict with the merchants in the Temple:

There in the Temple he found men selling cattle, sheep, and pigeons, and also the moneychangers sitting at their tables. So he made a whip from cords and drove all the animals out of the Temple, both the sheep and the cattle; he overturned the tables of the moneychangers and scattered their coins; and he ordered the men who sold the pigeons, "Take them out of here! Stop making my Father's house a marketplace!"
(Jn 2:14-16)

What can we learn about Jesus' character from this passage?
1. Let us consider Jesus' *attitude.* We can imagine the indignation on his face, the determined anger with which he drove out the cattle and pushed over the tables.

2. Jesus' *words* reveal the motives of his action. By speaking of the Temple as "my Father's house," he showed his respect for his Father, and for the place where he was worshipped. He objected to this house being made a marketplace—Jesus was inspired by zeal for the things of God. He was also thinking of the Gentiles who could pray only in this outer court.

3. The energy displayed in Jesus' *action* cannot be over-estimated—he cleared the whole Court of the Gentiles of the hundreds of merchants who were selling there. The vastness of the task and its unusual strictness make us marvel at the depth of his conviction. He carried out what only a very strong will and a very decisive personality could accomplish.

4. The *reactions of the others* confirm this last conclusion. Hundreds of cattle merchants and moneychangers bended to his will. They must have recognized in Jesus a moral superiority which they could not resist. Even the Temple officials, who protest to Jesus later on, do not dare to readmit the merchants in Jesus' presence!

What does this passage teach about Jesus' existential role in our lives? To answer this question well we have to scrutinize the text very carefully. Jesus' cleansing of the Temple is linked with his claim that he will "build up the house of God in three days" (Jn 2:19), and John tells us that Jesus was speaking of the temple of his body. To the Samaritan woman Jesus will explain that the old Temple has been abolished, and that people can henceforth worship the Father everywhere "in spirit and in truth" (Jn 4:21-24). The incident of the cleansing of the Temple shows us therefore that a new era of worship has arrived. The old manner of worship, with its many external rites and forms, is to be replaced by a more interior worship. Jesus himself will bring about this change. His sacrifice will replace the sacrifices of the past. He will be the new high priest. He will mediate a new covenant. His body will be the new temple through which we will bring more perfect worship to the Father. This is the existential role of Jesus which the passage wants to teach.

Knowing Jesus

We cannot be Christians if we do not "know" Jesus. It is especially in John's Gospel that this is stressed (see Jn 14:4-9, 20, 17:3). But what does it mean to know Jesus? When we speak of knowing someone, we mean first of all that we know something *about* that person and his character. In this sense we should know Jesus by having meditated on his character. The Gospels will help us in this. In fact, as Jerome says, "He who does not know the Gospels does not know Christ."

But knowing someone also means having made the acquaintance of that person and having a special relationship with him. This is the fullest sense of the word *knowing* when applied to Jesus. "The world" (that is, unredeemed man) "did not recognize" Jesus (Jn 1:10), but the apostles came to know Jesus as the Holy One of God (Jn 6:69) and as the "I Am Who I Am" (Jn 8:28). Their knowledge had made them Jesus' friends (Jn 15:13-15). They knew that the knowledge of Jesus would remain in them as long as his commandment of love would be their driving force (1 Jn 2:3, 3:24, 4:13).

Our knowing Jesus should be a similar kind of existential acquaintance. Jesus should mean everything to us. Through every means available to us we should imbibe his Spirit and his commandment of love. Then we will truly *know* Jesus in the biblical sense of the word. Then we will experience Jesus' character of love being realized again in our own lives.

FOURTEEN

Jesus Manifests His Power

IN THE FOREGOING CHAPTERS, we have had occasion to speak of how Jesus began to reveal his special position in many indirect ways: by calling himself greater than the Temple, by teaching with divine authority, by living a life of unparalleled holiness. A more direct revelation of his role lay in his miracles. Jesus' miracles were manifestations of God's power.

Miracles as Signs

When someone escapes from an accident by a hair's breadth, he may exclaim, "It was a miracle I didn't get hurt!" A poor student who receives good marks in an exam is said to have done "miraculously" well. In our everyday speech we often use the word *miracle* in such a weakened sense. We must, therefore, begin this chapter by asking ourselves what a miracle is in the technical sense of the word.

It is important for us to realize that not everything that is wonderful or extraordinary may be called a miracle. Three things are required to make an event a true miracle: the event must be visible; the event must go beyond the powers of nature (that is, it must have God for its author); the event must be the sign of a divine message. All three factors must be there; otherwise we cannot really call the event a miracle.

Perhaps we can illustrate this with a road sign. Suppose we find by the side of the road a signpost with the notice "No Parking." We have to obey the road sign; if we ignore it, the police may fine us. But what qualities should a road sign have to impose such an obligation? The same three qualities as the miracle: it must be visible; it must have been put up by the legitimate authority; it must be a clear sign by which I understand an order or a prohibition. Let us look at the three aspects one by one.

Visibility. It is obvious that a road sign does not put any obligation on me if I cannot see it, e.g., if it has been buried or put behind a tree. The same applies to a miracle. Miracles should be visible events such as we find in the Gospels— walking on water, the instantaneous cure of leprosy, the change of water into wine. Other things which we cannot see, however wonderful they are and however much they may require God's direct intervention, are not miracles in the true sense of the word. Examples are grace, the forgiveness of sins, the changing of bread in the eucharist, the ordination by which a person is set aside for God's service. These things are certainly extraordinary and they come about by God's own action, but we cannot see them and, therefore, they are not miracles. The local council may have passed a decision to forbid parking in a certain place, but as long as they have not put up a visible road sign I am not bound by it. God does many things in the secrecy of the heart and in the sacramental order—things we firmly believe in, since we know them from Christ's teaching—but we do not call these things miracles, as they are not visible to human perception.

Power and Authority. A traffic sign that was not put up by the local authority does not bind us either. Otherwise anybody might just scribble instructions on the wall or erect signposts. The same holds true for miracles. In order to be true miracles, they should go beyond the powers of nature. They should be such that only God, with his power and authority, could perform them. Raising a person from the dead, calming a storm, or healing a paralyzed man in a matter of seconds—these acts of Jesus certainly required God's direct intervention and, there- fore, we may call them true miracles. On the other hand, it is not necessary to hold that all Jesus' cures were miracles. His true miracles are those cures by which he did what goes beyond human power, such as restoring Malchus' ear (Lk 22:49-51) or giving sight to the man born blind (Jn 9:1-8).

Signifying a Divine Message. No road sign is put up for its own sake. It always aims at conveying a message, at pointing to something that is signified by it. As a matter of fact, that is why we call it a sign. We should remember that a miracle is always a sign. God performs no miracle without wanting to convey a message by it and through it, never for the sake of the event alone. Suppose that a journalist is travelling in a plane whose gas tank suddenly ruptures. God wants the journalist to be saved and supplies gas by creating it. May we call this visible event, which goes beyond the ordinary powers of nature, a miracle? No, unless it becomes at the same time a sign by which someone (perhaps the journalist) understands that God is communicating a message to him (perhaps of love and care). As a matter of fact, we know from the history of salvation, that God will not directly interfere with the normal course of events unless he wishes to communicate something to us. Every intervention of God in the Gospels is a sign, pointing to a truth which God wants to establish. When we read the account of a miracle in the Gospels, we should not stop at the mere fact. We always have to ask: What did Jesus want to signify by this miracle? What is he teaching by it?

Jesus' Miracles

Jesus' miracles are like public road signs which he erected so that all passersby might understand the message which he preached with divine authority. Jesus taught not only in words but also in deeds. An important part of his message is contained in the miraculous signs he worked. Jesus' divinity spontaneously manifested itself in the miraculous signs he performed. A survey of some of the miracles we see in the Gospels will help demonstrate this.

Raising the dead to life (4)	*Matthew*	*Mark*	*Luke*	*John*
His own Resurrection	28:1-20	16:1-20	24:1-53	20:1-29
Jairus' daughter	9:18-26	5:21-43	8:40-56	
The young man at Nain			7:11-17	
Lazarus				11:1-44

Power over inanimate nature (9)

Changing water into wine				2:1-11
Calming the storm	8:23-27	4:35-41	8:22-25	
Withering the fig tree	21:18-22	11:12-26		
Walking on water	14:23-33	6:45-52		6:16-21
Multiplying bread (1)	14:15-21	6:33-44	9:11-17	6:2-15
Multiplying bread (2)	15:32-38	8:1-9		
The big catch of fish (1)			5:1-11	
The big catch of fish (2)				21:1-13
The fish with the money	17:24-27			

Different kinds of cures (19)

The blind man of Jericho	20:29-34	10:46-52	18:35-43	
The blind man in Jerusalem				9:1-7
The blind man at Bethsaida		8:22-26		
The two blind men	9:27-31			
The leper in Capernaum	8:2-4	1:40-45	5:12-14	
The ten lepers			17:12-19	
The paralytic of Capernaum	9:2-7	2:1-12	5:18-26	

	Matthew	*Mark*	*Luke*	*John*
The paralytic of Bethzatha	5:1-15			
The woman with the flow of blood	9:20-22	5:24-34	8:43-48	
The man with the withered hand	12:9-13	3:1-5	6:6-10	
The hunchbacked woman			13:10-17	
The epileptic boy	17:14-18	9:14-27	9:37-43	
The man suffering from dropsy			14:1-6	
Simon's mother-in-law	8:14-15	1:29-31	4:38-39	
The Phoenician girl	15:21-28	7:24-30		
The Centurion's slave	8:5-13		7:1-10	
The Official's son				4:46-53
Malchus			22:49-51	18:10
The deaf mute		7:31-37		

Exorcisms (4)

	Matthew	*Mark*	*Luke*	*John*
The Gerasene	8:28-34	5:1-20	8:26-39	
The possessed man of Capernaum		1:23-28	4:33-37	
The dumb man	9:32-34		11:14-15	
The man who was blind and mute	12:22-32			

Foretelling the future (7)

	Matthew	*Mark*	*Luke*	*John*
His Passion and Resurrection	often	often	often	often
Peter's denial	26:30-35	14:26-31	22:31-34	13:36-38
Peter's martyrdom				21:18-19
The ass's colt	21:1-6	11:1-6	19:28-34	
Persecution of the church	10:17-23	13:9-13	10:3; 21:12ff.	
Growth of the church	26:13	14:9	24:46ff.	

	Matthew	Mark	Luke	John
Jerusalem's destruction (and other events)	24:1-20	13:1-19	21:5-24	

Jesus' miracles accomplished many things in the context of his mission. They were not simply displays of his power. Jesus' miracles had five important functions: they explained his mission; they revealed his divinity; they proved him to be the Messiah; they prepared the way for his sacraments; they began the world's renewal.

His Mission. Jesus' miracles were symbolic actions which revealed the nature of his mission. In daily life we often use symbolic actions to explain what we are doing. For instance, we hoist the flag on a national holiday to show that we are honoring the nation. And, by the symbolic action of hoisting the flag, we actually *do* honor the nation. The Old Testament prophets quite frequently expressed themselves by symbolic actions. When Jeremiah was sent to announce the destruction of Jerusalem, he took an earthen flask and smashed it to pieces in front of the people (Jer 19:1-10).

> Then the Lord told me to break the jar in front of the men who had gone with me and to tell them that the Lord Almighty had said, "I will break this people and this city, and it will be like this broken clay jar that cannot be put together again." (Jer 19:10-11)

Such a symbolic action was thought to be more than a mere demonstration to make something visual—the symbolic action itself was the beginning of putting the prophecy into operation. Jesus' miracles have to be considered such "symbolic actions."

During the last days of Jesus' preaching in Jerusalem, he performed a symbolic action that was meant to warn the Jewish people. On his way to the city, he went to a fig tree for its fruit. When he found only leaves, he cursed the tree and it withered

(Mt 21:18-22; Mk 11:12-26). It is obvious from the circumstances that Jesus performed this miracle with a spiritual purpose—it was not the time for figs (Mk 11:13) and a tree, without free will, cannot be punished. By cursing the tree Jesus warned the Jews that unless they produced fruit they also would be cursed. Read also the parable in Luke 13:6-9.

In the neighborhood of Jericho, Jesus cured Bartimaeus, a blind beggar. To understand the miracle we have to remember that, just before this event, Jesus had explained how he was to redeem mankind by his suffering, but the disciples had not understood. Luke repeats this three times.

> They did not understand any of these things;
> the meaning of the words was hidden from them,
> and they did not know what Jesus was talking about.
> (Lk 18:34)

In other words, the disciples were still blind. To help them understand, Jesus allowed the blind man to come to him and asked, "What do you want?" Anyone could guess what the blind man would want! Yet Jesus waited for him to exclaim, "Lord, that I may see!" Then Jesus said, "See! Your faith has made you well!" By this symbolic action Jesus demonstrated that he had come to make men see, that he could take away our blindness. But, like the blind man, we have to ask for it!

When Jesus prepared to call Peter, he explained, through a symbolic action, what Peter's work was to be. Peter had spent a whole night trying in vain to catch some fish. On Jesus' word he let down the net and caught such a great number that the net broke. Then Jesus said, "From now on you will be a fisher of men!" The miracle expressed very powerfully the meaning of Peter's mission—working to bring men to Christ, working at Christ's command and with his divine help, working with a guaranteed result. That was the meaning of the miracle.

The raising of Lazarus took place at the end of Jesus' public life. He had received the news of Lazarus' sickness in good time (Jn 11:3), and if he had wished he could have prevented

Lazarus' death easily enough (as the Jews also remarked, Jn 11:37). But Jesus allowed Lazarus to die, so that by raising him he could demonstrate a most important aspect of his mission (see his words in Jn 11:15). He wanted to prove by a symbolic action that all men would receive everlasting life through him.

> I am the resurrection and the life. Whoever believes in me will live, even though he dies, and whoever lives and believes in me will never die. (Jn 11:25-26)

The raising of Lazarus demonstrates this point more convincingly than words ever could. All the miracles of Jesus dramatically symbolize his whole mission of bringing salvation and life.

His Divinity. Jesus' miracles also reveal his divinity. The miracles were intended especially to help the Jews recognize Jesus' extraordinary character and his divine nature. When considering the miracles from this angle we have to take into account how the Jews would understand them. Life is a gift of the Creator. The origin of all life was always attributed to God as something belonging exclusively to his omnipotence. God gives and takes life as he wills. Of this the Jews were firmly convinced, and the Old Testament is full of references to it.

> When you turn away, they are afraid;
>> when you take away their breath, they die
>> and go back to the dust from which they came.
> But when you give them breath, they are created;
>> you give new life to the earth. (Ps 104:29)

> I, and I alone, am God;
>> no other God is real.
> I kill and I give life,
>> I wound and I heal. (Dt 32:39)

After Jesus had healed the paralytic, he discussed this giving of life.

"Just as the Father raises the dead and gives them life, in the same way the Son gives life to those he wants to. . . . Just as the Father is himself the source of life, in the same way he has made his Son the source of life." (Jn 5:21, 26)

Such a truly divine giving of life is implied in all the cures Jesus brings about. Jesus manifests his divine power over life or death not only when he raises the dead but in every healing!

Jesus' Identity. Jesus' miracles fulfilled the Old Testament promises, so that people might recognize him as the promised Redeemer. For many centuries the Jewish people had been prepared for the coming of the Messiah. Anxiously they awaited the coming of this promised Savior. They did not know precisely how he was to save them, but the prophets had sung repeatedly of the great works of liberation that the Messiah would undertake and by which they would recognize him.

> God is coming to your rescue,
>   coming to punish your enemies.
> The blind will be able to see,
>   and the deaf will hear.
> The lame will leap and dance,
>   and those who cannot speak will shout for joy. (Is 35:4-5)

> The Sovereign Lord has filled me with his spirit.
> He has chosen me and sent me
> To bring good news to the poor,
> To heal the broken-hearted,
> To announce release to captives
> And freedom to those in prison.
> He has sent me to proclaim
> That the time has come
> When the Lord will save his people. (Is 61:1-2)

Jesus himself preached in Nazareth on these latter words, showing how they were being fulfilled in him. For he came to preach the good tidings of salvation, which are demonstrated by the works of salvation (the miracles) which he does (Lk 4:16-22).

When John the Baptist sent two of his disciples to ask Jesus if he is the promised Redeemer, Jesus answered with a reference to these same prophecies (Mt 11:2-6).

> Go back and tell John what you are hearing and seeing: the blind can see, the lame can walk, those who suffer from dreaded skin diseases are made clean, the deaf hear, and the dead are brought back to life, and the Good News is preached to the poor. (vv. 4-5)

Jesus' miracles prove that the era of liberation, of salvation, has begun, especially for the poor and the lowly.

After mentioning the many cures which Jesus worked, Matthew points to a prophecy from Isaiah:

> But he endured the suffering that should have been ours. . . .
> Because of our sins he was wounded,
>   beaten because of the evil we did. (Is 53:4-5)

As we know, the prophecy announces that the Redeemer will die for our sins (Is 52:13-54:12). The illnesses of the people, the diseases which they suffer, are to be understood as symbolic of man's sins. Just as Jesus took away people's illnesses, so he will take away their sins by his vicarious death! Jesus' healing and curing is the beginning of his Messianic work of salvation—a salvation that will be primarily spiritual (Mt 8:6-17).

The Sacraments. Jesus' miracles prepared the way for his sacraments. Sacraments are external, visible actions or signs, by which an internal reality is expressed and brought about. If Jesus were to have instituted the sacraments without a visible and gradual preparation, his disciples would never have understood the nature of the sacraments.

When the paralyzed man had been laid at Jesus' feet, Jesus told him, "Your sins are forgiven." The bystanders could not see this interior forgiveness and doubted whether it had really taken place. Therefore Jesus told them, "I will prove to you, then, that the Son of Man has authority on earth to forgive sins!" He cured the man then and there! It was obvious to everyone that if Jesus, with divine power, could cure a paralyzed man, he could also forgive sins with the same power (Mt 9:1-8). Jesus passed on the power to work miraculous cures to his apostles (Mt 10:1). This was also a preparation. For just as he could give them power to heal external diseases (cures, which people could see), so he could give them the power to forgive men's sins (a cure, which people cannot see) (Jn 20:23). In this way Jesus gradually prepared the church for the sacrament of forgiveness and reconciliation.

Jesus had been preaching in the Temple on the light he was bringing to the world. To demonstrate his power to do so, he cured a blind man in a very special way—he anointed the man's eyes and sent him to the pool of Siloam to wash his face (Jn 9:7). The washing was a rite through which the man received salvation. In this way Jesus prepared the disciples for the new rite of washing, baptism, by which people were to receive the saving grace of his Passion. Without such a preparation they would not have understood the full meaning of his final instructions after his Resurrection.

> Go, then, to all peoples everywhere and make them my disciples: baptize them in the name of the Father, the Son, and the Holy Spirit. (Mt 28:19)

> "Go throughout the whole world and preach the gospel to all mankind. Whoever believes and is baptized will be saved. (Mk 16:15-16)

The meaning of baptism had been explained in Jesus' preaching (Jn 3:3-7), but also by Jesus' miracles.

It is difficult to see how the disciples could have understood the eucharist if they had not first been prepared for what it meant by many of Jesus' miracles. The miracles of providing the wine at Cana and the multiplication of the loaves were specially meant to lead up to this sacrament. In fact, after the multiplication of loaves, John has Jesus expressly announce, "I am the bread of life" (Jn 6:25-27). When the disciples later tried to understand what Jesus meant when he took bread and wine at the Last Supper, reflecting on these miracles helped them to understand the deeper significance of his words and actions there.

In a way we may say that the sacraments, because they are signs of the power of salvation, are continuations of Jesus' miracles.

Renewal. Jesus' miracles also indicate the renewal of the temporal world in which we live. His miracles were all acts of kindness and love by which he made the earthly lives of certain people happier. This "worldly" aspect of Jesus' miracles has a meaning, for it would imply the renewal also of the temporal world—already now during the period of the church militant, but especially later when man will be raised to new life, body and soul. Jesus' church continues this aspect of his miracles by the work it does in the fields of charity and social development. The church's service to mankind through its schools, hospitals, orphanages, and so on, springs from the same love with which Jesus healed the unfortunate and the sick of his time.

FIFTEEN

Jesus Reveals His Father

JESUS' TEACHING about the Father forms the core of the Gospel. Through his life, death, and Resurrection he revealed the Father to us and established a completely new relationship between him and us. Every day, and several times in the day, Christians turn to God and say, "Our Father, who art in heaven. . . ." Christ himself taught us to call God "Our Father," but in what sense can we really do so? What does Christ tell us of his Father and our Father?

Again, we live in an age when there is much renewed interest in the Holy Spirit. For many in centuries past and for many even today, he remains the almost forgotten Person of the Trinity. Who is this Holy Spirit? What is Christ's relationship with him? Where does he come into God's plan for our redemption? What can we learn of the Spirit from the Gospels? Furthermore, in our background study of the Gospels we cannot afford to ignore the context of Jesus' relationship with the Father and the Spirit—the Trinity. It is the very context of our life, for we are baptized and have our spiritual birth in the life of the Trinity. We are children of the Trinity.

Jesus and the Father

The first reference to the divine Fatherhood appears in Exodus, in a section which probably dates back to the ninth century B.C. God had decided to free and save his people from slavery in Egypt. He sent Moses to Pharaoh:

This is what Yahweh says, "Israel is my first-born son. I ordered you to let my son go to offer me worship. You refuse to let him go. So be it! I shall put your first-born to death." (Ex 4:22-23)

In this early period it is the people as a whole, and not each individual, that is the "first-born" of God. The idea is developed in other Old Testament books (e.g., Hos 11:1-8; Dt 32:4ff), but the clear and inexhaustible source for our full and rich concept of God's Fatherhood is to be found in Jesus' revelation of him in the Gospels. Before Christ, no man knew the Father, but Jesus has revealed the Father to us (Mt 11:27; Jn 1:18). It is in a spirit of prayer, therefore, that we ask Jesus, speaking to us through the pages of the Gospels, to reveal the Father to us even now. We are indeed privileged:

How fortunate you are to see the things you see! I tell you that many prophets and kings wanted to see what you see, but they could not, and to hear what you hear, but they did not. (Lk 10:23-24)

Let us read and reflect on some of the ways Jesus' words reveal the Father to us. Jesus continually spoke of the Father, and did his Father's will. So should we.

Matthew:

Love your enemies . . . so that you may become the sons of your Father. . . . You must be perfect—just as your Father in heaven is perfect. (5:44-45, 48)

Your Father already knows what you need before you ask him. (6:8—also Lk 12:30)

Not everyone who calls me "Lord, Lord" will enter the Kingdom of heaven, but only those who do what my Father in heaven wants. (7:21)

Whoever does what my Father in heaven wants him to do is my brother, my sister, and my mother. (12:50)

Luke:

No one knows who the father is except the Son.
(10:22; also Mt 11:27; Jn 6:46)

Do not be afraid, little flock, for your Father is pleased to give you the Kingdom. (12:32)

John:

Nor does the Father himself judge anyone. (5:22)

The Father . . . has made his Son to be the source of life.
(5:26)

No one can come to me unless the Father who sent me draws him to me. (6:44)

I talk about what my Father has shown me. (8:38)

As the Father knows me and I know the Father, in the same way I know my sheep and they know me. (10:14)

As for me, the Father chose me and sent me into the world. . . . The Father is in me and . . . I am in the Father. (10:36, 38)

Jesus knew that the Father had given him complete power; he knew that he had come from God and was going to God. (13:3)

I am the way, the truth, and the life; no one goes to the Father except by me. (14:6)

My Father will love whoever loves me; I too will love him and reveal myself to him. . . . Whoever loves me will obey my teaching. My Father will love him, and my Father and I will come to him and live with him. (14:21, 23)

I love you just as the Father loves me; remain in my love. If you obey my commands, you will remain in my love, just as I have obeyed my Father's commands and remain in his love. (15:9-10)

As the Father sent me, so I send you. (20:21)

Not all texts containing the word *Father* have been cited; there are just too many. Let us examine some of these texts more closely to see Jesus' revelation of the Father.

Jesus' Prayer to the Father

Jesus prayed to the Father and taught us to do likewise:

But when you pray, go to your room, close the door, and pray to your Father, who is unseen. And your Father, who sees what you do in private, will reward you. (Mt 6:6)

Jesus takes it for granted that we will pray; he does not say "you should pray," but "*when* you pray." No new formula is prescribed, no particular method. He leaves his listeners, the Jews, to the framework of prayer in which they had been brought up. The one essential thing is that prayer should put us in the presence of the Father and lead us into a life lived in total dedication to the Father (Jn 8:28-29).

Jesus tells us that our Father welcomes our requests because he loves us:

And so the Father will give you whatever you ask of him in my name. (Jn 15:16)

Ask, and you will receive. . . . Would anyone of you who are fathers give your son a stone when he asks for bread? Or would you give him a snake when he asks for a fish? As bad as you are, you know how to give good things to your children.

How much more, then, will your Father in heaven give good things to those who ask him! (Mt 7:7, 9-11)

Our Father is so anxious to be asked that he watches over us as a father watches over his favorite son (Mt 6:8). Jesus tells us that our prayer is to be first and foremost a loving, personal, and worshipful "being with" the Father, talking to the Father. To impress this upon us, Jesus teaches us to address God as *Abba* (an intimate Aramaic name, like "papa"). At most, the Jews would use the more formal and stiff title of *Ab*, meaning "Father." But Jesus uses, and wants us to use, *Abba*, meaning "Dad," to express our true, close relationship to the Father in heaven.

From time to time in the Gospels we get glimpses of the Lord's ongoing prayer to the Father. We find him absorbed in one or another of the petitions he himself taught us: "hallowed be thy name!" (Jn 12:28, 17:11); "thy will be done" (Lk 22:42); "forgive us our trespasses as we forgive those who trespass against us" (Lk 23:34); "lead us not into temptation but deliver us from evil" (Jn 17:15). It is no exaggeration to say this is the chief prayer of the Lord's life, full of all his strongest intentions and desires. All that he had and was he brought to the Father. The Lord prayed all night before he chose the disciples (Mt 14:23; Lk 6:12). He would often go away to lonely places and pray (Lk 5:16, 9:18, 28). He prayed in the garden of Gethsemane (Mt 26:36; Mk 14:32; Lk 22:39). He prayed on the cross (Mt 27:46; Mk 15:34; Lk 23:34). He prayed to the Father that we might be true to his name (Jn 17:11), that we might be one (Jn 17:21), that we might see God's glory (Jn 17:24).

Christ teaches us to pray to the Father through him:

I am telling you the truth: the Father will give you whatever you ask of him in my name. Until now you have not asked for anything in my name; ask and you will receive, so that your happiness may be complete. (Jn 16:23-24)

Our Father loves us as we are in union with Christ (Jn 16:27). Jesus is the way to the Father.

Jesus' Mission Is Doing the Father's Will

Christ's life-task was doing the work the Father gave him to do. Luke's Gospel brings this out vividly by the fact that the first and last words Jesus spoke are in total relation to the Father (Lk 2:49, 23:46). John also tells us that Jesus' last words were about fulfilling everything the Father wanted him to do (Jn 19:30). To reveal the Father to us is his chief work, and if today we do not really know the Father ourselves, then Christ's work is still to be done in us (Jn 17:3). Christ's whole mission is expressed in terms of his coming from the Father to us and of his returning to the Father with us:

> Before the world was created, the Word already existed; he was with God, and he was the same as God. . . . The Word became a human being and, full of grace and truth, lived among us. (Jn 1:1, 14)

> Jesus knew that the hour had come for him to leave this world and go to the Father. (Jn 13:1)

> There are many rooms in my Father's house, and I am going to prepare a place for you. . . . And after I go and prepare a place for you, I will come back and take you to myself, so that you will be where I am. (Jn 14:2, 3)

Christ's whole life aimed at showing us how to love the Father and to bear fruit:

> My Father's glory is shown by your bearing much fruit. . . . If you obey my commands, you will remain in my love, just as I have obeyed my Father's commands and remain in his love. (Jn 15:8, 10)

Christ's obedience to the Father revealed the obedience we should show in our own relationship with the Father:

I have come down from heaven to do not my own will but the will of him who sent me. . . . For what my Father wants is that all who see the Son and believe in him should have eternal life. (Jn 6:38, 40)

My Father is always working, and I too must work. (Jn 5:17)

I can do nothing on my own . . . but only what he who sent me wants. (Jn 5:30)

Is our spiritual life one of trying to please the Father, as Christ did?

The Father in the Parables

The parables also reveal the Father to us. Since much has already been said on the parables, it is only necessary to mention that if we read the parables with the intention of learning more of the Father, we will easily grasp new aspects of his personality. We see the mercy of the Father in the parable of the Prodigal Son (Lk 15:11). We see the Father's saving love for us in the parable of the Vineyard (Mt 21:33-46; Mk 12:1-12; Lk 20:9-19). In the parable of the Lost Sheep (Mt 18:12-14), we see our Father's concern lest any of us be lost to eternal life. In the parable of the Unforgiving Servant, we learn how the Father will treat us "if you do not forgive your brother from your heart" (Mt 18:21-35; see also the parable of the Wedding Feast, Mt 22:1-14).

Unity of Father and Son

We may get the idea that the Father and the Son are quite separate, but Christ also shows us his close and essential union with the Father. In many texts we see their unity (Jn 5:19, 26, 6:57, 10:38, 14:10, 11), but the strongest statement of all is "the Father and I are one" (Jn 10:30). Jesus always spoke of his own personal relationship to the Father as being different from our relationship with the same Father. Jesus is always the true, only,

and real Son of the Father—we are adopted sons and daughters
of the Father. This difference is brought out in such phrases as
"My Father and their Father, my God and their God" (Jn
20:17). When using the words "Our Father," Jesus was telling
us something, not addressing the Father in prayer himself. He
did not include himself in the prayer he teaches us, because his
relationship to the Father is something far superior and
intimate than our adoptive sonship.

SIXTEEN

Jesus Declares Himself

IT WAS ONLY after the Resurrection that the apostles came to the full realization of Jesus' divinity. In the light of their experience of him as the Risen Lord they understood better the many indirect ways in which he had shown his divine origin: the authority with which he taught, the power he displayed in his miraculous signs, the claims he made to being universal Savior and judge, and the special unity he enjoyed with the Father. Since all the Gospels were written after the Resurrection all its passages should be read with this "hindsight interpretation" kept in mind.

Jesus revealed himself gradually. Mark's Gospel still retains the stages: childhood anonymity, hidden ministry as preacher of the Kingdom, public proclamation of himself as the Son of Man, manifestation of his divine sonship through death and Resurrection. The reason for this gradual approach was two-fold: He knew his contemporaries would not be able to receive the full truth at once (Jn 16:25-28). But also, he himself as a true human being needed to grow naturally into his special role (Lk 2:52).

Describing all the implications of this process are beyond the scope of this book. However, we would miss a central part of the Gospel message if we were to pass over their presentation of Jesus as the one who lives from all eternity with the Father and the Spirit. We shall consider here some passages in which Jesus is presented as explicitly declaring his divinity—explicitly, that is, in a Jewish way of speaking. We will also consider what Jesus said about the Spirit, thus completing our survey of his teaching on the Trinity.

Jesus' Pre-Existence

During the feast of Tabernacles (Jn 7:2, 14), Jesus came to Jerusalem and preached in the Temple. The Jews directed the discussions to Jesus himself (Jn 8:52-58). When Jesus said, "Before Abraham was born, I am," with its overtones of Exodus 3:13-14, the Jews picked up stones to kill him (Jn 8:59). Jesus left the Temple, met the man blind from birth, and gave him his sight. The man was called before the Jewish leaders, where he defended Jesus (Jn 9:13-34), concluding with:

> What a strange thing that is! You do not know where he comes from, but he cured me of my blindness! We know that God does not listen to sinners; he does listen to people who respect him and do what he wants them to do. Since the beginning of the world nobody has ever heard of anyone giving sight to a blind person. Unless this man came from God, he would not be able to do a thing. (Jn 9:30-33)

Jesus touched upon a very difficult doctrine when he spoke about his own divinity. He proved his claim with a stupendous miracle, and by the nature of the miracle (giving sight, giving light) he indicated that the gift of faith will be given to those who want to see. Read the discussion with the Pharisees in John 9:39-41.

The Divine Judge of All Mankind

When Jesus cured the paralytic at the pool of Bethzatha, a dispute developed about Jesus' healing on the Sabbath (Jn 5:16). During the ensuing discussion, Jesus said a number of striking things (Jn 5:18-23):

—The Son can do nothing by himself; he does only what he sees the Father doing.

—As the Father raises the dead and gives them life, so the Son gives life to men, as he determines.

—The Father does not judge anyone, but has given it to the Son to judge.

—It is the Father's will that all should pay the same honor to the Son as to him. To deny honor to the Son is to deny it to the Father who sent him.

Jesus claimed that the power to judge and give life is shared by Father and Son. The Son is absolutely equal to the Father, exercising the same divine activities, deserving the same honor. He appealed to the miracle as a proof of his claim:

> The deeds my Father gave me to do, these speak on my behalf and show that the Father has sent me. And the Father who sent me, also testifies on my behalf. You have never heard his voice or seen his face. (Jn 5:36-37)

Moses had given a rule for discerning the true from the false prophet:

> If you say in your heart, "How may we know the word which the Lord has not spoken?"—when a prophet speaks in the name of the Lord, if the word does not come to pass or come true, that is a word which the Lord has not spoken.
>
> (Dt 18:21-22)

Jesus appealed to this rule:

> I have come with my Father's authority, but you have not received me. . . . Do not think, however, that I am the one who will accuse you to my Father. Moses, in whom you have put your hope, is the very one who will accuse you. If you had really believed Moses, you would have believed me, because he wrote about me. (Jn 5:43, 45-46)

Jesus was also referring to the Messianic promise given by Moses in the same text:

> The Lord your God will raise up for you a prophet like me. ... Whoever will not listen to his words, it will be required of him! (Dt 18:15)

Jesus claimed to be equal to the Father. He is the prophet spoken of by Moses. The Jews should apply the rule laid down by Moses and judge the truth of his word by his miracles.

Jesus Is One with the Father

On the feast of Dedication, Jesus had a discussion with the Jewish leaders in Solomon's Porch (Jn 10:22ff). In the course of the conversation Jesus said, "I and the Father are one." When the Jews picked up stones to kill him and said, "You are only a man, but you are trying to make yourself God," Jesus began to question them:

> I have done many good deeds in your presence which the Father gave me to do; for which one of these do you want to stone me? ... Do not believe me, then, if I am not doing the things my Father wants me to do. But if I do them, even though you do not believe me, you should at least believe my deeds, in order that you may know once and for all that the Father is in me and that I am in the Father. (Jn 10:32, 37-38)

Jesus withdrew from Jerusalem, but very soon afterwards he performed one of his greatest miracles, the raising of Lazarus (Jn 11). This miracle showed Jesus' power to give life (which only God can) and prepared the way for Jesus' Resurrection. It clearly proved to many Jews that Jesus could only be working with God's sanction.

> Many of the people who had come to visit Mary saw what Jesus did, and they believed in him. (Jn 11:45)

A large number of people heard that Jesus was in Bethany, so they went there, not only because of Jesus but also to see Lazarus, whom Jesus raised from death. So the chief priests made plans to kill Lazarus too, because on his account many Jews were rejecting them and believing in Jesus. (Jn 12:9-11)

The people who had been with Jesus when he called Lazarus out of the grave and raised him from death had reported what had happened. That was why the crowd met him—because they heard that he had performed this miracle. (Jn 12:17-18)

At each stage, Jesus' self-declaration becomes clearer, and each person is forced to choose how he will respond.

Jesus Is God

The Jewish leaders had arrested Jesus. They took him to their supreme court, the Sanhedrin, and tried to accuse him of a sin worthy of death (Mt 26:63-64; cf. also Lk 22:66-71). He was asked a question under oath:

> [The high priest said] "In the name of the living God I now put you under oath: tell us if you are the Messiah, the Son of God."
> "So you say. But I tell all of you: from this time on you will see the Son of Man sitting on the right of the Almighty and coming on the clouds of heaven!"

Jesus' claim to be the "Son of Man" is based on Daniel 7:13ff.

> Behold, with the clouds of heaven there came one like a son of man. . . .
> And to him was given dominion and glory and kingdoms,
>   that all peoples, nations and languages should serve him;
> his dominion is an everlasting dominion.

It is obvious from the text that the Son of Man has a divine status. Moreover, Jesus said that he will sit at God's right hand, which implies the same thing (see Mt 22:41-45). It is clear that the high priest and the scribes took Jesus' words to mean a claim of divinity. For it was not blasphemy to call oneself the Messiah, and doing so did not deserve death as a punishment.

It should be noted that Jesus spoke about this coming of the Son of Man as a warning. He was thinking not of the Last Judgment alone, but also of the destruction of Jerusalem, which was to be the type and symbol of the Last Judgment. Jesus spoke of them together (Mt 24-25). Forty years later the Romans conquered the city and totally destroyed it. Innumerable people were killed by famine, disease, and the sword; the remnant of Jerusalem's inhabitants, about 97,000 people, were taken to Rome and sold as slaves. The Christians, warned by Jesus' prophecy, had left the province of Judea in time and had settled in Pella, on the other side of the Jordan. God confirmed the words of Jesus and showed the high price of denying his claims.

Some Difficult Texts

When the rich young man came to Jesus he asked, "Good Teacher, what must I do to receive eternal life?" Jesus replied, "Why do you call me good? No one is good except God alone!" (Mk 10:17-18). "Rabbi" or "Good Master," was an especially flattering way of addressing someone; Jesus would not accept this type of flattery. He did not deny that he can be called good or that he himself is God. This passage is like the story of a famous American scientist who visited an Italian museum. The guide—who had no idea with whom he was speaking—was addressing the American time and again as "Eccellenza." The scientist got irritated and asked: "Why do you call me *excellenza*? Only famous people are called *excellenza*?" He did not deny that he was well-known, but he could not bear to be flattered by a man who did not know him. Jesus' reaction was similar to this. Jesus never stopped people who sincerely confessed their faith in his divinity (Mt 16:16; Jn 20:28), but he did not want empty flattery.

"Eternal life means to know you, the only true God, and to know Jesus Christ, whom you sent" (Jn 17:3). Was Jesus distinguishing God from himself? Did he thereby deny that he is God? Jesus distinguished between the Father and himself as two persons within God, but as regards divinity he put both persons on the same level. To gain eternal life one has to know both the Father and the Son. We know them in two stages—by natural revelation (by which we know the Father through considering creation) and by the supernatural revelation of Jesus (by which we know the Son, sent by the Father). Jesus' words mean that eternal life will be given those who accept both revelations, of the Father as Creator and the Son as revealer of the Trinity. He did not deny his divinity with these words, but taught his divinity through them.

At the Last Supper Jesus said, "If you loved me, you would be glad that I am going to the Father; for he is greater than I" (Jn 14:28). If the Father is greater than Jesus, then is Jesus not God? Jesus did not mean that the Father is greater from the point of view of divinity, but that the Father is the Person on whom the Son as Son totally depends. Whenever Jesus spoke about the Father, he always stressed that the Son receives from the Father, and that the Son receives *everything* (the whole divinity) from him—divine action, life in himself, divine authority, divine honor. God could not give these things to someone outside the Godhead, for they express the divine nature itself. The Father is "Father" because he passes on the whole divine nature to the "Son." Father and Son share the same nature, but the Father as Father gives, the Son as Son receives. The Father lives totally in giving all to the Son; the Son lives totally in receiving all from the Father. By the statement quoted above, Jesus meant that if the disciples realized how Jesus lived completely by dependence on the Father, they would be glad for the reunion.

Jesus grew up in Nazareth "both in body and in wisdom, gaining favor with God and men" (Lk 2:52). If Jesus is God, how could he advance in wisdom? We should not forget that Jesus was truly man. He was like us in all aspects. He ate like us;

he worked like us; he was tired like us. When he was beaten he suffered and felt pain, just as we would. His appearance to other men was like that of any human person. Jesus also could acquire knowledge as a man. Things he knew by his divinity could yet be learned by his humanity. It is quite a different thing to possess infinite knowledge as God, and to store newly acquired knowledge in the human memory. In this way Jesus could truly be said to advance in wisdom when he was a boy. As God, Jesus possessed everything; yet, as man, he received gifts from his fellow men.

Jesus and the Spirit

The Holy Spirit is God's supreme gift to us (Lk 11:13). Until we have received him the work of Christ in us remains incomplete. Without his sanctifying presence, all of Christ's teaching and suffering would have no saving effect on us. Christ's passion and death would remain distant events in the world's history. We would not be God's children (Rom 8:15). We would still be separated from both Christ and the Father (Rom 8:9). We see how incomplete was Christ's work in the apostles before the Spirit came to them. The apostles had been with Jesus for three years and were still too weak to appear at the crucifixion. They had three years of class with the best teacher and still did not understand his message. Jesus said, "You need someone else. You need the Holy Spirit. Wait here until he comes, and then you will know what I meant when I told you all these things" (see Jn 14:25-26).

We can never know the Spirit in the same way that we can know the Father and the Son. The Son offers himself to us in his humanity, identical with our own. Through his words, deeds, and attitude he reveals himself to us. The Father is invisible, but his presence is tangible when we study his Son. To know his Father it suffices to watch Jesus closely (Jn 14:9). The Spirit is different. He has no face, not even a name that makes us think of a familiar person. The very word *spirit* is rather elusive; we get only a partial image from it. The word is *ruah* in Hebrew, *pneuma* in Greek, and *spiritus* in Latin, but in each language it is only a common noun meaning "breath." It can refer to the breath of the wind or to the breath of respiration. How, then, can we know the Spirit?

> He is the Spirit, who reveals the truth about God. . . . You know him, because he remains with you and is in you.
>
> (Jn 14:17)

To know the Spirit is first of all to experience his action in us, to make oneself docile to his inspirations. That is why in the Gospels we are never presented with a visual image of him (the dove at the Lord's baptism is a symbol of his coming), but in its pages he is always shown at work. It is through the action of the Spirit as found in the Gospels and in our own lives that we come to know this divine Person.

The Work of the Spirit in Jesus' Life

The Incarnation. We see the action of the Holy Spirit in salvation at the very Incarnation of the second Person of the Trinity. To Mary the angel said:

> The Holy Spirit will come on you, and God's power will rest upon you. For this reason the holy child will be called the Son of God. (Lk 1:35)

In Matthew 1:20, the text implies that the Holy Spirit is the father of the child. The angel's words, "The Holy Spirit will come on you," refer to the Old Testament manifestation of God in the cloud (*shekinah*) and in the glory (*kabod*). The face of Moses shone with this divine glory; the cloud "came over" Mount Sinai at the great Covenant scene. It rested on the ark during the tent days and, later on, overshadowed the inner sanctuary of the Temple of Solomon during the dedication ceremony. This same divine presence comes over Mary.

The Visitation. We see that Elizabeth's child, John, was to be filled with the Spirit even in his mother's womb (Lk 1:15). The child leapt with joy at Mary's greeting (Lk 1:44). The Holy Spirit was also at work in Elizabeth, and she greeted Mary with "You are the most blessed of all women, and blessed is the child you will bear!" (Lk 1:41-42). The Spirit worked in Zechariah (Lk 1:67), and in Simeon as well (Lk 2:25-27).

The Lord's Baptism. Matthew 3:13-17; Mark 1:9-11; Luke 3:21-22; John 1:29-34—we know the texts well enough. Let us look more closely to see the work of the Spirit in Christ's public life. The coming down of the Spirit on someone always denotes that God leads that person on to fulfill a real task. We see how the Spirit came down on the artisan Bezalel (Ex 31:3, 35:31); on the judges Othniel, Gideon, Jephthah, and Samson (Jgs 3:10, 6:34, 11:29, 13:25); on Saul (1 Sm 10:6-10). It was foretold that in a special way the Spirit of God would be with the Redeemer (Is 11:1ff, 61:1ff). The Spirit coming down on Christ, then, means that the Spirit now moved Christ to do his Messianic task, given by the Father.

The Spirit is the bond between Father and Son bringing to the Son the Father's love (the voice declares this love). The Father now dwells in the Son by his Spirit, the bond of love between them. In the strength of the Spirit, everything the Son does—all miracles, all cures, all sayings and deeds, every-thing—can be said to be the work of the Father—"I can do nothing on my own authority . . . but only what he who sent me wants" (Jn 5:30). If we understand the unity of will, of life, of love between Father and Son properly, we see that this unity is only through the presence of the Holy Spirit. Hence little is said explicitly about the Spirit in the public life of Jesus. The evangelists preface his whole public life with this coming down upon him of the Holy Spirit and thereby take for granted that all else is done through the same Spirit.

The Giving of the Spirit to the Church

But in Jesus' public life he had received the Spirit only for himself. Through his real baptism on the cross (Lk 12:50), the

Son wins the Spirit for us, his church. That is why he said to the apostles that it is better for them (and for us) that he leave them:

> But I am telling you the truth: it is better for you that I go away, because if I do not go, the Helper will not come to you. But if I do go away, then I will send him to you. (Jn 16:7)

New Testament writers agree that the giving of the Spirit was withheld until after the Resurrection and exaltation of Jesus.

Only John and Luke tell the story, and their accounts complement each other. John puts Jesus' appearance to Mary Magdalene and his appearance to the apostles on one day (Jn 20:1-18), with the giving of the Spirit that same evening:

> It was late that Sunday evening. . . . Jesus came. . . . Then he breathed on them [remember, spirit means "breath"] and said, "Receive the Holy Spirit." (Jn 20:19-22)

Luke tells us that the second giving of the Spirit was fifty days afterward (Acts 2:1ff).

The Sin Against the Spirit (Lk 12:10)

The sin of saying "evil things against the Spirit"—that is, the sin of a person who rejects and dismisses the clearly evident signs of the Kingdom's arrival and resists the fully known truth—will not be forgiven. This is because the basic disposition of sorrow for sin is just not there and cannot be there. It does not mean that God does not want to forgive this kind of sin.

The Trinity in Christian Teaching

Jesus reveals himself to us as the Christ, the Son of God. He reveals the Father to us, and his unity with the Father. He also reveals the Spirit to us. But notice that Jesus reveals the Trinity to us in a very personal way. The notion of the Trinity that has been most common in our classes and in our spiritual lives has

often been an impoverished one. Perhaps we excused ourselves
by saying the Trinity was a great mystery, that we did not even
have to try to understand. Of course, we could not even have
known about the Trinity unless it had been revealed by God
through Christ, but, precisely because it has been revealed, God
wants us to understand, as far as we are able, what it means. It is
all too easy to fall into mathematical explanations of the Trinity
concentrating on "three" and "one," but the Trinity is God
himself. Rather than explaining the Trinity to ourselves as if it
were *something,* we should let Christ introduce us to the Trinity
as *Someone.* We should meet the divine Persons in their unity
and in their diversity, the only way in which they choose to be
known.

SEVENTEEN

The Heart of the Mystery

JESUS PREDICTED his suffering, death, and Resurrection many times (Mt 16:20-23, 17:22-23, 20:17-19, etc.), the sacrifice by which he reconciled mankind to his Father. Jesus saw in his Passion a fulfillment of Old Testament prophecies. To understand why he had to suffer and die, we can do no better than study his own teaching on the matter, concentrating on three important texts.

First, in his dispute with the priests in the Temple, Jesus narrated the parable of the owner of the vineyard who wanted to collect his revenue from unwilling tenants (Mt 21:33-46; Mk 12:1-12; Lk 20:9-19). When his servants returned empty-handed, the owner sent his only son, whom the tenants killed.

> Surely you have read this scripture? "The stone which the builders rejected as worthless turned out to be the most important of all." (Mk 12:10)

The Jews were going to kill Jesus, although he was God's only Son. But they did not realize that by rejecting Jesus and making him suffer, they would be instrumental in making him the cornerstone of salvation, as described in Psalm 118 (read the whole psalm).

Second, in the context of teaching his disciples selflessness, Jesus adduced his own life as a model: his disciples are to be "like the Son of Man who did not come to be served but to serve

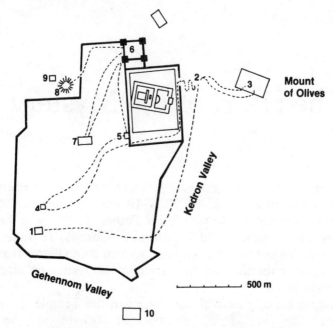

1. The house of the Last Supper
*2. Kidron Valley crossing (Jn 18:1)
*3. Garden of Gethsemane
4. House of Caiaphas
5. Hall of the Sanhedrin, where Jesus was officially con-demned to death (Mt 27:1; Lk 22:66)
6. Fortress of Antonia
7. Herod's palace
*8. Calvary
*9. Jesus' tomb
10. The Blood Acre, associated with Judas' suicide

Jerusalem: Jesus' passion and death

and to give his life to redeem many" (Mt 20:28; Mk 10:45). Thus he applied to himself the prophecy of Isaiah 52:13-53:12 that the Servant of Yahweh will suffer to save others from their sins.

He endured the suffering that should have been ours. . . . because of our sins he was wounded. . . . We are healed by the punishment he suffered. . . . he willingly gave his life.

(Is 53:4, 5, 12)

In the third passage, Jesus links his death to the new covenant. God had promised a new covenant with his people, in which they would receive forgiveness of sins and experience his intimate presence among them (Jer 31:31-34). But the sealing of such a covenant required sacrificial blood (Lv 17:11). The Covenant on Sinai, too, had been ratified with blood (Ex 24:6-8). Jesus saw his Passion as the sealing of God's New Covenant: "This is my blood, which seals God's covenant, my blood poured out for many for the forgiveness of sins" (Mt 26:28; see also Mk 14:24; Lk 22:20). The fact that Jesus died as the Passover lambs were being slaughtered in the Temple confirms that he was the new paschal lamb sacrificed for us.

We will study the mystery of Jesus' death and Resurrection more fully later, but for now, we will concentrate on factual background information regarding Jesus' Passion and death.

We will first consider the principal scenes of the Passion. The map in Figure 1 contains a reconstruction of the route Jesus travelled from the time of the Last Supper until his death and burial. Some of the localities have been identified with certainty (indicated with an asterisk ★). For other places, there are good historical and archaeological arguments, but we do not possess the same certainty.

Time-Scheme of the Passion. Jesus' opponents acted with terrible swiftness! Probably no more than fifteen hours elapsed between his arrest and death.

Thursday
11:00 P.M.—Arrest
11:30 P.M.—First interrogation before Annas.
12:00—First (unofficial) trial in Caiaphas' house before a select group of Pharisees.
Friday
2:00 A.M.—Jesus is remitted to custody.
6:00 A.M.—A hurried session of the Sanhedrin to have Jesus officially condemned to death.

> *6:30 A.M.*—Jesus is brought before Pilate. The Jewish
> leaders successfully oppose all Pilate's attempts to
> hold up the case (including the visit to Herod).
> They force the issue until Pilate gives the order to
> crucify Jesus (11:00 A.M.?).
>
> *12:30 P.M.*—Jesus is crucified.
>
> *3:00 P.M.*—Jesus dies.

Clearly the Pharisees wanted the whole thing over and done
with before Jesus could get popular support from the large
crowds that would be moving about. "We must not do it during
the festival," they said, "or the people will riot" (Mt 26:5).
Probably they had decided to kill Jesus on the day before the
Passover, as people would be too busy with their preparations
to take much notice. They summoned false witnesses (Mt
26:59-60); they rushed an official trial in the Sanhedrin (Mt
27:1), probably invalid because Jesus was given no chance to
call his own witnesses; they forced Pilate, who plainly declared
Jesus innocent on juridical grounds (Jn 19:4), to condemn Jesus
for political reasons (Jn 19:12-16). Jesus' condemnation to
death was unjust from all points of view, but the Jewish leaders
were blinded, and our judgment about them should follow
Jesus' prayer, "Forgive them, Father! They don't know what
they are doing" (Lk 23:34).

During the days preceding his sufferings Jesus was preparing
for the great sacrifice he was to bring about through his death. It
was with this in mind that he had gone up to Jerusalem (Lk
9:51), and three times on this journey he foretold his Passion.
When he raised Lazarus from the grave, he wished to announce
his own Resurrection.

On the Sunday before Passover, Jesus spoke to the people at
Bethany about his coming Passion:

The hour has now come for the Son of Man to receive great
glory. I am telling you the truth: a grain of wheat remains
no more than a single grain unless it is dropped into the
ground and dies. If it does die, then it produces many

grains. . . . When I am lifted up from the earth, I will draw everyone to me. (Jn 12:22-24, 32)

On Wednesday he predicted that in two days "the Son of Man will be handed over to be crucified" (Mt 26:2).

On Thursday morning, he sent two apostles to prepare for an early pasch because "My hour has come" (Mt 26:18).

During the Last Supper, Jesus frequently referred to his imminent death. He said that he was happy to have this meal before his death (Lk 22:15), because this was to be the last time for him to drink wine until the Kingdom of God had come (Lk 22:18). He explained that he was going back to the Father who sent him (Jn 16:5-30). And when instituting the eucharist, he anticipated his Passion by his words, "body to be sacrificed for you" and "blood to be shed for you" (Mt 26:26-28; Lk 22:19-20).

In the Garden of Gethsemane Jesus felt all the anxiety and suffering of a human heart just before the terrible trial. He freely submitted himself to it in the spirit of sacrifice (Mt 26:36-44). The Passion did not come as a surprise to Jesus:

I am willing to die for them [my sheep]. . . . No one takes my life away from me. I give it up of my own free will.

(Jn 10:15, 18)

Jesus in the House of Caiaphas

After Jesus had been arrested in the Garden of Gethsemane, he was taken to the house of Caiaphas the high priest. Where was this house? What did it look like? We cannot determine its exact location or its shape to the last detail, but to some extent the house can be reconstructed. The Gospels contain quite a few elements of description, and we know fairly well from archaeology what houses of important people looked like in Jesus' time. In Figure 2, we have a free reconstruction, accurate enough to help us understand the Gospel texts.

Gate (no. 1)—One entered the house by a gate, usually

leading into a small porch. The gate was watched by a gatekeeper or, at times, by a watchdog. Caiaphas' house had a maidservant as gatekeeper, and she had apparently been told to keep disciples of Jesus out of the house.

> Simon Peter and another disciple followed Jesus. That other disciple was well-known to the High Priest, so he went with Jesus into the courtyard of the High Priest's house, while Peter stayed outside by the gate. Then the other disciple went back out, spoke to the girl at the gate, and brought Peter inside. The girl at the gate said to Peter, "Aren't you also one of the disciples of that man?" (Jn 18:15-18)

Porch (no. 2)—The gatekeeper's question causes Peter to deny Christ for the first time. Mark, too, mentions that Peter denied Christ when "he went outside into the porch" (Mk 14:68); obviously he also means the porch into which the gate is set.

Courtyard (no. 3)—Having entered, one came into a courtyard, surrounded by galleries or porticoes. Chickens would often scramble around in these open courtyards during the day. Perhaps the cock that crowed was one of these household animals. The Gospel accounts tell us that on the night of Jesus' arrest there was a fire in the middle of the courtyard, where the servants and soldiers were warming themselves.

Fire (no. 4)—Peter joined this group and faced more trouble. They accused him of being Jesus' disciple. One man thought he had seen Peter in the Garden of Gethsemane (Jn 18:26). Others noticed from his accent that Peter was a Galilean (Mt 26:73). Peter denied the Lord three times (Mt 26:69-75; Mk 14:66-72; Lk 22:55-62).

Annas' Room—Jesus was taken first to Annas for a private interview. We may well imagine that this first investigation took place in a kind of parlor at the entrance of the house (no. 5), or, perhaps, in the living quarters of the high priest's family (no. 6). We know how Annas tried, without success, to intimidate Jesus (Jn 18:12, 19-23).

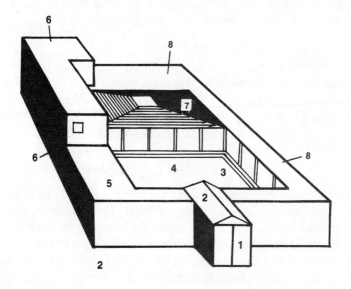

Fig. 2. The house of Caiaphas

Council Room (no. 7)—In the center of the house there was an official hall for functions such as dinners and meetings. The Romans called it *triclinium* (or *atrium* if it were used for everyday business). No doubt Caiaphas had gathered some chosen members of the Sanhedrin in his hall for their first attempt to find an accusation against Jesus (Mt 26:57). This was not an official court session, since these could only be held after sunrise, but only a preliminary investigation held to expedite the session in the morning. We know that the council must have sat in the way customary at the time, in a half circle with the high priest in the middle. Jesus stood opposite the high priest. This explains a touching passage in Luke's Gospel.

[Peter, in the courtyard, had denied Jesus.] At once, while he was still speaking, a rooster crowed. The Lord turned around and looked straight at Peter, and Peter remembered that the Lord had said. . . . Peter went out and wept bitterly.

(Lk 22:61-62)

Jesus' Prison (no. 8)—After the preliminary trial Jesus was kept in custody. Probably he was tied to some pillar in one of the servant's quarters (no. 8). We know how he suffered from the insults and beatings the guards and the members of the Sanhedrin inflicted on him (Mt 26:67-68; Lk 22:63-65).

Jesus in Pilate's Civil Court

In the early morning the Sanhedrin met officially to decide on Jesus' death (Mt 27:1). They probably held this meeting in the official hall next to the Temple, the normal place for such meetings. As far as we can tell from the evidence, they made two decisions—that Jesus should be killed, and that he should be accused of rebellion against Rome and therefore be executed by the Romans.

The Jewish leaders took Jesus immediately to Pilate's place in the Fortress of Antonia. Having passed through the main gates they stood on a little square, called *lithostrotos* ("paved stones"). Archaeological excavations have identified this locality beyond any doubt (see Fig. 3, no. 4). On this square there was a tribunal (no. 5) with a special place for the judgment seat (Jn 19:13). It would seem that Pilate would normally have heard the accusations inside (no. 6?), but the Jews refused to go inside the house of a pagan because it would have defiled them for the rest of the day and meant they could not eat the Passover (Jn 18:28). Note the attitude of worrying about an external defilement while having an innocent man condemned to death!

The Jews had decided to accuse Jesus of political rebellion. Of course, they added all kinds of other accusations (see Jn 18:29-32; Mk 15:3-5), but only to make things look worse:

We caught this man misleading our people, telling them not to pay taxes to the Emperor and claiming that he himself is the Messiah, a king. (Lk 23:2-3)

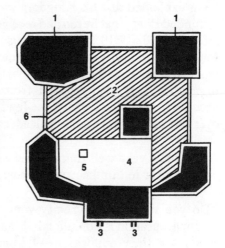

1. Towers
2. The soldiers' quarters, known as the praetorium.
3. Entrances through a fortified gate.
4. The lithostrotos or "paved stones." Here Jesus was tried, scourged, and crowned with thorns.
5. The judgment seat.
6. Inner room where Pilate withdrew to confer with Jesus.

Fig. 3. The plan of the Fortress of Antonia

Pilate knew that this accusation was false on several scores. He had his own information service. He was responsible for political tranquility in the country and had surely gathered information about Jesus as soon as Jesus grew popular. He must have known Jesus' respect for authority, even Roman authority, for, contrary to what nationalists would do, Jesus made friends with tax collectors (Matthew, Zacchaeus) and with the Roman officer at Capernaum. When asked about taxes, Jesus had officially stated that one should pay the emperor what belongs to the emperor (Mt 22:15-22). He must have received reports of Jesus' refusal to be taken for a political Messiah. By this time, Jesus had convincingly enough demonstrated the spiritual and religious nature of his mission, and Pilate knew that he was no political rebel.

Jesus did not reply to any of the accusations, but Pilate had personal conversations with Jesus at various stages of the case. Jesus did not want to discuss any particular accusation (Mt

27:11-14). As to the fundamental question of political kingship, Jesus explained that his Kingdom was "not of this world," and reminded Pilate that he too had received his authority from God (Jn 18:33-38, 19:10). From his discussion with Jesus, Pilate found that Jesus was a deeply spiritual man, of extremely strong character, ready to die for his convictions, but with no political interests. Pilate also realized from the beginning that the accusation was false, because the Jews would never have handed over one of their real political leaders to the Romans.

> He knew very well that the Jewish authorities had handed Jesus over to him because they were jealous. (Mt 27:18)

"Do you want me to crucify your king?" (Jn 19:15) meant "Your accusation is ridiculous!" Finally the Jews admit the real reason for their opposition—"He claimed to be the Son of God!" (Jn 19:7). Pilate knew, therefore, that the priests wanted Jesus killed for purely religious reasons, and that the accusation of rebellion was merely a pretext.

All through the trial, Pilate declared Jesus to be innocent:

> You brought this man to me and said that he was misleading the people. Now, I have examined him here in your presence, and I have not found him guilty of any of the crimes you accuse him of. . . . There is nothing this man has done to deserve death. (Lk 23:14-15)

> Look, I will bring him out here to you to let you see that I cannot find any reason to condemn him. (Jn 19:4)

> But what crime has he committed? (Mk 15:14)

He even tried in many ways to prevent Jesus' death. He sent Jesus to Herod, who could have summoned Jesus to Galilee (Lk 23:6-12). He proposed Jesus as the prisoner to be released for Passover, hoping that the people would go against the priests (Lk 23:13-16). He had Jesus scourged and humiliated (Mt 27:26-31), hoping that the people would have compassion on him when they saw him in that state (Jn 19:4-7). Pilate finally gave in when the Jews threatened to denounce him to the emperor (Jn 19:12-16). While permitting Jesus to be crucified, he repeated that he was convinced of Jesus' innocence and washed his hands in public.

> I am not responsible for the death of this man! This is your doing!" The whole crowd answered, "Let the punishment for his death fall on us and on our children!
>
> (Mt 27:24-25)

The religious leaders forced Jesus' condemnation by using Pilate's fear of political trouble.

The Crucifixion

The Romans inflicted crucifixion only on non-Romans and slaves, and only for certain major crimes—murder, robbery, betrayal, and rebellion; it was considered the most cruel and barbarous death possible. Since the official sentence under which Jesus was condemned concerned rebellion, or political insurrection, the punishment was crucifixion. But crucifixion was a very unexpected way of killing Jesus. The punishment for blasphemy and for violating the Sabbath—the crimes often imputed to Jesus—was stoning, and many of the Jews who knew that the high priests wanted to kill Jesus probably assumed he would be stoned through a popular turmoil, as Stephen was. The disciples, too, must have been surprised when Jesus repeatedly foretold that the high priests would "hand him over to the Gentiles [Romans] who would make fun of him, whip him, and crucify him" (Mt 20:19). John especially points to this.

> [Jesus told the crowd in Bethany] "When I am lifted up from the earth, I will draw everyone to me." (In saying this he indicated the kind of death he was going to suffer.)
>
> (Jn 12:32-33)

[Pilate said during the trial] "Then you yourselves take him and try him according to your own law."

They [the Jews] replied, "We are not allowed to put anyone to death." (This happened in order to make come true what Jesus had said when he indicated the kind of death he would die.) (Jn 18:31-32)

By choosing death on a cross as the means of saving mankind, Jesus made it the symbol of every man's self-sacrifice (Mt 16:24).

Some particulars about the crucifixion will be helpful.

The Cross-beam—The cross consisted of a vertical pole and a cross-beam. It was this cross-beam which the condemned person was to carry to the place of execution.

Erecting the Cross—There were two ways of fixing someone to the cross. In the first, the whole cross was laid flat on the ground, the victim's hands and feet were nailed to it, and then the whole cross was raised. In the other, the vertical pole was erected, the person's hands were nailed to the cross-beam, and the cross-beam was then set upon the pole.

Jewish Privileges—Although crucifixion was done by the Romans, there were a few special practices in Palestine. One was the offering of drugged wine (to mitigate the pain) by some good people (Mk 15:23). Another was that the person was not left naked, but was allowed to wear a loincloth.

Publicity—The execution was a public one. Therefore it was carried out on a small hill on the side of a busy road. The name of the hillock was Calvary or Golgotha (Mt 27:33). There was also a public inscription in three languages proclaiming the reason for the execution. Pilate had written "Jesus of Nazareth, the king of the Jews," and he refused to change it into anything else (Jn 19:19-22).

Certitude of Death—Once the order for execution had been given, the procurator was responsible for carrying it out. He was not allowed to let the person escape. For that reason, there were soldiers on guard near the cross, to insure that the victim actually died. These soldiers broke the legs of the two persons crucified with Jesus to hasten their deaths, but since Jesus was already dead they did not break his legs. They did, however, open his heart with a spear (Jn 19:31-37). Before Pilate released the body to Joseph of Arimathea, he summoned the centurion for an official report on Jesus' death (Mk 15:42-44).

The Site of Jesus' Tomb

The narratives of the Resurrection presuppose that we can visualize the location of Jesus' tomb. Calvary lay outside the walls of Jerusalem, and the sepulchre of Joseph of Arimathea lay in a small garden just behind it. We know from excavation and from ancient records that there was a small valley between the rock of Calvary and the rock from which Joseph's tomb had been cut. Figure 4 shows the city wall (1), the hill of Calvary (2), and the tomb (3). Since Joseph of Arimathea was a well-known figure in Jerusalem, the fact that Jesus had been buried in his grave provided a very clear identification that could not easily be lost to tradition. Family graves, especially those near the town, were known to everyone.

Figure 5 will help us understand what the entrance to the grave looked like. The tomb had been cut out of the rock and its entrance closed up with a wall made of stones and cement (3), leaving only a small opening through which one could enter (2). This opening could easily be closed by rolling a round stone (1) in front of it. It was easy for the high priests to watch the grave, since they not only put soldiers on guard but "made the tomb secure by putting a seal on the stone" (Mt 27:66)—a rope was sealed with wax to the stone and to the wall next to it, so that it could later be seen if anyone had moved the stone. Because the stone in front of Jesus' tomb was very large (Mk 16:4), the pious women who came to anoint Jesus' body asked themselves, "Who will roll away the stone for us?" (Mk 16:3).

Figure 6 shows the inside of the tomb, which consisted of various small rooms (2, 4) cut from the solid rock (1). The rooms were connected by small openings similar to the front opening (3, 5). Jesus' body was placed in the tomb on a stone couch cut

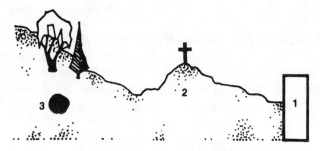

Fig. 4

Fig. 5

Fig. 6

Jesus' tomb

out from the wall (6). The entrance of the pious women (Mk 16:1-8) and the subsequent visit of Peter and John (Jn 20:1-10) give the impression that Jesus' body had been put in the first room (4). But a study of the customs of the time and archaeology tell us that it was more likely that his body had been put in one of the interior rooms (2). The outer room (4) was, perhaps, more of a small entryway where the apostles saw the linen clothes (Jn 20:5-7).

The testimony of the empty tomb was stressed in the preaching of the early church, so we can expect some consciousness of its location to have been maintained.

30-70 A.D.: During this period the apostolic community itself remained in Jerusalem. Herod Agrippa built a new wall in 43 which included Calvary and the Sepulchre in the city.

70-134: After the destruction of Jerusalem few people lived in the city, but both Jews and Christians kept going up to it on pilgrimage, and the small settlement of inhabitants maintained its traditions.

135-324: After the second Jewish revolt (132-134), Emperor Hadrian wanted to rebuild Jerusalem as a pagan city. He called it *Aelia Capitolina*. Knowing the veneration of the Christians for the site of Calvary and the Sepulchre, Hadrian decided to build a pagan temple on top of it. The small hillock of Calvary was raised, with rubble and earth, to a terrace on which a sacred grove to Venus and Cupid was planted. South of the grove a large rectangular area was cleared as a *forum* (marketplace square for public meetings). The area of the Sepulchre was covered for a similar purpose. This arrangement did not stop the flow of pilgrims, however; they knew that their sacred places were underneath the pavement.

325-613: When Emperor Constantine had finally put an end to the persecutions of the Christians, his mother, Queen Helena, went to Palestine and assisted personally in the excavation of the sacred places. Golgotha and the Sepulchre were found intact. Constantine then ordered that beautiful shrines should be built over them. The rock surrounding the tomb was cut from all sides to make it round, and over it a round church was constructed. This building was called *Anastasis* (Resurrection). Calvary itself was cut to size, making a platform of 18 feet by 15 feet. It was enclosed in a courtyard with marble pillars with steps leading to its top. The flooring was all mosaic and remained in the open until about 420 when a dome was built over it.

614-1140: These splendid Byzantine buildings were destroyed by Chosroes, a Persian king. Temporary repairs were done by Modestus, an abbot, and the sanctuaries remained in this state more or less unaltered during the Muslim invasions.

1140-1808: The crusades brought in the beginning of a new period as the crusaders built a huge basilica that united all the holy places. This basilica had to be restored frequently on account of later wars (1244, 1310, 1400, 1719), but it has retained its original form to some extent.

1808: A fire destroyed the dome of the Sepulchre. New buildings were erected which, with the Crusaders' basilica, form the present shrine. Both archaeology and the descriptions of thousands of pilgrims throughout the centuries confirm the locality of Calvary and the Sepulchre.

The Descent into Hell

In the Apostles' Creed we say that prior to his Resurrection Jesus descended into hell. What does this mean? Obviously, we do not profess to believe that Jesus went into the place of eternal punishment in our contemporary theological usage. We must not confuse the hell of the eternally damned with *Sheol*, "the place of the dead," the home (in Jewish theology) of all the dead. The Old Testament universe had three parts.

1. Heaven: the place where God is and lives, separate from where men are.
2. Earth: the place where man lives and works and makes his life. It has been given to him by God, and he is its lord with power and dominion over all other creatures.

3. Sheol: the place of the dead. The Jews imagined it to be under the earth. All the dead went to Sheol, good and bad alike (Ps 30:9, 89:48; Ez 32:17-32). The word *Sheol* was translated into Greek by the word *hades,* from which the English word *hell* comes.

The Jews gradually developed, under God's revelation, a theology about the fate of the dead. At first there seems to have been no special place for the good; all were mixed together. Later, they said that the good waited in peace in Abraham's presence (see the parable of the Rich Man and Lazarus, Lk 16:22). Later still, they came to a resurrection of the body (though this was not universally accepted).

When we say that Jesus descended into hell we mean only (in the terminology of the Bible) that he was truly dead; he was no longer in the "land of the living" but went down into the "land of the dead." He had taken upon himself everything that being man included, even death. When Jesus rose, therefore, he rose from among the dead. He is now the Lord of both the living and the dead, and shall come to judge both the living and the dead. The descent into hell is not a geographical journey but theology in very human words (read Acts 2:23-36; Eph 4:8-10). Sheol, the prison of the dead, is now unlocked by Christ, who has the keys (Rv 1:18, 20:1).

The Events of the First Easter Day

The Gospels do not provide an orderly, unified account of the marvelous events of the first Easter. Each Gospel narrates these events differently. What follows is an attempt to describe what happened on Easter in a chronological way, using the four Gospel accounts. This attempt has its imperfections. In some cases, we simply do not know how events unfolded. It is, in fact, something that the Gospel writers did not try to do. They were more concerned to proclaim one mighty fact—he is risen!

There is no description in the Gospels of this stupendous

event of the Resurrection itself. The earthquake and the angel rolling away the stone (Mt 28:2) are probably a later interpretation. Such happenings would, in any case, be only peripheral to the fact itself of Jesus returning fully alive in body and soul.

The Gospels witness to two fundamental facts regarding the day of Easter. On that day Jesus' tomb was found empty. And on the same day he appeared to his apostles and to some disciples. Although some details in the accounts may be literary or theological elaborations, we can reconstruct from them a plausible sequence of events.

Dawn: Women Come to the Tomb. At about 6:00 A.M., Mary Magdalene, Mary the mother of James, and Salome the mother of the sons of Zebedee (and possibly others) came to the tomb to anoint the body of Jesus. They had hurriedly done some anointing on Friday (Jn 19:40), but had not finished. They prepared spices and ointments at home (Lk 23:56), but since they could not use them on the Sabbath they waited until dawn of the following day (Lk 24:1-2). On the way to the tomb they asked themselves, "Who will roll away the stone for us?" (Mk 16:3). Obviously they did not know the tomb was sealed and guarded. (There had been no guard when Joseph of Arimathea, Nicodemus, and the women buried the body of Jesus: Mt 27:62; Mk 15:47; Jn 19:39; it was not posted until Saturday.) When the women came to the tomb they found the stone rolled back and the tomb empty (Lk 24:3).

Mary Magdalene Tells Peter and John. When Mary saw the empty tomb, she was so overcome that she ran back to tell Peter and John that someone had stolen the body (Jn 20:2). Mary ran a long distance back from Calvary to Jerusalem, probably to the room of the Last Supper.

Women See the Angel. While Mary was running to Jerusalem to tell Peter, two men in shining clothes (Lk 24:4) or "the angel who rolled back the stone" (Mt 28:5) told the women who had remained at the Sepulchre that Christ was risen:

> Now go and give this message to his disciples, including Peter: "He is going to Galilee ahead of you; there you will see him, just as he told you." (Mk 16:7)

But the women were so frightened that they told no one at the moment (Mk 16:8). They ran off in fear.

Peter and John at the Tomb. It was still early in the morning when both disciples ran to the tomb. John arrived first, but Peter went in ahead of him and saw the linen clothes lying wrapped up in one place. He and John believed what Mary Magdalene had told them, that the tomb was empty, but they still did not believe in the Resurrection. They were puzzled and went home (Lk 24:12; Jn 20:3-10). These stories of the women circulated among the disciples (Lk 24:22-24).

Jesus Appears to Mary Magdalene. Mary slowly returned to the tomb. The two disciples had left her behind when they ran ahead. She did not go home with them but stayed at the tomb, weeping over the theft of the body (Jn 20:11-18). When Jesus appeared to her and said, "Woman, why are you crying? Who is it you are looking for?" she thought it was the gardener. He said, "Mary!" and she recognized the risen, glorified Jesus. Overjoyed, she threw herself at his feet and embraced him. Jesus did not forbid her to hold on to him, but merely said something like this:

> Don't waste time holding on to me. I am not here to stay. I'm on my way back to the Father. Go tell this good news to the others. "I go back up to Him who is my Father and your Father, my God and your God."

So Mary Magdalene told his disciples that she had seen the Lord, and that he had told her this.

The Appearances. This is the first appearance of the risen Jesus, but by no means the only one. The accounts of the appearances of the risen Lord can be schematized:

Appearances	Matthew	Mark	Luke	John	1 Corinthians
1. To Mary Magdalene		16:9		20:11-17	
2. To the holy women	28:9				
3. To Peter			24:34		15:5
4. To the disciples on the road to Emmaus		16:12	24:13-33		
5. To the apostles with Thomas absent		16:14	24:36-43	20:24-29	
6. To the apostles with Thomas present				20:24-29	15:5
7. To the disciples at the Sea of Tiberias				21:1-14	
8. To the apostles	28:16-17	16:14			
9. To more than 500					15:6
10. To James					15:7
11. To the apostles (see Acts 1:4-9)		16:9	24:44-52		15:7
12. To Paul (see Acts 9:17-27, 22:14-19, 26:16)				15:8	

The first five appearances occurred on the very day of the Resurrection, beginning with the appearance to Mary Magdalene at about dawn or sunrise (6:00 A.M.) and ending with the one to the disciples on their way to Emmaus at dusk. The sixth, to Thomas and the other apostles, took place on the following Sunday, a week later. Apart from the Ascension appearance (no. 11 above) we do not know the dates of the other appearances.

The Meaning of the Resurrection: The Paschal Mystery

Sometimes the Resurrection of Jesus is seen only as the greatest proof of his divinity. But the Resurrection is more than an argument to prove that Christ is God. It is the mystery of our salvation. Too often we tend to think of Christ as saving us only by his death, but the Resurrection is just as real a part of our salvation. Let us try to understand the full meaning of Christ's Resurrection in the total Paschal Mystery. ("Mystery" here is used not only in the sense of a truth beyond our full understanding, but also, and especially, as a divine action accomplished among men.)

Christ's death and Resurrection are inseparable. They form one redemptive work although they are two historical events. By becoming man, Christ took on our sinful human condition, the condition of a human nature closed by sin to the Spirit of God. But Christ died to that sinful human nature. By his death on Calvary, in perfect love and obedience to his Father, he passed over out of the body of sin to go to his Father. But his death did not complete that pass-over: Jesus had yet to take us with him to his Father. Unless we are with the Father, even though dead to sin, we are still not redeemed. The journey was completed only when Jesus rose and returned to the Father. Only with the Resurrection is the path to our Father in heaven really complete; we are saved not only by Jesus' death but also by his Resurrection (Jn 16:19-22).

This divine work of Christ dead and risen for us we call the Paschal Mystery, or the pass-over mystery of our redemption.

The Paschal Mystery in Our Daily Lives

The Paschal Mystery must be lived by each one of us. Christ's death and Resurrection must continue their effect in the life of the person in grace. We must die with Christ to our former, sinful nature, and thereafter remain continually risen with Christ. Our sinful state of death must be constantly annihilated by Christ's death, and our life in the Spirit must be constantly renewed and restored by Christ's Resurrection. We can do this only because we have become part of the true vine, members of Christ's own body, and as such have a continual share in his death and Resurrection (Jn 15:1-4).

This dying with Christ and rising again with him takes place first of all in baptism. Baptism is not merely something that happened to us a long time ago. Every day we live out our baptism, and everything else in our lives finds its foundation in that.

> For surely you know that when we were baptized into union with Christ Jesus, we were baptized into union with his death. By our baptism, then, we were buried with him and shared his death, in order that, just as Christ was raised from death by the glorious power of the Father, so also we might live a new life." (Rom 6:3-4; see also Col 3:1-4, 2:12)

This dying and rising again with Christ takes place at every liturgy, particularly on Sunday, the day of Resurrection, the little Easter, as we celebrate the memorial of the Lord's death and Resurrection. The true celebration of the liturgy means not only understanding what is going on, but living out our Paschal sacrifice. When Christ gave the disciples a mission in the world (Mt 28:18-20; Mk 16:15-18; Lk 24:47-48; Jn 20:21-22; Acts 1:8), he sent them forth as part of his own Passover. We too are called to mission as part of our sharing in the Paschal Mystery.

EIGHTEEN

Gospel Formation: The Lord's Prayer

THE GOSPELS of Matthew, Mark, and Luke are so alike that many of the passages can be laid side by side and their similarity seen at a glance. For this reason, they are usually referred to as the synoptic gospels—from the Greek *sun-optein*, meaning "to see together." Compare Matthew 3:17, Mark 1:11, and Luke 3:22. When such parallel passages are laid out side by side the similarities become very obvious. But, at the same time, this also highlights the significant differences. This question of similarities and differences is called "the synoptic problem." The basic question gives rise to even deeper questions. Which of the different versions is the original one? Is it not a bit unnecessary to have three inspired versions when they are all saying the same thing? In fact, do such parallel passages contain the same message, or do we have to look for a specific teaching in each one of them individually?

Because of the great similarities among the Gospels of Matthew, Mark, and Luke, where there are substantial differences we are faced with questions of historicity, and accuracy. What we have done so far has been aimed at increasing our understanding and appreciation of the Gospels. This other concern may seem too technical to be worth going through, but every serious reader of the Gospels ought to be aware of the problem with the synoptic Gospels and have seen at least once how the scholars deal with it.

In each of the next three chapters, we will be looking at one of the passages in which the synoptic problem arises and in each passage resolve the problem somewhat differently, which will be helpful in further reading of the Gospels. Once we have a working knowledge of this technique or process we can then use it to analyze other Gospel passages, to extract as much meaning as possible. This will also give us a deeper insight into what is meant by the truth of the Gospels.

In this chapter we will compare, contrast, and analyze the Gospel versions of the Lord's Prayer, not only because it is such an important prayer, but because this will serve as an example of how Gospel passages were handed on from Jesus' own teaching, through the instructions of the early church, through the writings of the evangelists, to our own day. As with many other passages in the synoptic Gospels, it is obvious that they are closely related. As we examine the characteristics of the two texts, we will try to determine how it is that we have these two versions. In these few pages it will not be possible to go into all the details—whole books have been written on this topic—but we can go into the more obvious and most important features.

In analyzing a passage our approach should be objective and scientific. There are three stages. First of all, we begin by making observations; we gather as much information as we can about the texts with all their particular features. From these observations, it should then be possible to draw up a working hypothesis—that is, a logical reconstruction, consistent with our observations, of how these passages came into existence. Finally, on the basis of this hypothesis, we draw exegetical conclusions and are brought nearer to the meaning of the text. This is exactly the way all scientific investigation is conducted. From careful observation of the way metals expand and contract according to temperature, a scientific hypothesis that metals increase in volume when heated has led to many practical conclusions—for example, thermostats, and the need to leave a space between railway lines to allow for the effects of temperature differences.

First Observation

There are very noticeable similarities between the extant Greek texts of the Lord's Prayer in Matthew and Luke. Here are the two versions, in an English translation which faithfully reflects the Greek original, laid out in parallel for easier comparison (Mt 6:9-13; Lk 11:2-4):

Matthew: Our Father in heaven: May your holy name be honored;

Luke: Father: May your holy name be honored;

Matthew: may your Kingdom come; may your will be done on earth as it is in heaven.

Luke: may your Kingdom come.

Matthew: Give us today the food we need (for today/for tomorrow).

Luke: Give us day by day the food we need (for today/for the next day).

Matthew: Forgive us the wrongs we have done, as we forgive the wrongs others have done to us.

Luke: Forgive us our sins, as we forgive everyone who does us wrong.

Matthew: Do not bring us to harsh testing, but keep us safe from the Evil One.

Luke: And do not bring us to hard testing.

Statistically, we can compare the words in the two Greek versions as follows:

	Total Words	Identical Words	Almost Identical	Extra or Different Words
Matthew:	58	25	7	26
Luke:	38	25	10	3

The similarities far outweigh the differences.

Moreover, the style of expression in both texts is not what we would normally expect in Greek. For example, the expression "May your holy name be honored" is extremely unusual in Greek, and yet we find that exact same construction in both Matthew and Luke.

Further, there is the Greek term *epiousion* which occurs in both texts, and which is so rare that there has always been disagreement as to what exactly it might mean. This is why in the passage above we have given alternatives:

today: the food we need/for today/for tomorrow

day by day: the food we need for today/for the next day

This is the only time this word occurs in the Bible. Moreover, in all the thousands of secular Greek writings that are known to us the word has been found only in one other text of uncertain date. This is why the early Fathers of the church found it difficult to give this phrase an exact meaning. Some said it should mean "for today or for tomorrow"; others, "necessary." An expression we sometimes use, "in time," has something of the same ambiguity.

These observations lead to our first hypothesis: The only reasonable conclusion consistent with the degree of similarity that we have discovered, especially given the use of the unique Greek compound, is that both Matthew's version and Luke's version are derived from one common Greek original. Perhaps an example will help to clarify the argument. Imagine you are a teacher and you have given the class an essay on a specific topic. You find that in two of the essays more than half the words and expressions are identically the same. Moreover, both pupils use a word like "membranaciousness." We could safely conclude that, whether directly or indirectly, both essays have been at least partly copied from one and the same original text.

Second Observation

Though the only extant texts we have are in Greek, the style of language and expression is Aramaic. This observation is based on a linguistic analysis of the texts.

The thought patterns underlying the way the prayer is expressed in both Matthew and Luke are consistent with the background of Jewish belief. It was the Jews (not the Greeks) who were waiting for the coming of God's kingdom. To ask God for "food we need/for today/for tomorrow" is part of the Jewish heritage. It echoes the experience of the Jewish people in the desert, where God gave manna, enough to satisfy their needs for each day (Ex 16:4). Similarly, "do not bring us to hard testing" is an echo of the temptations of the Jewish people in the desert: "Why are you putting the Lord to the test?" (Ex 17:2; see also Nm 20:2-13ff; Dt 8:2ff).

The grammatical constructions used in the prayer also point to an Aramaic original. To give one example: in Greek sentence construction, the verb occurs after the subject; in Aramaic, the verb begins certain sentences. Here the double phrase "May your name be honored; may your kingdom come" is expressed as "May [it] be honored your name; may [it] come your Kingdom." In normal Greek grammar the order in each of the phrases would be inverted. However, the order corresponds exactly to what it would be in Aramaic:

jitgaddas   *semak*
May [it] be honored your name

tete   *malkutak*
may [it] come your Kingdom.

It is also very difficult to see what sort of meaning "May your name be honored" would have in Greek. To a Greek way of thinking, to ask that God's name be made holy would automatically imply that until now his name was not holy (otherwise there would be no need to make the request). The same phrase

אבונא דבשמיא

יתקדש שמך

תאתא מלכותך

יהוא צבינך כמא בשמיא

כנמא בארעא

הב לן לחמא רמסתנא ביום

ושבק לן חובי

כמא אבן שבקכא לחיבי

וץ תעלן לנסיונא

אלא פצא יתן מן בישא

אמן

A reconstruction of the Lord's Prayer in Aramaic

in Aramaic/Hebrew is an idiomatic expression with a very precise meaning. The expression "name" stands for the person himself. So, for example, in the Old Testament we find God saying that he will demonstrate the holiness of his name (Ez 36:22ff), meaning that he will prove himself to be holy by his deeds. Applying the same idiom to this phrase the request becomes "God, may your holiness be shown [to us] by your deeds."

This observation leads to our second hypothesis: The typically Jewish thought patterns, the grammatical construction, and the meaning of the expressions all indicate an original Aramaic version. Indeed, we are obliged to presuppose an Aramaic original if much of the prayer is to have any real meaning.

Again, a fictitious example may illustrate our reasoning more clearly. Suppose you came across the following extract from a story written in English: "While Uncle Moon was shining bright Lalitha said to Nageswarrao, "Husband, tomorrow to your eldest brother let us go." Because of the strangeness of the language we would immediately expect that the original story had been written in another language and literally translated into English. In fact, the original here was the Indian language Telegu. Not only is the ordering of the words foreign to us, but the thought-patterns lying behind it, too—the expression "Uncle Moon," saying "husband" impersonally instead of calling him by name, etc.

Third Observation

There are differences between the versions of the prayer that Matthew gives us and the one that Luke gives us.

Matthew's text has seven petitions, Luke's has five.

Matthew quotes Jesus as saying "Our Father in heaven," whereas in Luke's version he says only "Father."

Matthew adds "May your will be done on earth as it is in heaven," which Luke omits.

In Matthew the request for food is for "today" whereas in Luke it is "day by day."

In Matthew we have to ask forgiveness for "the wrongs we have done," whereas in Luke it is for "our sins."

In Matthew the measure of our forgiveness is "as we forgive the wrongs others have done to us," whereas in Luke it is "as we forgive everyone who does us wrong."

Matthew concludes the prayer with the request "but keep us safe from the Evil One," which Luke omits.

Thus we have a third hypothesis: The best way to understand these differences is to attribute them to the specific and distinct purpose of each evangelist.

Matthew wrote his Gospel principally for Jews. "Our Father in heaven" is a turn of phrase very congenial to a Jewish way of praying. They often address their prayer to God as "Father," but always qualify it to emphasize his difference from fathers on earth. For example, Jews would pray "Father, our king!", "Father, our God!", or "Our Father in heaven." To accommodate this Jewish style of prayer Matthew depicts Christ as giving us the prayer as we would say it. That is to say, God is "Father" to Jesus in a far stronger sense than for us. So Matthew adds the extra phrase "in heaven" to make this distinction.

"May your will be done on earth as it is in heaven." Because the Jews already had fixed ideas of the kind of Kingdom that the Messiah would bring, namely, a political kingdom that would liberate them from Roman rule, Matthew adds this extra phrase so that his Jewish readers will understand "May your Kingdom come" in the way that Jesus meant it. In other words, Matthew is emphasizing that the Kingdom we request in the prayer is a heavenly one, not an earthly one.

Luke begins simply, "Father," expressing a personal relationship that no Jew would dare. This is consistent with many other episodes in Luke's Gospel where Christ speaks about God as "my Father" (Lk 10:21, 22, 22:42, 23:46). We find Paul explaining to the churches in Rome and Galatia (Gentile communities) that through Christ all Christians have become

God's children in a special way, which is why they can pray "Father, my Father" (Rom 8:15; Gal 4:6). Luke, then, is giving us the prayer as it was recited by the early Gentile Christians.

Luke also clarifies for Gentiles what Matthew calls "wrongs" by saying explicitly "sins," and later on in the same phrase he adds that we should forgive "everyone."

Similarly, what Jews would understand implicitly in "give us today. . . ." Luke makes explicit by saying "give us day by day. . . ."

The textual differences between Matthew and Luke, then, do not imply a difference in meaning. The meaning of both versions is the same, but there are differences of formulation and of emphasis to accommodate the mentality to which the text is addressed.

Fourth Observation

Another substantial difference between Matthew and Luke is the different contexts in which each evangelist places the prayer in his Gospel. Luke records the occasion as well as Jesus' words; in Matthew it is more loosely related to general teaching. Luke introduces the prayer as follows:

> One day Jesus was praying in a certain place. When he had finished, one of his disciples said to him, "Lord, teach us to pray, just as John taught his disciples."
> Jesus said to them, "When you pray, say this: 'Father . . .'"
> (Lk 11:1-2a)

Matthew does not explicitly record the occasion of Jesus teaching the prayer but sets it within the context of the Sermon on the Mount, linking it (as does Mark) with Christ's teaching on prayer and on forgiveness:

> This, then, is how you should pray: "Our Father in heaven. . . . Forgive us the wrongs we have done, as we forgive the wrongs that others have done to us. Do not bring us to hard

testing, but keep us safe from the Evil One."

If you forgive others the wrongs they have done to you, your Father in heaven will also forgive you. But if you do not forgive others, then your Father will not forgive the wrong you have done. (Mt 6:9-15)

This part of Matthew is parallel to Mark 11, where Jesus is also instructing his followers about prayer:

And when you stand and pray, forgive anything you may have against anyone, so that your Father in heaven will forgive the wrongs you have done. (Mk 11:25)

Thus, our fourth hypothesis is that the context in Luke, and not Matthew, is the original one.

Luke preserves a standard way of presenting Jesus' teaching. Whenever it seemed appropriate (the occasion), Jesus would speak his mind on the subject briefly (Jesus' word). This word would then be explained by him at length (instruction). Of these, Jesus' word was the most important. The disciples would have learned it by heart. The occasion and the explanatory instruction were often recorded but not always. Consequently, we can safely presume that the fact that Luke does record the occasion in this instance means it is important for a correct understanding of Jesus' word. In this case, we learn from the context in which Luke places it that Christ meant this to be a model of prayer.

Although the prayer appears within Matthew's Sermon on the Mount, a close examination shows that it appears in a section which interrupts the flow of a longer statement by Christ. We may reasonably conclude that the prayer did not originally belong to the context of the Sermon on the Mount but that it has been edited into its present position. It is easy to see why it has been inserted at this point. Jesus is talking about how religion ought to be practiced properly and gives three examples—almsgiving, prayer, and fasting. Quite naturally, this prayer has been added. This is how this section of chapter 6 of Matthew breaks down:

1. *Introduction (6:1):*
   Do not perform your religious duties in public so that people will see what you do.

2. *First example—on almsgiving (6:2-4):*
   "So when you are about to give alms, do not send a trumpeter ahead of you . . . do it in secrecy. Then your Father, who sees what you do in secret, will reward you."

3. *Second example—on prayer (6:5-6):*
   "So, too, when you pray do not be like the hypocrites. . . . Pray to your Father in secrecy. Then your Father, who sees what you do in secret, will reward you."

4. *Interruption:*
   (6:7-8): Do not pray with many meaningless words.
   (6:9-13): "This, then, is how you should pray: 'Our Father . . . .'"
   (6:14-15): Teaching on forgiveness

5. *Third example—on fasting (6:16-18):*
   "So, too, when you fast, do not imitate the gloomy-faced hypocrites. . . . When you fast [do it] in secrecy. Then your Father, who sees what you do in secret, will reward you."

Many other sayings of Jesus pronounced on other occasions are similarly inserted by Matthew into the Sermon on the Mount. You might like to study this on your own, comparing what Matthew says with the parallels in Luke.

To summarize, the relationship we find in the Gospel texts can arise from any one of the following reasons: Jesus' teaching is linked to the historical occurrence which prompted it (e.g., Lk 11:1-2a, 2b-4); the link may have arisen in oral tradition (e.g., Mt 6:9-13, 14-15—this particular example is worked out more fully later); sometimes the Gospel writer himself links texts because they share a common theme (e.g., Mt 6:7-15 is inserted between v. 6 and v. 18).

In the course of analyzing two texts of the Lord's Prayer as presented by Matthew and by Luke, we have amassed enough information to hypothesize a history of the prayer.

27-30 A.D. At the disciples' request (cf. Lk 11:1-2), Jesus taught them to pray in the language they spoke; we refer to this as the "Aramaic original." Jesus also taught them other aspects of prayer, e.g., that we have to forgive others.

30-50. After the Resurrection, the apostles preached about Christ and his teaching, which included what he taught them about prayer. So the Aramaic original was passed on by oral tradition, together with an explanation of the occasion of its formulation.

50. In Aramaic Matthew, to emphasize the importance of Christ's teaching on prayer, the Lord's Prayer was put with the rest of his most important teaching within the Sermon on the Mount. Aramaic Matthew was principally for Jews, so its expression was typically Jewish, retaining much of the Aramaic original, including the link with forgiveness (Mt 6:14-15).

64. Mark did not include the text of the Lord's Prayer in his Gospel. Oral tradition was still strong, and perhaps he assumed that every Christian was already familiar with the text. However, he did retain teaching on forgiveness (Mk 11:25).

65. Meanwhile, for the benefit of Gentile converts, the Aramaic text of the Lord's Prayer was translated into Greek. It was a translation and consequently much of the style, language, and underlying thought-patterns were distinguishably Aramaic. This Greek translation was included when the Aramaic Matthew was translated into Greek.

Pre-70. Luke wrote his Gospel specifically for Greek converts, adapting and explaining Christ's teaching as he felt necessary. He, too, included the then current Greek version of the Lord's Prayer, but clarified some of the expressions and phrases so as to make the prayer more intelligible for the Gentile converts, and placed it in the context of other sayings of Christ on prayer.

Pre-100. A document we know as the "Didache" (literally, "instruction") gives the text of the Lord's Prayer, together with the recommendation that it be said "three times a day." It follows the Matthean version, with one final addition—"For yours is the power and the glory for all ages" (Didache 8:2-3).

Pre-200. In his writing, Marcion gives another form of the Lord's Prayer based on the Lucan version but with some free adaptations. This shows that the early Christians used it as a model for prayer in their own words, rather than as an absolutely fixed formula.

> Father,
> your name be made holy.
> *May your Holy Spirit come upon us and purify us.*
> Keep giving us from day to day *your* daily bread.
> And forgive us our sins,
> for we ourselves forgive everyone in debt to us.
> And *do not let us be led* into temptation.

We reconstructed this probable history backwards. By comparing and analyzing existing texts, we were able to hypothesize in principle an underlying Aramaic original for the Lord's Prayer. Some scholars, especially Joachim Jeremias, have taken this one stage further and have tried to re-translate the prayer into Aramaic. Here is such a reconstruction:

> *Abba*
> Father
>
> *jitqaddas*   *semak*
> may [it] be honored your name
>
> *tete*   *malkutak*
> may [it] come your Kingdom
>
> *lahman delimhar*
> bread for today

hab lan   joma den
give to us day this

useboq   lan hobain
forgive us our sins

kedisebaqnan   lehajjabain
as we forgive those sinning against us

welan   ta'elinnan   lenisjon
and do not lead us into temptation. ·

Even if you have no familiarity whatsoever with Semitic languages, you cannot help but notice the way it is laid out in parallel phrases, the natural rhythm in the phrases, the rhyming (in particular between lines two and three, and six and seven). Try sounding out the Aramaic aloud, and these features become even more obvious.

General Conclusions on Historicity

Reviewing the history of one passage prompts some general questions about the way in which the Gospel writings and their message have been handed on. How accurate are the texts we have today? Where there are differences, which are we to believe, if any? And especially the question: Have the Gospels preserved Jesus' own words?

A secular example will help us formulate an answer. When the late President de Gaulle was visiting Romania in 1968, student demonstrations demanding radical change broke out in France. De Gaulle flew back to Paris immediately and made an important statement, a portion of which was reported in three different ways.

De Gaulle said, "Amelioration—si; un chien-lit—non!"

De Gaulle said, "Improvement—yes; a dog's bed—no!"

De Gaulle said, "Improvement—yes; confusion—no!"

Which version gave De Gaulle's own words?

The first report gives the precise French words, and therefore, is exactly identical to the original utterance. (In Scripture scholarship, this is what is known by the technical expression *ipsissima verba*—literally, "the very same words.") Such extreme accuracy in reporting is very commendable, but its value is limited. It will only convey what was meant to those who understand French. If we do not know the language, such accuracy can present only the external shell of the words with no guarantee that the meaning is being transmitted.

The second report translates the French original, and, in its quest for accuracy, renders a literal translation. To someone who speaks no French at all, such a report is, perhaps, an improvement on the first, but this is still no guarantee that the meaning will be conveyed. In this case, quite the opposite, because idiomatic expressions literally translated are still shells of words and devoid of any real meaning.

The third report converts the French idiom into plain English, giving us a dynamic equivalent of the original words. In so doing, the original words have been altered, or have even disappeared, but the meaning of the original has been accurately preserved.

In answer to our question—which report gave De Gaulle's own words—we might answer, "In their own way, all of them!" But, it should be clear that a more valid question would be, which report conveys his words best? We would have to say the third report is the one which gives us most accurately what De Gaulle said, in the sense that we are sure of understanding what he meant. Throughout the Gospels, we find reports of all three types.

In some cases, the *ipsissima verba* are reported, even to the extent of being preserved in the original Aramaic:

"Eli, Eli, lama sabachthani?" (Mt 27:46)

"Talitha, qumi!" (Mk 5:41)

"Ephphatha!" (Mt 7:34)

In some cases, we have literal translations of the original utterance:

"May [it] be honored your name" (Mt 6:9b)

"May [it] come your kingdom" (Mt 5:10a)

"Tradition of the elders" (Mt 15:2; Mk 7:5)

Modern biblical translations usually adapt the extant Greek in this form into the third type.

In some cases, we have dynamic equivalents of the original words. For instance, Luke changes Matthew's "debts" to "sins." This accurate equivalent ensures that we will understand that Jesus is talking about moral debts rather than fiscal debts.

What value, then, can we attribute to direct quotations in the Gospels? Luke often explicitly says, "He [Jesus] said to them. . . ." Does this way of quoting mean we have the exact words of Jesus? Again, a secular example will help. Imagine that a large steel firm has a customer who has regularly failed to pay his bills. The firm has determined to bring him to court. Just as the court proceedings would have begun, they are postponed for political reasons. The managing director decides to take advantage of this, and goes off for a vacation. Meanwhile, the situation changes and a member of the firm is sent to update the managing director. When the director hears the new developments, he says, "Right! Let the fireworks begin! Further procrastination would be anything but advantageous to us." The messenger sends the following telegram to the firm: "MD says go ahead. Further delay harmful." If we compare the original comment and the subsequent telegram, only one word of the original remark survives, but we are obliged to admit that the messenger has provided a very accurate equivalent.

So, too, in the Gospels. When the evangelist begins "Jesus said . . . ," in some privileged instances we do have the very words (*ipsissima verba*) of the original utterance. More often, we are given dynamic equivalents, which have been phrased so that we can grasp what Jesus wanted us to understand. For example, with the word *daily bread,* Jesus presupposes that his Jewish listeners will automatically think back to the experience of manna in the desert. Jesus is saying to pray that God will look after us in the same way, but, if you take only the literal expression and had no familiarity with manna, it would seem as if we are being told not to pray for bread for next week. Luke was aware of this possibility of a literal translation misleading his readers, and expresses what Jesus meant by using the words "Give us day by day the food we need. . . ."

Why was the original Aramaic prayer that Jesus himself taught lost? Put that way, it sounds as if the church was rather careless. But the fact that this happened teaches us a very important point about how teaching was passed on. If it had been part of Jesus' original intention that his followers should use exactly and only the very words he gave them, then the church would certainly have preserved them. Jesus and the apostles were deeply concerned, not about formulations, but about the correct interpretation of his teaching—not necessarily the words themselves, but the message they carry. Which is better: that Christians should be reciting a formula of words from a language long since dead, or that Christ's words come alive in the language and understanding of each of us? Inspiration does not mean that the external words were dictated by the Holy Spirit, but that the church, under the guidance of the Holy Spirit, in its teaching accurately handed on the meaning of what it received from Jesus. From the very earliest days, the actual wording was adapted to suit the culture and understanding of the recipients.

Which of the versions of the Lord's Prayer is it best to use—Matthew's, Luke's, or a translation of the Aramaic original? That is the wrong question to ask. Praying does not mean reciting words by heart, but praying according to the pattern that Jesus gave us. According to that pattern, we should praise God, pray for the extension of his Kingdom, pray for our own needs, ask for forgiveness of our sins, pray for final perseverance. A free prayer, based on the pattern of the Lord's Prayer might be:

Father,
you are worthy of all honor, praise, and glory.
May your plan of salvation be fully realized throughout the whole world.
May all men acknowledge you as their creator and their Father.
Father,
help with our daily needs.
Give food to the hungry;
give work to the unemployed;
support the poor and the lonely.
Please,
forgive us our sins.
We know that you demand charity from us,
and we cannot be your friends
if we are at enmity with others.
We realize we should be merciful to others,
just as you are towards us.
We are conscious of our own weakness.
We know that we often fall into temptation.
Please, give us the strength to live up to our good resolutions and keep us from what may harm us.

It is by making the Lord's Prayer personal that we do what Christ told us: "This is how to pray . . ." (Mt 5:9; Lk 11:2).

NINETEEN

Gospel Formation: The Fig Tree and the Cleansing of the Temple

THE NEXT EPISODE we will analyze occurs during the last week of Christ's ministry. According to Matthew and Mark, after the triumphal entry into Jerusalem, Jesus cursed a fig tree and proceeded to cleanse the Temple. Luke places his reference to the fig tree earlier in Jesus' ministry, but records the cleansing of the Temple as occurring in this last week, as do Matthew and Mark. We can represent the three Gospel versions schematically.

Event	Matthew	Mark	Luke
1. Triumphal entry into Jerusalem	21:1-11	11:1-10	(19:28-38)
2. Entry into the Temple	21:12a	11:11a	
3. Return to Bethany		11:11b	
4. Curse of fig tree		11:12-14	(parable of the fig tree, 13:6-9)
5. Cleansing of the Temple	21:12-13	11:15-17	(19:45-46)
6. Children's praise	21:15		

Event	Matthew	Mark	Luke
7. High priests and scribes decide to kill Jesus	21:15-16	11:18	(19:47-48)
8. Jesus returns to Bethany	21:17	11:19	
Curse of fig tree	21:18-19b		
9. Withered fig tree	21:19c-20	11:20-21	
10. Explanations: power of faith; power	21:21	11:22-33	
of prayer; pray	21:22	11:24	
with forgiveness		11:25	
11. Controversy with high priests, scribes, and elders over Jesus' authority	21:23-27	11:27-33	(20:1-8)

Even a glance at the above schema highlights certain fundamental differences in the accounts.

First Observation

There are noticeable differences among the synoptic accounts of the fig tree episode.

The versions of Mark and Matthew are closer to each other than either of them is to Luke's version. Both Matthew and Mark describe the event of Jesus cursing the fig tree and the subsequent miracle of its withering. Luke, however, records only a fig tree parable, absent in Matthew and Mark, and separates the parable from the cleansing of the Temple.

Further, there are differences between Matthew and Mark in their account of the cursing and the miracle. What is unique to each evangelist is printed in italics.

Matthew 21	Mark 11
On his way back to the city early next morning, Jesus	The next day, as they were coming back *from Bethany*,

was hungry.
He saw a fig tree by the side
of the road and went to it,

butfound nothing on it
except leaves.

So he said to the tree,
"You will never again bear
fruit!"

The disciples saw this and
were astounded. "How did
the fig tree dry up so
quickly?" they asked.

Jesus answered, "I assure
you that if you believe *and
do not doubt, you will be able
to do what I have done to this
fig tree.*
And not only this, but you
will even be able to say to
this hill, "Get up and
throw yourself in the sea,"
and it will.

Jesus was hungry
He saw *in the distance* a fig
tree *covered with leaves,* so he
went *to see if he could find
any figs on it.*
But when he came to it, he
found only leaves, *because it
was not the right time for figs.*
Jesus said to the fig tree,
"No one shall ever eat figs
from you again!"
*And his disciples heard him.
At once the fig tree dried up.*
(Cleansing of the Temple)
(Jesus and the disciples
return to Bethany.)
*Early next morning, as they
walked along the road, they
saw the fig tree. It was dead
all the way down to its roots.
Peter* remembered what
had happened and said to
Jesus, "Look, Teacher, the
fig tree you cursed has
died!"
Jesus answered them, "Have
faith in God.

I assure you that whoever
tells this hill to get up
and throw itself in the sea
*and does not doubt in his
heart, but believes that what
he says will happen,* it will
done for him.

If you believe, you will receive whatever you ask for in prayer."	For this reason I tell you: when you pray and ask for something, believe that you have received it, and you will be given whatever you ask for."

The most obvious difference is that Matthew's account has only one part; when Jesus curses the fig tree, it dries up immediately. Moreover, this follows the Temple cleansing. Mark, on the other hand, explicitly records that Jesus returns to Bethany twice (11:11b, 19), so that the event is spread over three days. In addition, the actual cursing of the fig tree and then the seeing it withered are a day apart, and these two moments in the story are separated by the Temple cleansing.

There is also a noticeable difference of approach. Mark fills out his account with a welter of factual details; Matthew's account, by contrast, cuts through these details to give a simpler and shorter account.

Second Observation

Matthew often simplifies narrative in his Gospel. Three examples from elsewhere in the Gospels illustrate this point.

First, Luke tells us that the Roman officer sent friends to Jesus to say: "Sir, don't trouble yourself. I do not deserve to have you come into my house" (Lk 7:6). Matthew, however, tells the story as if the Roman officer himself came. "When Jesus entered Capernaum, a Roman officer met him and begged for help. . . . 'Oh no, sir,' answered the officer, 'I do not deserve to have you come into my house'" (Mt 8:5).

Conclusion: Matthew simplifies the story by cutting out the intermediary persons.

Second, Mark and Luke narrate that Jesus commanded the two disciples who were going to prepare for the Last Supper, that they were to follow a man carrying a jug of water. This man would bring them to the house where they could prepare the Pasch (Mk 14:12-14; Lk 22:7-11). But Matthew reports Jesus as saying: "Go to a certain man in the city . . . and tell him. . ." (Mt 26:17-18).

Conclusion: Matthew simplifies the story by omitting out the incident of the man carrying the jug of water.

Third, from Luke we learn that Jesus drew the statement on the Greatest Commandment from the lips of the scribe. The scribe says: " 'Love the Lord your God . . .' and 'Love your neighbor as you love yourself.' " Jesus then approved of this answer (Lk 10:25-28). Matthew puts the words directly into Jesus' own speech: "Jesus answered, 'Love the Lord your God. . . . Love your neighbor as you love yourself' " (Mt 22:37-39).

Conclusion: Matthew simplifies the story by putting the doctrine directly in Jesus' own mouth, omitting the attempted answer of the scribe.

We can therefore hypothesize that Mark, not Matthew, gives account closest to historical events.

Third Observation

Jesus' cursing of the tree is to be understood not only as an example for trust in prayer, but also as a symbolic action concerning Jerusalem.

Tradition has linked Jesus' words on trust in prayer to the cursing of the fig tree. (See Mt 21:21-22; Mk 11:22-24.) No doubt, this exhortation of Jesus did belong to Jesus' explanatory discussion on the following day. But the cursing of the fig tree had a symbolic meaning regarding Jerusalem. This is clear from the context:

—Jesus looked for figs although he knew that it was not the time for figs (Mk 11:13). He must, therefore, have had another reason.

—It is stressed that the tree had many leaves but no fruit (Mt

21:19; Mk 11:13). The tree is obviously the symbol of a person who shows *outward* virtue without real sanctity.

—Jesus was on his way to Jerusalem (Mt 21:18). He would examine Jerusalem for true fruits of sanctity, but would only find leaves (Mt 21:12-13; etc.). The curse of the fig tree, therefore, was a warning to Jerusalem. If it did not produce fruit, it would be destroyed (see Mt 21:43; 23:37-39; etc.).

—This symbolic meaning would have been even more apparent to the disciples because John the Baptist, in reference to Jesus, had said, "The axe is ready to cut down the trees at the roots; every tree that does not bear good fruit will be cut down and thrown into the fire" (Mt 3:10).

We may, therefore, conclude that the apostles (and the evangelists also) understood the symbolic meaning of Jesus' action. They saw in it a warning to Jerusalem.

Concerning the original event itself, we may hypothesize as follows: Jesus cursed the fig tree when on his way to cleanse the Temple. It was a symbolic warning to Jerusalem. On the following day, when passing again, the disciples expressed surprise at the efficacy of Jesus' curse. Jesus then taught about the power of prayer.

These various elements were carefully transmitted, and when the evangelists committed them to writing, they each presented these elements in a way which suited their purpose and their audience.

Mark related the event in his Gospel as he found it in Peter's teaching and, as we have observed, gave the historical account.

Luke, however, was writing for Gentile converts who were not used to the symbolic actions of prophets. The cursing of the fig tree might have been misunderstood by them; therefore Luke omitted the incident. But he presented it as a parable.

In harmony with his common procedure, Matthew abbreviated the narration. He placed the cleansing of the Temple immediately after the glorious entry into Jerusalem, thereby condensing what happened in two days to a one-day event.

Because of this, he also had to simplify the story of the tree. Both the curse and the explanation of the withering up are put together as if they happened on one day.

General Conclusions: Facts and History

Quite a few aspects of our reconstruction need further discussion, but it may be more efficient to restrict our attention to one focal question. This question concerns the accuracy of historical narratives. Have the evangelists been accurate when writing down the deeds of Jesus?

By way of example we may recall that Jesus did *not* enter Jerusalem triumphantly and cleanse the Temple on one day. It was only on the day following the cursing that the withered tree was seen by the disciples.

Matthew, however, puts both deeds of Jesus on the same day. Matthew states that the tree withered at once.

Didn't Matthew, by his simplification, falsify the facts? If the tree was only seen withered the next day, how could he say that it "withered at once"?

Yet we should not confuse "simplification" with "falsification." Falsification always presupposes an intent to deceive the listener or reader. Simplification involves no such intent. It is usually necessary to simplify in order that the reader will have a more correct understanding. Simplification means cutting out details, but only in the interest of conveying the substance more accurately.

When Pope John Paul II visited Mexico, the journey itself lasted many days, and the pope met and spoke to thousands of people in a very busy schedule of meetings and appointments. A complete report of all the details would be covered only by several volumes. But journalists were restricted to selecting what they thought were the most significant details. They had to simplify, and did it according to the special purpose of each individual journalist and the paper or magazine he or she represented. The reporter for *The Times* might try to highlight points of interest to British readers. A fashion magazine might show more interest in how the president's wife was dressed to meet the pope at the airport, or details of the menu at an official reception. A typical journalistic report might read:

> The Holy Father left the president's house at eight o'clock. He shook hands with the president and his wife, waved to the crowds, and then stepped into his official car. His car moved away at the head of a motorcade, followed by ten more cars full of dignitaries. People cheered the pope all along the route.

Someone might accuse the journalist of deliberate falsification because: the pope shook hands with several other people besides the president and his wife—he shook hands first with the hostess, the president's wife, and only then with the president; he waved to the crowds as soon as he came out, before shaking hands with the president, as well as after; he whispered something to his private secretary before stepping into the car; the car was not at the head of the motorcade because an escort of police motorcycles led the way; etc. Technically, all of these additional details are correct, but we would not condemn the newspaper report as false. We accept that in the interest of conveying what is important, unnecessary details will be omitted.

The same is true of the evangelists in their reporting of events from the life of Christ. Luke changed the miracle story into a parable not to deceive his readers but to simplify those aspects which might have confused them. Similarly, Matthew's condensing the account into one day is not a deliberate falsification to mislead readers, but rather to highlight the meaning of Jesus' words and actions.

At the same time, we should not confuse wealth of detail with accuracy of reporting. Most often in everyday living and reading we deal only in terms of historical accuracy, and we might be tempted to judge a report's accuracy not only on the truth of the details it contains but very often on the amount of detail. Imagine what a twentieth-century journalist might have reported if he had been in Capernaum when Jesus cured the Roman officer's slave.

The day began ordinarily enough. At a quarter to eleven, Jesus sat on a stone in the corner of the market place. There was quite a crowd around him, notably some merchants from Massabah, who happened to be in the city on business, and who were curious to see what this wandering preacher they had all heard about was really like. Jesus was talking about the need to renounce wealth and to be satisfied with God's providence. Jochanan, the leader of the visiting merchants, and a man reputed to be involved in dishonest trade, kept distracting the audience by shifting his mule backwards and forwards. A woman was so caught up in what Jesus was saying she dropped the basket of chickens she was carrying and this caused quite a stir. Just then some scribes who had been lurking on the fringe of Jesus' audience for some time took advantage of the interruption to move into the center of the group. They had been sent by Publius Quartus, they announced, a Roman officer stationed in the town. One of the scribes, whom I could not follow properly because of his terrible Galilean accent, spoke highly of Publius. The others kept interrupting him, muttering their assent and trying to outdo him in praise. Publius, they stressed, had spent half a talent of his own money for the reconstruction of the synagogue. Then they explained that Publius was worried about Anammelek, one of his slaves, who was seriously ill. They asked Jesus to visit the house, explaining that Publius himself had explicitly requested it. Jesus stood up and made ready to go to the officer's house in the Roman quarter of the city, when more messengers arrived from Publius on their master's behalf. They had been sent to say it was not necessary for Jesus to come all the way to his house. Could he not cure from this distance? . . .

This account seems much fuller than what Matthew tells us in his Gospel, because of the wealth of extra details it adds. But, that is exactly the point; those details are *extra*. Examine the above account carefully and extract the essential points: the Roman officer asks Jesus for help; he has such great faith that he tells Jesus it is not necessary to come to his house; Jesus cures the servant and praises the Roman officer's faith. Matthew's version trims out unnecessary extras about the bystanders and intermediaries, so as to focus our attention on only those circumstances which are important. Not only despite the inaccuracy of detail, but because it is uncluttered by unnecessary extras, Matthew's report is truer to the theological meaning which, after all, is what he is trying to impart.

We have studied the account of the fig tree in Mark and Matthew. What do these two evangelists want to teach us about Jesus cursing the fig tree? What do they—under inspiration—want us to remember and believe? Are they much concerned about the smaller details? Manifestly, they are not. Matthew does not seem to worry whether Christ did it on one day or two. This by itself is a great lesson to us. *The Holy Spirit apparently does not want us to get lost in details.* Details such as how old the fig tree was and how high, whether there were more trees or only one, whether it belonged to this person or that, are not part of Christ's message. In fact, although knowing such details might satisfy our curiosity, it would not help our faith.

Accepting the material fact of the sign alone would, of course, not do justice to the Gospels either. *Jesus' curse of the fig tree has a meaning.* It is this meaning that matters. It was to convey this meaning that the evangelists recorded the event. As we have seen before, the cursing of the fig tree is connected with Jesus' judicial power. Jesus came to examine the worship in the Temple. He would find it a purely external show without true inner devotion: leaves without fruit. "These people . . . honor me with their lips, but their heart is far from me" (Mt 15:8; cf. 21:12ff; 23:1ff). Jesus' terrible severity, expressed in his drying-up the fig tree, serves as a warning to Jerusalem—and also to us! For we also, like the Pharisees in the Temple, may make our prayer and religious life an "external show" without true inner love for God. Jesus' words in the gardener's parable

(Lk 13:6-9) prove that he is willing to give us some respite for true conversion, but he will ultimately judge us. Jesus' curse of the fig tree forces us to acknowledge Jesus as our judge. It also makes us examine our consciences to see whether we are producing real fruit and not only leaves.

TWENTY

Gospel Formation:
The Dispute about Tradition

TO UNDERSTAND the teaching of the Gospels more fully, we must take into account the long and complicated history of the Gospels themselves. The Gospels, as we have them, reflect all the stages through which Jesus' message came to us: the historical circumstances of Jesus' own teaching; the way this was presented in the oral catechesis of the early church and the particular pastoral stress it may have received; the way this came to be formulated into fixed and memorized traditions; the particular style and purpose of each evangelist. We do not have space here to study the Gospel texts in their entirety nor to go extensively into how they came to have their present form. But we can go some way to gaining an insight into the various aspects of the formation of the Gospels and the factors which influenced that formation.

When confronted with any Gospel text, the first thing we ought to remember is its context. This means not only that we have to take into account where in the particular Gospel it happens to fall, but that we have to go beyond to the original context or occasion in Jesus' life. This has a technical name, *Sitz-im-Leben,* a German phrase which means literally "the situation-in-life." You yourself may have had the experience of someone quoting back to you your own words, but with a completely different meaning because they have been taken out of the context in which you spoke them. For example, an expression used lightheartedly with a friend might be a joke, but if reported coldly to an enemy, could seem like an insult! The same applies to Jesus' own words. For example, when Jesus said, "You are the light of the world," unless we know whether he was speaking to the Pharisees, to a crowd of ordinary listeners, or privately to his disciples, we might not understand what he meant. The original *Sitz-im-Leben* helps us to understand why Jesus uses this particular expression, these words and not other ones.

Apart from the Gospel context of the original *Sitz-im-Leben,* there is another context which usually influences the Gospel context, namely, the *Sitz-im-Leben* of the early church when this episode was being committed to writing. For example, at the time Luke was composing his Gospel the particular *Sitz-im-Leben* which influenced his writing was the need to explain Jesus' teaching to Gentile converts with a Greek mentality. So, for example, to make clear what Jesus meant by "forgive us our debts," he puts it as "forgive us our sins" (Lk 11:4).

In this chapter, we will try to understand how to apply this particular technique by studying one example of how a Gospel text was formulated by Jesus, how it was handed down by the apostles, and how it was committed to writing by the evangelists. Again, we will make our analysis as objective and scientific as possible, with observations, hypotheses, and exegetical conclusions.

The relevant passages from Matthew and Mark have been translated as literally as possible.

Pharisees and scribes from Jerusalem then came to Jesus and said, "Why do your disciples break away from the tradition of the elders? They do not wash their hands when they eat." He answered and said, "Why do you break away from the commandment of God for the sake of your tradition? For God said, 'Honor your father and your mother' and 'Anyone who curses father and mother must be put to death.' But you say, 'If anyone says to his father or mother: "Anything I might have used to help you is dedicated to God," he is rid of his duty to his father and mother.' For the sake of/through your tradition you have made null and void the word of God. Hypocrites! Rightly Isaiah prophesied of you: 'This people honors me with their lips but their heart is far from me; in vain do they worship me, giving as teaching only the commandments of men.'" (Mt 15:1-9)

The Pharisees gathered around him, and some of the scribes who had come from Jerusalem, and noticing that some of the disciples were eating with unclean hands, that is, un-washed—for the Pharisees, and all the Jews, do not eat without washing their hands as far as the elbow, following the tradition of the elders; and when they return from the marketplace, they do not eat without purifying themselves; and there are many other traditions they observe concerning the washing of cups and pots and bronze dishes—and the Pharisees and scribes asked him: "Why do your disciples not respect the tradition of the elders, but eat with unclean hands?" And he said to them, "Rightly Isaiah prophesied of you, hypocrites, as it is written: 'This people honors me with their lips but their heart is far from me; in vain do they worship me, giving as teaching only the command-ments of men.' Putting aside the commandment of God, you cling to human traditions." And he said to them, "Rightly is it you put aside the commandment of God to keep your own traditions? For Moses said, 'Honor your father and your mother' and 'Anyone who curses father and mother must be put to death.' But you say, 'If a man says to his father or mother: "Anything I might have used to help you is *corban*" (that is, an offering), then he is forbidden to do anything for father or mother. So you make null and void the word of God for the sake of/through your tradition which you have handed down, and you do many such things." (Mk 7:1-13)

First Observation

The original context of the passage is the conflict with the Pharisees and the scribes about adhering to the tradition of the elders.

In addition to the fact that Matthew and Mark explicitly use the expression *tradition of the elders* (Mt 15:2; Mk 7:3, 5; see also Mt 15:3, 6; Mk 7:4b, 9, 13), there are very clear references to what constituted part of this tradition:

The "washing of hands" (Mt 15:2; Mk 7:2-5) does not refer to a washing for hygienic purposes, but for ritual. Mark hints at how highly complicated this ritual cleansing tradition was and, in fact, it involved some 600 prescriptions. Neglect, however slight, of one of these rendered a person defiled. Given that the whole passage revolves around this Jewish ritual, the context cannot but be Jewish.

Further, there is a reference to how many Jews sidestepped the demands of their religion. Both Matthew and Mark refer to it, but Mark actually uses the Jewish technical expression— *corban*. Whenever they vowed something to God in this way, they could obviously not give it to someone else. But some used this as a loophole, a cast-iron excuse for not giving to others things they ought really to have given. Moreover, if the vow was made in a vague manner, no immediate obligation followed from it. The particular example that both Matthew and Mark use is that of someone who normally would be bound to support his needy parents. Making a vague vow and promising to God "anything I might have used" meant he could no longer give to his parents. But since the vow was too vague to impose a direct obligation, he did not give it to the Temple either. None of this would make sense except in the Jewish context.

Again, the whole style of the argument, which depends on scriptural quotations, presumes that not only those involved in the episode, but also those for whom the Gospel was written, would be familiar with these quotations. This too, therefore, points to a Jewish, and indeed a rabbinical, context.

This hypothesis is confirmed by the fact that Mark (because he is writing for the church in Rome and his Gospel will be reaching Gentile converts as well) feels obliged to explain at length some of the traditional practices of the elders (7:3-4), and Luke (writing for Gentiles) omits this episode completely.

Second Observation

The way in which Mark and Matthew have the passage in common suggests that both draw from sources that go back to an oral tradition.

We should, first of all, notice the remarkable agreement in many formulations. The quotation from Isaiah, for example, is exactly the same (Mt 15:7-9; Mk 7:6-7). This is all the more remarkable since the quotation deviates somewhat from the standard Greek translation (the Septuagint).

Yet, there are also many small differences which cannot be explained by the redaction of the evangelists alone. For example: Matthew says, "*God* commanded: Honor your father," etc. (Mt 15:4). Mark says, "*Moses* commanded: Honor your father," etc. (Mk 7, 10). Matthew says, "Why do your disciples *transgress* the tradition of the elders?" (Mt 15:2). Mark says, "Why do your disciples *not walk according to* the tradition of the elders?" (Mk 7:5). Matthew has (i) honoring parents; (ii) quotation from Isaiah. Mark has (i) quotation from Isaiah; (ii) honoring parents. In these and more such differences there is no reason to accept that they were all effected by the evangelists. Matthew and Mark must have drawn from sources that already contained these small differences.

The agreement and the small differences can only be explained by the fluctuation in oral, memorized texts. Written texts do not allow of any changes of this kind, but memorized texts could have many small differences, such as whether "God" commanded or "Moses," whether the texts said "transgressing" or "not walking according to," whether this passage or that came first, etc.

We hypothesize, therefore, that the two versions in Matthew and Mark draw from sources which go back to an oral, memorized tradition. It was a common tradition because of the close parallels in the two accounts. It was an oral, memorized tradition because the small differences between Matthew and Mark are those which would arise naturally in passing down an oral tradition by memory.

Third Observation

The present form of the Greek text in Matthew and Mark suggests that the original oral, memorized formulation was in Aramaic.

The terminology used proves this abundantly. Mark still uses the original *corban* (Mk 7:11). Furthermore, the other terms such as "defiled" hands (Mk 7:2), "tradition of the elders" (Mt 15:2; Mk 7:5), to "transgress" (Mt 15:3), to "make void" (Mt 15:6; Mk 7:13) and to "walk according to" (Mk 7:5) make no sense in Greek. Their meaning becomes clear if we understand that they are literal translations of rabbinical Aramaic terms. The terms permeate the passage to such an extent that an Aramaic original must be assumed.

The Aramaic origin can also be illustrated from the constructions in the passage. The turn of phrase "Rightly did Isaiah prophesy" (Greek: *kalos*) is strange in Greek. But we understand it fully when we remember the Hebrew (and Aramaic) construction *hetib*, literally, "to make it good to do something"—i.e., to do something rightly. Another clear example we may see in the sentence construction of Mark 7:2 and 5: "seeing some eat . . . *and* the Pharisees asked." The *intermediate "and"* (between the main clause and the subsidiary ones) goes contrary to Greek idiom, but is characteristic of Aramaic.

Since some of these features are present both in Matthew and Mark we must conclude that the oral, memorized tradition that preceded their sources was formulated in Aramaic.

Fourth Observation

We can recognize in the versions of Matthew and Mark the characteristics (rhythm, structure, key words, mnemonic helps) of a memorized formulation.

The Jews used to memorize the teachings of famous scribes. The whole system of teaching was geared to this. For hundreds of years the teaching of the rabbis (*Mishnah, Talmud*) were not written down at all, but simply learned by heart and so handed on. We have excellent proof in the Jewish sources of the accuracy of this system of retaining knowledge.

To make it easier to learn texts by heart the matter was arranged in a way that would easily cling to memory and imagination. We find such characteristics of memorized texts in the dispute with the scribes:

—Jesus' reply to the scribes is repeated three times: once in the general opening statement, and twice in the refrain.
—The scribes' question and Jesus' reply is the same word, "why" (*Maduao*), which people would easily remember.
—Moreover, in both arguments we find the opening word "Rightly" (*Hebi*) and the key word "honor" (*kabad*). This links both arguments.
—The Aramaic must also have been rhythmic. We can still see this in some parts, as in Matthew 15:1-3.

Again we come to the conclusion that an Aramaic memorized formulation must have preceded the sources underlying Matthew and Mark.

On the basis of this observation, here is a reconstruction of the passage in its oral form for memorization. Note the repetition of "Why" and the use of "break away"—the same verb as in the scribal question—as a mnemonic aid; the general statement of Jesus' counter argument, which is taken up in the refrain/chorus; the repetition of "Rightly" as a mnemonic aid.

Introduction

Pharisees and scribes from Jerusalem
then came to Jesus and said,
   "Why
   do your disciples break away
   from the tradition of the elders?
   They do not wash their hands when
   they eat."
He answered and said,
   "Why
   do you break away from the
   commandment of God?
   For the sake of/through your human
   tradition
   you make null and void the word of
   God."

First recital

And he said to them,
   "Rightly
   is it you put aside the commandment
   of God
   to keep your own traditions?
For Moses said,
   'Honor your father and your
   mother' and
   'Anyone who curses father and
   mother must be put to death.'
But you say,
   'If a man says to his father or
   mother
   "Anything I might have used to help
   you is *corban*" he is rid of his
   duty to his father or mother.'"

Refrain/chorus

> "So for the sake/of through your
> tradition
> you make null and void the word of
> God.
> And you do many such things."

Second recital

And he said to them,
> "Rightly
> Isaiah prophesied of you, hypocrites,
> as it is written,
> 'This people honors me with their
> lips but their heart is far from me;
> in vain do they worship me,
> giving as teaching only the
> commandments of men.'
> For you clean the outside of the cup
> and of the plate but inside they/you
> are full of extortion and greed!"

Refrain/chorus

> "So for the sake of/through your
> tradition
> you make null and void the word of
> God.
> And you do many such things."

Fifth Observation

There are many indications that the original Aramaic formulation may be that of Jesus himself, memorized by the disciples.

The structure of the passage is consistent with oral, memorized tradition. When the rabbis debated religious and theological questions and reached a conclusion, they would then pass this on within the context of a general structure with an introduction indicating the topic discussed, the conclusion, and the argument to back up the conclusion. This is exactly the structure of the passage we have been analyzing. We can easily imagine that Jesus, having been involved in a lengthy and perhaps detailed debate with the Pharisees from Jerusalem, would subsequently express his arguments to his disciples in the classic form which they could readily memorize.

Moreover, the content of the passage focuses on Jesus' doctrine. Whereas after the Resurrection attention is focused on Jesus' person, the preaching before the Resurrection simply proclaims Jesus' teaching. Further, in this passage the force of the argument depends on two quotations from the Old Testament and not on the authority of the risen Jesus, as revealer of God's will. The episode presents Jesus fighting the Pharisees on their own grounds. He proves his superiority as a rabbi, and provides his disciples with excellent scribal arguments against objections. For all these reasons, we can safely assume that the passage belongs to the preaching of the period before the Resurrection.

Finally, the vision of God and of morality is so strong, so direct, and so contrary to the accepted vision of the time that it would be more consistent to ascribe it to one outstanding leading thinker than to an amorphous community such as the early Christians. In other words, our analysis points to Christ himself as the author of this passage.

Overall Hypothesis

Using all the evidence we have amassed we can summarize how this passage came to have its present form.

Some important scribes and Pharisees came to Jesus and accused him of not observing the tradition of the elders. Jesus replied at length. Later, Jesus discussed the argument with his own disciples. Since they were likely to meet similar opposition in their own preaching Jesus formulated his arguments for them in a way they could easily remember and repeat. Jesus' replies to the Pharisees would be passed on in this form by word of mouth. After the Resurrection they were equally relevant to the whole dispute between the converts and their practice of religion, and the Jews and their practice of theirs. When Christianity began to attract Gentile converts, a three-fold adaptation was necessary: the text had to be translated into Greek (the universal language of the time); many references had to be explicitly explained (as in Mk 7:3-4); and the texts had to be committed to writing since Gentiles were not used to an oral tradition. The same passage reached Matthew and Mark in only slightly different forms, and because of its usefulness and relevance to the communities for whom they were writing, they included it in their Gospels. As always, each evangelist made minor adjustments so that the passage conformed to his own style and purpose.

In these last three chapters, we have concentrated on individual passages to illustrate techniques of analysis which you yourself may subsequently apply elsewhere in the Gospels. However, it is not always possible to reconstruct Jesus' original teaching or to detect an oral tradition underlying every passage in the Gospels. Some passages were not formulated until after the Resurrection, in the early days of the church. As particular problems arose the apostles saw that some words or deeds of Jesus, which had not been formulated in pre-Resurrection oral tradition, were relevant for the church of their time. They would make this a part of their teaching, and when the evangelists came to write the Gospels, they would take note of this teaching.

By and large, though, the stages we have outlined in the formation of the passage on the dispute between Jesus and the Pharisees are very representative of how the bulk of the synoptic tradition was formed.

Summary: The Stages of Gospel Formation

From what we have seen in this and previous chapters we can now make a more general description of how the Gospels were formed. Modern writers on the Gospels often presuppose that we know about this process of Gospel formation, and they normally use certain accepted terms. Care has been taken to include most of these terms in the following survey.

27-30 A.D. Jesus preaches in Palestine. He announces the arrival of the Kingdom of heaven. His teaching follows the well-known pattern of prophetic instruction. Rather than treating the subject systematically he speaks about different aspects of the Kingdom as circumstances demand and appropriate occasions arise. Jesus selects disciples who receive personal instruction. As with his prophetic instruction, his personal instruction is not abstract and theoretical, but direct and concrete. These disciples learn certain words and sayings by heart. There is no evidence that Jesus asked them to commit any of this to writing, nor is there evidence of any writing by these disciples during that period. Jesus simply acts, teaches, and gives special explanations to his disciples. Included in this teaching is the promise that, at the right time, his Spirit would enlighten them and instruct them as to what to teach. The period of Jesus' own teaching is known technically as the "ministry of the historical Jesus."

30 A.D. The apostles start to proclaim Jesus as Messiah. An outline of what they preach can be found in the many sermons recorded in the Acts of the Apostles. From those outlines, we gain some insight into what is known as the "oral catechesis" in the apostolic church. As with Jesus' own preaching, this oral teaching is not systematic, but corresponds to the needs of the particular people to whom it is addressed. So, for example, when speaking to people who had been disciples of John the Baptist, they would recall John's testimony about Jesus (Mt 3:10-12; Mk 1:7-8; Lk 3:15-18), in an effort to persuade them to accept Jesus (Acts 19:1-7).

A short complete section of apostolic teaching is known technically as a "pericope." The specific context in which such a passage took shape and was formulated is known as its *Sitz-*

im-Leben. The disciples repeated these pericopes over and over again in order to commit them to memory. In this way the pericopes gradually came to have a fixed form. Then various passages were strung together, often with some kind of key theme or similarity to provide the logical link. Most often they would be put together in the pattern of apostolic *kerygma* (preaching)—Jesus' miracles, his sayings, his death, and his Resurrection. This oral catechesis, because it was preaching about Christ, makes no attempt to give a detailed, chronological, "photographic" account of Jesus, but rather presents him as the Messiah, the Savior, the Son of God. Everything that Jesus said and did was understood in the light of the Resurrection. The Jesus that is presented in the teaching of the early church is known technically as "the Christ of faith" (in contrast to the historical Jesus mentioned above).

40 A.D. Written Documents. For the benefit of preachers and catechists, parts of the oral catechesis were quite quickly committed to writing. Collections of documents recording what Christ said and did began to circulate within the church. Although the original ones are no longer extant, scholars have been able to reconstruct two such written sources by analyzing the texts we do have. The first is known technically as *Urmark* or "original Mark" and often shortened to *M*. The Gospel of Mark is almost entirely based on this source, but all three evangelists drew from it when composing their Gospels. The second is referred to as *Q*, the initial letter of *Quelle*, the German word for "source." Matthew and Luke both drew on this source.

50 A.D. Literary Composition. When the growth of the church called for a more uniform and complete presentation of its teaching, some talented, zealous preachers set about accomplishing this work. Each wrote in very definite and concrete circumstances, with his own particular viewpoint, his own distinct purpose and personal preferences. Mark and Luke wrote for Gentile Christians, Matthew for Jewish Christians.

Mark concentrated on Jesus' deeds, Matthew and Luke carefully recorded many of Christ's shorter sayings. Each evangelist had his own themes and according to his own literary abilities arranged and presented the matter available to him in his own way." This arranging is known technically as "literary composition."

Matthew, Mark, and Luke—drawing from the same written sources, M and Q—have many passages in common, technically called "parallel passages." In contrast, where one evangelist records something not found in the others, it is referred to as a "proper passage." It is important to note, however, that even in parallel passages we can detect the literary preference and thematic preference of each evangelist. Remember, too, that Q and M are hypothetical reconstructions, although most scripture scholars would say that we can be almost certain that these existed. It is safe to presume that the evangelists had other written and possibly unwritten sources from which to draw material but lack of evidence means that this is only guesswork, however reasonable.

Because each evangelist presents Christ in a slightly different manner you will sometimes see references to the "Christ of Matthew," "the Christ of Luke," "the Christ of Mark," "the Christ of John," "the synoptic Christ."

This is a brief look at the way the Gospels came to be. We can only scratch the surface here. Indeed, we will never exhaust the study of the Gospels for they are the living word of God. It is well worth devoting your life to this study, for the Gospels are life itself.

Index